KABBALAH:
FOR THE PERPLEXED

Continuum Guides for the Perplexed

Continuum's Guides for the Perplexed are clear, concise and accessible introductions to thinkers, writers and subjects that students and readers can find especially challenging. Concentrating specifically on what it is that makes the subject difficult to grasp, these books explain and explore key themes and ideas, guiding the reader towards a thorough understanding of demanding material.

GUIDES FOR THE PERPLEXED AVAILABLE FROM CONTINUUM

Mysticism: A Guide for the Perplexed, Paul Oliver

Forthcoming in Religious Studies:

The Baha'i Faith: A Guide for the Perplexed, Robert H. Stockman
Confucius: A Guide for the Perplexed, Yong Huang
Daoism: A Guide for the Perplexed, Louis Komjathy
Jainism: A Guide for the Perplexed, Sherry Fohr
Mormonism: A Guide for the Perplexed, Robert L. Millet
New Religious Movements: A Guide for the Perplexed, Paul Oliver
Sikhism: A Guide for the Perplexed, Arvind-Pal Singh Mandair
Spirituality: A Guide for the Perplexed, Philip Sheldrake
Sufism: A Guide for the Perplexed, Elizabeth Sirriyeh
Zoroastrianism: A Guide for the Perplexed, Jenny Rose

KABBALAH: A GUIDE FOR THE PERPLEXED

PINCHAS GILLER

continuum

Continuum International Publishing Group
The Tower Building   80 Maiden Lane
11 York Road   Suite 704
London SE1 7NX   New York, NY 10038

www.continuumbooks.com

British Library Cataloguing-in-Publication Data
A catalogue record for this book is available from the British Library.

ISBN: HB: 978-1-4411-1119-7
      PB: 978-1-4411-1032-9

Library of Congress Cataloging-in-Publication Data
Giller, Pinchas, 1953-
Kabbalah: a guide for the perplexed / Pinchas Giller.
    p. cm.
    Includes index.
    ISBN 978-1-4411-1032-9—ISBN 978-1-4411-1119-7
1. Cabala—History. I. Title.

BM526.G475 2011
296.8′33—dc22
                          2011008347

Typeset by Newgen Imaging Systems Pvt Ltd, Chennai, India
Printed and bound in India

For Mel Reisfield

CONTENTS

LIST OF ILLUSTRATIONS

PREFACE

It is a little bit ironic that the title of this series is "Guides for the Perplexed," as the original *Guide for the Perplexed* of Maimonides has been the *bete noir* of kabbalists since its composition. Yet the Continuum Press chose this title for their series of accessible books about difficult subjects, and Continuum has been unfailingly supportive in this endeavor, particularly Tom Crick and Kirsty Schaper. Many thanks to Kirsty for recruiting me and for supporting the project.

I am indebted to the readers of initial drafts: Rachel Blatt, Jonathan Bubis, John Carrier, Nosn Crane, Ron Goldberg, Steven Henkin, Joshua Jason, Jessica Kendler, Shaul Magid, Erica Miller, Sarah Newman, Sarah Michelle Shulman, Howard Tilman, Scott Westle and Elliot Wolfson for their comments and feedback. Rick Levine, in particular, reviewed the entire manuscript exhaustively prior to its submission. I am grateful to Chaim Singer-Frankes, who prepared the chart of the sefirot, and Gabriel Botnick, who adopted the charts from the arcane work *Kelalei Hathalat he-Ḥokhmah*. All errors are, needless to say, mine alone.

Pinchas Giller
Los Angeles, 2011

CHAPTER 1

WHAT IS KABBALAH?

JEWISH METAPHYSICS

Kabbalah is best described as the *inner* part of traditional Judaism. It is a tradition that goes back more than two millennia, one that has produced thousands of books and many movements, mystical circles and communities. Throughout its history, Kabbalah has been located squarely in the context of Jewish religious practice: the laws, traditions and lore of conventional Judaism. It has been

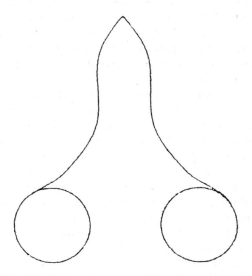

Figure 1.1 The Third Eye, from a traditional commentary to the *Sefer Yezirah.*

KABBALAH: A GUIDE FOR THE PERPLEXED

a force in Jewish history, but it is mainly a source of nourishment for the Jewish consciousness. Jewish scholars tend to speak of Kabbalah in historical terms. This view is ultimately unsatisfying to those who are curious about incorporating Kabbalah into their lives, for Kabbalah is born out of the tensions and dynamics that exist within conventional religious Judaism.

It is most useful to think of Kabbalah as the official metaphysics of Judaism, the aspects of Judaism that lie beneath present reality and cannot be proven by logic or the evidence of human senses. Taken this way, the immediate subjects of Kabbalah are the soul and its afterlife, the structure of Heaven and the underworld, the creation of the world and what will happen at the end of time. For all of these questions, there are vast and complex traditions and practices that access the power and knowledge of kabbalistic realities.

Most religions other than Judaism have these ideas as part of their mainstream traditions. For example, Christians imbibe a heavy dose of metaphysics as part of their basic beliefs. Catholic children are instructed in the processes of their souls and inculcated with images of the afterlife, its rewards and punishment. Pentecostal Christians have an elaborate myth of what will occur when the Messiah comes, an expanded reading of the book of Revelations, replete with rivers of fire, multiheaded beasts, the punishment of the unbelievers and the "rapture" of the faithful. Hindus and Buddhists have a strong understanding of the career of their souls, particularly the *karma* that attaches to them when they sin and which will burden them in their next incarnation.

Conventional Judaism seems oblivious to these concerns. Jewish philosophers have criticized the metaphysical systems of other religions as indicating a low spiritual level, a culture of gratification and a morality based on Divine reward. The very this-worldliness of Judaism, and its emphasis on actions, through the *mizvot*, is seen as a great virtue. It is a source of pride for many Jews that Judaism is mainly concerned with individual behavior and responsibility, as opposed to obtaining some reward from God. Indeed, many Jews are critical of other religions for their other-worldliness. "Don't be like servants working for a reward; be like servants working for no reward!" admonishes the great law code of Judaism, the *Mishnah* (*Avot* 1.3). The metaphysical understandings of Judaism, the dynamics of what goes on under the surface of day-to-day reality, are suppressed throughout the religion. The

Mishnah (*Hagigah* 2.1), when discussing mysticism, expresses this reticence as follows:

> Whoever speculates on these four things, it would have been bet-
> ter if he had never come into the World: what is above and what
> is below, what is before and what is after!

The kabbalistic tradition completely undermines the sentiments of this statement. Kabbalah is *extremely* concerned with "what is above, what is below, what is before and what is after." "Above" is Heaven in all of its glory, where God dwells in a throne room at the apex of a series of palaces, each of which is staffed by a bureaucracy of ministering angels who are assigned to various tasks. "Below" is the underworld, as horrific and varied as that of Dante. Implicit in the existence of Heaven and Hell is the idea that the souls of the living are fated to go to one place or the other. If one accepts the existence of the divine realms, one must accept that human beings have a soul *at all*, which has seldom been the concern of main-stream Jewish teachings. As for "what was before," this refers to the creation of the World. For kabbalists, the events of the first three chapters of Genesis are not a sufficient description of the creation of the world on which to base a theology. In order to create the world, God had to make a space for a universe of finite, imperfect creations, "un-Godly" by definition. The dynamics of this creation are viewed as a very complex process by the kabbalists and con-sume thousands of pages of dense theory in the kabbalistic library. Finally, with regard to "what is after," Kabbalah subscribes to the Jewish view that the world is, in fact, perfectible, and that the prob-lems of the present world would be resolved in the messianic age. The task of the individual is to work toward the *tiqqun*, or "fixing" of the world, epitomized by the coming of the Messiah.

The average Jewish schoolchild does not have these metaphysi-cal concepts at his or her fingertips, as would his or her classmates who are raised in other religions. These ideas are not studied in advanced schools of Jewish learning, the rabbinical schools, yeshivot, or Israel programs. Yet these underlie many Jewish prac-tices and are the basis for many of the most compelling aspects of Jewish life.

The very word "kabbalah" comes from the Hebrew word *le-kabel*, meaning, "to receive." Kabbalists believe that all of their traditions

3

are received from an earlier source, initially from a revelation from God, which is then passed along in a chain of transmission among cognoscenti. Because it is viewed by its practitioners as the original Judaism, Kabbalah paradoxically sees itself as the part of Judaism that is the least innovative. Originally, kabbalists believed that Kabbalah could never grow through new revelations, but must be a demonstrably early tradition. This was the position of the twelfth-century kabbalist, Rabbi Moshe Ben Naḥman (Naḥmanides), who was apt to bring discussion of a given kabbalistic topic to a halt with the exclamation, "we have no tradition for this!"

Kabbalistic ideas have customarily been kept away from the masses. Over the centuries, Kabbalah has undergone periods in which it was preserved for the cognoscenti and elites. At other times, kabbalistic ideas were widely circulated and kabbalistic teachings inspired various social and religious movements. A view has persisted which maintains that mystical realities were to be reserved until one was 40, "with a full belly of Jewish learning." Yet many great kabbalists, such as Isaac Luria and Rabbi Naḥman of Breslav, died in their mid-thirties. When great movements sparked by mystical ideas led to bad results, the Jews blamed the influence of Kabbalah and banned it as "dangerous." Nonetheless, there have been periods when Kabbalah left its cloister and became the popular theology of Judaism.

TRADITIONAL KABBALISTS VERSUS SCHOLARS OF KABBALAH

In this "post-modern" age, Kabbalah is in ascent while philosophy, the great vehicle of modernity and enlightenment, is in eclipse. Yet the rise of interest in the Kabbalah has been accompanied by new sensibilities, based on the research of modern scholars. The twentieth century saw much research into the history of Kabbalah, led by the late Professor Gershom Scholem of the Hebrew University. In their writings, Scholem and his students told the great story of Kabbalah to the modern world. Scholem saw Kabbalah as beginning when ideas from the late Biblical period developed into full-fledged mythologies during the time of the Talmud, from about 200 BCE to 500 CE. These mythologies were then reworked by medieval European kabbalists in the twelfth century. The early medieval kabbalists wrote new mystical works, culminating in the kabbalistic

4

"bible," the *Zohar*. The *Zohar* spread throughout the Jewish world and inspired a mystical renaissance in the Galilee hill town, Safed. There, according to Scholem, strong messianic impulses developed in response to the trauma of the recent Spanish Expulsion in 1492. Finally, kabbalistic teachings erupted into historical movements, such as the infamous heresy of the false messiah Shabbatai Zevi and the popular movement of Hasidism. Throughout the history of Kabbalah, according to the scholarly view, Kabbalah changed, evolved and even "modernized."

Such an understanding would horrify a traditional kabbalist. Kabbalists don't believe in the development of Kabbalah; they believe that the truths of Kabbalah were *always* there. The main task for mystics is to uncover and recover what was common knowledge to humankind in earlier periods of history. One Safed kabbalist even stated that when the world was created, there was no sky. A person standing on the earth could look up and simply see God and the workings of Heaven clearly, with no obstruction. According to traditional Kabbalah, in the beginning of time mystical ideas were accessible to everyone and known to all of humankind. Subsequently, however, humanity went through a series of calamities in their relationship with God. These calamities included the fall in the Garden of Eden, the Flood, the building of the golden calf and the destruction of the two temples in Jerusalem. Each catastrophe obscured the relationship between humanity and God. Kabbalists began to develop theologies of calamity, declaring that, for instance, the Flood never ended. Humanity is spiritually drowning, and the flood is but a metaphor for the confusion and upheavals of contemporary history. The Safed kabbalist Moshe Cordovero compared the world to a ruined building that the builder had neglected. The infrastructure of the building began to collapse and the stairwells and passages between the various wings of the building became clogged. Another Safed kabbalist, Isaac Luria, described a world that had suffered a structural flaw that had caused it to rupture and collapse.

Whatever the metaphor that they employed, kabbalists felt that they had the job of repairing the results of the catastrophe. However the mystics defined the problem, they all agreed that the essential truths of Kabbalah had been revealed at the creation of the world, but had been put away to be recovered by the kabbalists themselves. Hence, for traditional kabbalists, it is heretical to think that kabbalistic ideas "developed," as they were all present at the creation of the world.

Their different understandings of the nature of Kabbalah leave scholars and traditionalists at an impasse. Traditional kabbalists don't think that they have much to learn from the professors. At the same time, academic scholars of Kabbalah seem most comfortable with the works of kabbalists from prior centuries, avoiding encounters with living kabbalists, who are bound by the strictures of various types of orthodoxy.

In my studies of contemporary kabbalists, I have learned that there is much that one cannot know. The person standing next to me in a synagogue may be in a state of mystical ecstasy, but I can't enter his mind to see, and the adept may, in fact probably will, be hostile to questions. This begs another question of authenticity, namely, the effect of scholarly writing on Kabbalah and its tacit dissemination into the traditional communities.

The late pietist Rav Moshe Besdin used to define the problem as follows, "There are people who learn *about* it, and there are people who learn *it*. We are the people who learn *it*, not *about* it." For all mystics, this kind of radical subjectivity is part of their mysticism. Existentially, they must see the world without scholarly detachment in order to *be* mystics. Yet modern Jews ought not to be willfully naïve about the conclusions that the academy has reached (although there are some who try). A failure of contemporary Western Judaism is that when congregants ask a spiritual question, their Rabbi is apt to respond with an academic answer. That answer, while being true on a certain level, is not the truth that the congregant was looking for. The academy does not provide satisfying answers about the meaning of Kabbalah in the life of a modern Jew. There are accounts of Scholem himself being disarmed by questions about the relevance of Kabbalah to modern individuals. To this day, many scholars, particularly of the Israeli school, will retreat from personal questions with the disclaimer, "Well, at the end of the day I'm just a historian." This view is inadequate, because presently the Jewish population is curious to try this at home.

KABBALAH AS NORMATIVE JUDAISM

Although kabbalistic ideas may seem obscure and exotic to contemporary Western Jews, they were essential to normative Judaism until fairly recently. Throughout Jewish history, the intellectual emphasis of mainstream Judaism has swung between the metaphysical, mythic ideas characteristic of Kabbalah and a philosophical rationalism completely opposed to those ideas. Maimonides, the exemplar of philosophical rationalism, asserted that one could not know God and what God *is*, but could only know what God is *not*. In Christian Spain and across the Pyrenees in Provence, mystics responded by teaching that God had attributes that poured out of Heaven and into the reality of the human experience. As the situation of medieval Spanish Jewry slid into chaos, culminating in the Expulsion of 1492, Kabbalah emerged as the basis of many Jews' belief. For American Jews who trace their ancestry to the "Ellis Island/Lower East Side" wave of immigration at the turn of the

Figure 1.2 The letter *Aleph*, comprising the name YHVH, from Moshe Cordovero's *Pardes Rimmonim*.

twentieth century, nascent mystical beliefs probably died with their great-grandparents. The last vestiges of such beliefs might be an elderly relative's muttered *kin eyna hora*, a spell meant to banish the "evil eye" from alighting on the recipient of a compliment.

Yet many Jewish practices originate in Kabbalah. The entire special ritual of the Friday night synagogue service, particularly the welcoming of the "Sabbath Bride," originated with the kabbalists of Safed. The custom of holding the cup for the Friday night benediction in the palm of the hand is proposed on the first page of the *Zohar*. The *Zohar* is also the source for the welcoming of the seven guests, Abraham, Isaac, Jacob, Moses, Aaron, Joseph and King David, into the festival booth on the holiday of Sukkot. Every Jewish ritual has a specifically kabbalistic way of doing it, so that the ritual is a way of channeling and addressing Divine energies.

People come to me sometimes and ask, "What can I do that is kabbalistic?" I answer that the most kabbalistic acts are the basic rituals of religious Judaism: wearing a prayer shawl and the tefillin, reciting the *Shema'* prayer in the morning and evening, preparing the Sabbath table, participating in the synagogue rite, keeping the Sabbath and Festivals and shunning forbidden foods and sexual liaisons. These are the building blocks and prerequisites of the kabbalistic lifestyle. Amulets, red strings, "holy" water, crystals or other new age accoutrements are irrelevant to the lifestyle of authentic kabbalists.

When I was a teacher in Jerusalem, my secular students would sometimes hunt down kabbalists in the community. They would come back telling me that at a certain point in the encounter, the teacher had stressed that they could not go forward in Kabbalah without observing traditional Judaism. I was unsurprised, because detaching kabbalistic practice from traditional Judaism would be like performing an operation with instruments that are not sterile.

The fact that Kabbalah is such a normative part of Judaism is related to another popular misconception about mysticism in general. The general public seems possessed of the notion, reinforced by the popular culture, that mystics are great social rebels, or anti-establishment figures. This has been true in only a small percentage of cases. For every figure such as the Christian Marguerite Porète, burned at the stake for her heresy, or Sufi mystic Al Hallaj, crucified for the same reason, there have been hundreds of cases like that of Teresa of Avila, who founded the Carmelite nuns, or

Francis of Assisi, who successfully fought his excommunication by the Catholic Church. Mystics are usually members of the religious establishment, or supporters of that establishment at the bottom level. This was certainly the case in Kabbalah. Such major kabbalists as Nahmanides, Isaac Luria and the Gaon of Vilna were also authorities in Jewish law. In fact, mysticism generally comes out of the friction of a "high church" of rules and regulations, rubbing up against the religious impulses of a loving individual who is immersed in those practices, their symbols and the mythos attached to them. Mysticism tends to begin within the walls of an established tradition and then transcends those boundaries.

At the same time, there is very little mysticism produced by movements that reduce their religious beliefs down to a few essentials. As a demonstration of this, a publisher recently collected a few hundred titles that were viewed as the "Classics of Western Spirituality," mainly the mystical writings of Western religion. Few of these works were produced by Protestants, who have pared their theology down to what they consider the "essence" of Christianity. The vast majority of mystical systems have come out of the Catholic, Celtic, Eastern Orthodox, Orthodox Jewish and classical Muslim traditions. Mysticism doesn't flourish in a reductionist, reformed context. It requires the mysteries and spiritual infrastructures, the restrictions and repressions, the loamy spiritual soil of a secondary tradition, as the context in which to grow.

DOES EVERYBODY HAVE TO BELIEVE IN KABBALAH?

The structure of Jewish belief and practice is that the religious practice is fairly set, while the mind is free to roam. Maimonides, who set conventional Judaism in place nearly a thousand years ago, stressed that there were only 13 ideas that Jews had to believe in, even though they were impossible to prove through the evidence of the senses. These were largely givens about God, the truth of the Torah, and the beliefs in the resurrection and the coming of the Messiah. Otherwise, the way that a person filled in the gaps in Jewish tradition was really up to them. Indeed, most literate Jews are comfortable with the fact that there are various, contradictory explanations for the nature of biblical events in the lore known as *midrash*. Ultimately, Jews may see the stories of the Bible and the teachings of the religion in multiple ways. Since the beliefs of

Kabbalah are so absolute, Jews who are unfamiliar with these traditions are often puzzled. They might wonder, "If this is the inner reality of Judaism, do I have to buy in?"

The most widely known kabbalistic understanding is that there are four levels of meaning to existence. These are the simple meaning (*peshat*), the hints and allegories within meaning (*remez*), midrashic traditions that are attached to them (*drash*) and the secret mystical understanding (*sod*). The wisdom to address the truth of existence may come through reading the symbols that come one's way.

Ultimately, the acceptance of Kabbalah by individuals really begins with the acceptance of their own potential inner divinity, the holiness of their souls. Follow this reasoning: If God exists, then what is the point of human existence except to know God? Humans are the only beings that know there is a God, recognize the possibility of holiness and yearn for transcendence. So the impulse to enter the world of Kabbalah begins not with belief, but with a knowledge, that which the ancients called *gnosis*, of the existence of a separate reality that lies within the phenomenal world, forming the basis of the real existence that is beneath this present world of pain, suffering and illusion. With this knowledge, one can begin to understand something of the Kabbalah.

CHAPTER 2

KABBALAH: A BRIEF HISTORY

The history of Kabbalah is not the doctrine itself, and the presentation of kabbalistic history has been the source of an odious pseudo-intellectualism. The result of this academic emphasis is that it is possible to study and even write about the whole history of Kabbalah without knowing anything of its inner nature. There is an enormous gap between people who are looking for the spiritual meaning of Kabbalah, the person looking to establish the historical truth of Kabbalah's development and the cocktail party conversation that is so rife regarding its historical developments and "major trends." Perhaps such is the case with all academic fields.

Nonetheless, Jews live in history and derive lessons from it. Jews *remember* in a very muscular way. So, in order to understand something of Kabbalah, one must understand something of the forms it took in the four great historical periods of Judaism. These are the time of the Bible (c. 1800 BCE–c. 500 BCE), the time of the Second Temple and the composition of the Talmud (c. 500 BCE–500 CE), the Middle Ages (500 CE–1848 CE) and modernity. Kabbalah is essentially a product of the end of the biblical period and its history flourishes to the end of the Middle Ages, with movements of renewal unfolding up to the present.

It is fair to say that Kabbalah began when prophecy ended. The activities of the prophets and their acolytes did not simply cease with the activities of the last prophets accredited by the Bible. Prophetic activity continued after the last three "accredited" prophets, Haggai, Zachariah and Malachi. This "unaccredited" prophetic activity seems to have evolved into the mystical activity of the Rabbis of the Talmud in the Second Temple Period. This ancestor of Kabbalah came to be called "Merkavah" mysticism, after the visions of the Merkavah, or celestial chariot. Its content consisted of descriptions of mystical ascents through a series of heavenly palaces, and descriptions of the angelic hosts who dwell there, and, especially, their songs and prayers.

The early mysticism of the Talmudic period reemerged in the twelfth century in three locales: Provence, Gerona and the Rhineland. Each of those communities produced ideas that were, in turn, shuffled into the central kabbalistic work, the *Zohar*, which appeared in Spain in the late thirteenth century. The *Zohar* spread through the Jewish world and attained particular prominence in the Galilee hill town of Safed in the sixteenth century. Ideas developed by the Safed kabbalists, in turn, influenced mystical movements that carried into modernity: Hasidism in Eastern Europe and the traditions of the North African and Middle Eastern communities. The *Zohar* also set a tone of religious romanticism, along with the empowerment of a new kind of spiritual elite. The heroes of the *Zohar* were not the unworldly rabbis of the study hall and the dank ghettos of medieval Europe, but wandering holy men whose activities resembled nothing so much as Zen monks and Franciscan friars. This new model of rabbinic activity became the norm for the successive generations of mystics in Safed and, eventually, the Hasidism of Eastern Europe.

THE OLD RELIGION

The upshot of this is that Kabbalah is one of the guardians of what might be called "the old religion," that is to say, the traditions that bubbled through the ancient world at the end of paganism and at the same time as the emergence of Christianity. There was, throughout the ancient world at that time, a growing disaffection with the individual rites of the pagan cults that dominated every civilization. With the conquest of the known worlds by Alexander and the Romans, cult after cult failed to work for its adherents. An idea came into being that its gods had deserted the World, that the gods had lost their powers. People were becoming disenchanted with their ancient religions. The old Gods and their cults were no longer "working" for them, literally, as they allowed their believers to be vanquished and ruled by the great cosmopolitan states of Greece, Rome and Persia.

In this milieu, people began to conceive of a world from which God has departed, an empty, Godless world ruled, if at all, by a governor, known widely as the Demiurge. The new religions which spoke of God as having departed the world were called Gnosticism, and they took many forms, telling, for instance, the tale of the great God Mani who had departed the world but left behind sparks of divinity, which the spiritual seekers could gather. In any case, the Gnostic cultures comprise something that I would call "the old religion," the religion that came before the present Judaism that we have before us.

This idea may have begun in Judaism itself, whose canon seemed to point to a Gnostic progression. The evolution of God's role in the world seemed to be in the direction of gradually withdrawing from human affairs. Gnostic tendencies are evident in many of the renegade circles that are described by historians of late antiquity. A Gnostic statement about the evil of the phenomenal world would be the idea that this world is so debased that if God sent his son into it, humankind would turn and kill the child. This existential statement was a step that Judaism never took. From the mythic familiar god of Genesis, to the lawgiver and covenant maker of the Torah, to the angry spurned husband of the later Prophets, God stayed in dialogue with the Jews, if angrily. Toward the end of the Hebrew Bible, God is reputed to toy with humans such as Job, and to even be oblivious to the human condition and its attendant need for morality in Ecclesiastes.

In telling these stories, the Merkavah mystics were part of a phenomenon that distinguished the ancient world. From the settlements of the Theraputae in the Nile River Valley, to the shrine that would eventually be called St Catherine's Monastery in the Sinai desert, up the Jordan river valley to the Essene settlements in Qumran and the Gnostic community at Mar Sabba near Bethlehem, a line of Gnostic influence stretched from Egypt to Jerusalem. Similar doctrines arose further north, in the fertile crescent in Syria and Mesopotamia, where the Manichean and Zoroastrian religions flourished. In all of these locales, an old esoteric religion flourished that was eventually forced out by the high church of Christianity and the sword of Islam.

Kabbalah preserves the old religion in many ways. For instance, in the Torah, the "scapegoat," the goat that is sent out from the Temple on the Day of Atonement, bearing the sins of Israel, is sent out to "Azazel in the wilderness." Now most Jews think of Azazel as a place in the desert. But the books of Enoch describe a moment, at creation, when three angels, the "watchers" snuck down to earth as part of the "fallen ones" described in the sixth chapter of Genesis. Of these, one became Azazel, literally a demon who eats sin, who is fed every year on the Day of Atonement. This is the role of Azazel in the *Zohar*, as well. So we see that elements of the old religion, expunged from Judaism, but last seen in the Merkavah, reenter Judaism through the *Zohar* and the Kabbalah.

As I stated before, Kabbalah began when prophecy ended. That is to say, the students of the last accredited Hebrew prophets, Haggai, Zechariah and Malachi, didn't know that their masters were going to be remembered as prophets while they, the students, weren't. At the time, they went along and did their thing, which probably consisted of meditation, speculation over the political fate of the Jews and mystical visions of God and the heavenly host, about which the people of the time knew more and more. They got their ideas from their new access to the Bible, which had been organized and propagated in the Babylonian exile by Ezra, the scribe, who, in order to save Judaism from extinction, popularly replaced the cult of the Jerusalem Temple with a cult of the sacred book. Jews began to be scattered abroad in many lands, but besides yearning for Israel and the Temple, they began to channel their spiritual urges into a new interest in their literature and its ideas.

As a result of this new interest in the sacred books (not yet the "Bible" as we know it from our motel room night tables) they learned many things. For instance, from their study of the Creation of the world, they realized that there was more to the story than just the seven days of creation described in Genesis 1. The events of Genesis 2 fit only roughly into the creation story of the first chapter, and the scribe/prophets knew that they had to fit the two stories together and draw conclusions from the distinctions between the two stories. Moreover, in combing through the holy books that were being collected, copied and sanctioned by Ezra and his students, the new "non-prophets" took note of hints of other creations, traditions, tales of a great primordial battle between God and the "spirit of the Deep" that took place before the first day of creation (alluded to in Gen. 1.3, "the spirit of Elohim hovered over the face of the Deep.") There were also disparate references to God as a sky rider, much like the Greek god Apollo, who rides across the sky in a chariot and lays out the sky as his cloak. These allusions also contained hints about the structure of heaven and the way that God lived there. The book of Isaiah (chapter 6) described the throne of God as being in the Jerusalem Temple, while the book of Job described a heavenly court, in which angels attended to God and occasionally cooked up mischief, as did the "wanderer" (Hebrew: Satan) in the case of Job. All of these hints and allusions in the Biblical texts had to be combined and their differences reconciled in order to work out the true narrative of creation and the actual structure of the present Heaven where God lived, most of the time.

THE WORK OF CREATION AND
THE WORK OF THE CHARIOT

The earliest doctrines that can confidently be called Kabbalah originated in speculations on the mechanics of creation and the origins of the Universe. These traditions emerged at the moment of transition from the end of prophecy and the beginning of Kabbalah and were commonly known as the Creation and Chariot Traditions (*Ma'aseh Bereishit* and *Ma'aseh Merkavah*). The Creation and Chariot Traditions arose from the need, in late antiquity, to systematically understand a number of passages in the Bible.

The *Ma'aseh Bereishit*, or "works of the creation" tradition consisted of combining the biblical creation accounts, such as the variant accounts of Genesis 1 and 2, Psalm 104 and Job 38–41, the "voice from the whirlwind." These accounts of the creation were the proof texts for *Ma'aseh Bereishit*, which combined these accounts in an attempt to construct a coherent Creation tradition.[1] *Ma'aseh Bereishit* stems from a basic problem in the Bible's presentation of the creation of the world, namely, that there was not one creation story, but many. The first chapter of Genesis obviously told one story, but the fourth verse of the second chapter seemed to tell a different one. In Genesis 1, the world seemed to be created out of nothing in seven days, while in the Genesis 2, the world was created in one day out of preexistent matter (the "unformed, void" world). In Genesis 1 man "male and female," were created together at the same time, while in Genesis 2, Eve was taken from Adam's side and called "Isha" to his "ish," "woman" to his "man." Another creation tradition seemed to tell of the generations of man in chapter 5 of Genesis. Then, a second, mysterious tradition, of God as an Apollonian sky rider fighting back the power of "the deep," the primordial springs of water under the earth, seems to haunt the later sections of the Bible, particularly in Psalm 104, Proverbs and Job. Linked to this concern for the true, embellished account of the processes of creation was an interest in the structure of Heaven. Again, the Bible presented many tantalizing hints: the throne room of Isaiah 6, the heavenly court of the Book of Job, the multiple firmaments of Psalm 104, but there was no set cosmology. Another interest of the creation traditions was angelology. How to square the anonymous messengers of Genesis and Exodus with the flaming seraphim of Isaiah 6, the mythic beasts that draw Ezekiel's chariot and the full-fledged characters Michael and Gabriel of other Babylonian sections of the Hebrew Bible such as Daniel, Ezekiel and Ezra? How deeply to expand the postbiblical tradition of Enoch, who ascends to heaven and transforms into the angel Metatron? The reconciliation of these various contradictory traditions was the preoccupation of the *Ma'aseh Bereishit* tradition.

The Merkavah, or "chariot" traditions, originated in the descriptions of the divine chariot in Ezekiel 1. It is unclear as to whether the Merkavah writings that are extant reflected the activities of a school of prophecy at the time, but certainly with the circulation of the book of Ezekiel many prophets and pietists of the early exilic period were meditating, hoping for a glimpse of the chariot. Eventually, it would seem that the chariot came to be viewed as a vehicle for carrying them to the palaces of God. These "chariot" traditions evolved into the traditions of successive Palaces, or *Heikhalot*, through which the adherent ascended to the various levels of Heaven. Later, the *Zohar* would reinterpret the Palaces of the Merkavah tradition in terms of the *sefirot*. Hence, *Ma'aseh Bereishit* and *Ma'aseh Merkavah* carried Jewish mysticism from its earliest stages at the end of the prophetic period into the Second Temple Period, the vaunted time of Rabbis of the Talmud and the rise of Christianity. Merkavah motifs continued into the *Zohar* and are inextricably woven in to the fabric of subsequent Kabbalah.

Many of these accounts are retained in the sacred books that did not make it into the Bible, which Jews and Christians call the *Apocrypha* and *Pseudepigrapha*. Many Jews have some familiarity with the idea of the nonbiblical books; they are aware, for instance that the tales of the Maccabees whose exploits are celebrated in the popular holiday Ḥanukah, are not detailed in the Bible (although they are included in some Christian versions of Scripture). Similarly, the Apocrypha is full of accounts that draw on the *Ma'aseh Merkavah* and *Ma'aseh Bereishit* traditions. One of the most compelling is the tale of Enoch or Ḥanoch; a man who the Bible says "walked with God, and was not, for God took him" (Gen. 5.24). Ḥanoch was accepted into Heaven by God and transformed into an angel, named Metatron, who had an important role in subsequent Kabbalah. It is ironic that certain Christian sects preserved the books of Enoch as part of their Bible (one can even see accounts of the transformation of Enoch in the technicolor books of Bible stories left in pediatrician's offices in Middle America) while his tale plays no functional role in exoteric, popular Judaism.

Merkavah influences did seep into popular Judaism in a not-unexpected way. The Rabbis of the Talmud, when asked who had written the accredited version of the morning and evening prayers, credited the "men of the Great assembly," a shadowy group that has never been historically documented. Yet it is clear that certain sections of the standard Jewish prayers originated with the Merkavah mystics. The morning prayer, "He who illuminates the land and all who dwell in it . . ." includes references to the angels ministering in the Temple as described in Isaiah 6, mixed in with references to the beasts that pull the Merkavah, all attending the wonder of the sun's rising in the morning, which is described as the ongoing "Ma'aseh Bereishit." More to the point, many of the hymns of the prayer service, such as the songs "Lord, Master" (*El Adon*), "The glory and the Faith" (*ha-Aderet ve-ha-Emunah*) and the closing hymn "It is upon us to praise the Lord of All" (*Aleinu*) were discovered among the early Merkavah texts.[2]

This last fact bears some further comment. The Merkavah texts were lost for the better part of history, and all that was known of them was through allusions in later kabbalistic works. All of that changed in the nineteenth century, when the elders of the great synagogue in Cairo decided to clean the attic, where every used book and instance of Hebrew writing had been put away (as the Cairene Jews were very fussy, and not only did not dispose of prayers upon which the name of God has been written, but did not dispose of any Hebrew writings at all). A young Rumanian scholar in the employ of Cambridge University, Solomon Schechter, obtained the manuscripts of the *genizah*, or storeroom, for Cambridge. Back in England, as he pieced together what he had, he was astonished to find the answers to many of the greatest riddles of the Early Kabbalah.

For instance, there is an enigmatic passage in the Talmud that tells the story of the "four who entered the Pardes." The word *pardes* literally means an orchard but, of course, it resembles the Latinate "paradise." Three of the four Rabbis who attempt the entry, Ben Azzai, Ben Zomah and Elisha Ben Abbuyah, come to bad ends, while only Rabbi Akiva, the fourth, "enters in peace and departs in peace." Moreover, the rabbinic versions of the story only record one remark of Rabbi Akiva's, namely, "when you come to the stones of pure marble, do not say 'Water, Water.'" In the *genizah* fragments, Schechter found descriptions of the celestial palace, the chambers of the Merkavah, through which the adventurers would travel, and, particularly, at the sixth gate, pillars of pure marble so highly polished as to look like crystal, or even columns of water, which were guarded by jealous angels who, if they heard of their gate being misunderstood, would stone the adventurer to death. This passage, which had been lost in a pile of papers in the attic of the Cairo synagogue, explained something that had not been fully understood by generations of readers of the Talmud!

The real meaning of the *Pardes* narrative had been lost because the early Kabbalah of the Merkavah went underground. The traditions of the Merkavah mystics were suppressed and their practices ceased to be popular or even documented among the Jews. With the transfer of Jewish life to Babylonia, the destruction of the Jerusalem Temple and the oppression of the Byzantine Empire and the Muslim conquest, Kabbalah went underground, not to reemerge historically for 500 years, until it flourished again in Medieval Europe.

EARLY KABBALAH

And then, nothing. The ancient world fragmented, after a series of catastrophes, Jewish settlement in Israel ceased and Merkavah teachings were forced underground. The "Dark Ages" had begun, and the Jewish world fragmented. With the exception of Babylonia, whose leaders, the Gaonim, operated a sort of clearing house for rabbinic advice and authority, the Jews struggled to establish themselves in the hard new realities of life after the collapse of the Roman Empire.

Merkavah, for the most part, were forced into secrecy as well, as the world of Jewish mysticism struggled through an enormous dry spell. Yet many of the ideas of the Merkavah culture spontaneously came back, in the eleventh century, in three disparate locales: Provence, in France, Gerona in Spain and the Rhineland in what is now Germany. Each one of these areas interpreted Merkavah ideas and added to them.

THE GERMAN HASIDISM

Each one of these groups put their own particular spin onto the ideas of the Merkavah. The pietists of the Rhineland were called the *hasidim*, or saints of Ashkenaz. The German ḥasidim had a grim, doom-laden view of reality. Their worldview was best evoked by the paintings of Hieronymus Bosch or the plague wanderings depicted in Bergman's film *The Seventh Seal*. Death stalks the living at every turn and the world of the dead was an abode of dread and danger. This dread is expressed in the widely circulated ethical will of Yehudah ha-Ḥasid, the leader of the movement. According to that document, the dead were liable to try to lure the living over into the netherworld. For the German ḥasidim, the living were to be protected from the machinations of the dead.

Another characteristic of the doom-laden worldview of the German ḥasidim was the idea, presented in R. Eliezer of Worms' *Sefer ha-Rokeah*, of graduated repentance. The idea that *teshuvah*, or repentance, wipes the spiritual ledger clean in one fell swoop is a nuance of Rabbinic Judaism that runs counter to human nature. Psychologically, human beings are more prone to punishing themselves with guilt for their transgressions. According to the Rokeah, every serious sin ought to be compensated by a rigorous series of fasts and afflictions, such as rolling naked in the snow or in brambles. These pietistic practices spread though Medieval Europe and the Middle East, but subsided as a cultural norm after a number of people died in the midst of radical acts of repentance.

Many of the ideas of *Sefer Hasidim* were eventually incorporated into the code of Jewish law and into popular practice. One example is the custom of Ashkenazic Jews not to name a baby after a living relative. In fact, the German ḥasidim displayed a great horror of the evil eye, and any anomaly in nature or society, such as the birth of a deformed livestock or a tree that bore fruit twice in one season, was viewed as demonic and ought to be destroyed.

TWO WORKS AND THEIR IMPLICATIONS

The other two locales in which Kabbalah reemerged were Provence, in France and Gerona, in Spain. The two spontaneous revivals owed much to the existence of two little books, which had passed through the Dark Ages of Kabbalah unscathed. The first, the *Sefer Yezirah*, or "Book of Creation," was only 1,600 words long. Nonetheless, the current printed edition runs to hundreds of pages, because it bears commentaries by every great Jewish intellectual from Sa'adiah Gaon in the ninth century to the Vilna Gaon a thousand years later. The *Sefer Yezirah* is written in the terse style of the great Jewish law book, the Mishnah. It describes how the world was created based on the Bible's assertion that the instrument of Creation was God's speech, or, specifically, the 22 letters of the Hebrew alphabet (Hebrew, of course, being the Divine language).

Figure 2.1 The letter Aleph, comprising the ten sefirot and the "hands" mentioned in *Sefer Yezirah*, from Moshe Cordovero's *Pardes Rimmonim*.

In addition to the letters are ten forces, refereed to as the ten *sefirot*, realms or numbers. Read simply, these ten sefirot described in the mysterious *Sefer Yezirah* might be merely the ten integers of the base-ten system. It might be a kind of Pythagorean mysticism, for in the ancient world the science of mathematics was perceived as a kind of magic. The combination of letters and sefirot interested another group of scholars of the period, the *Iyyun* or contemplation circle, a group so shadowy and mysterious in its provenance that we do not even know its origins. The *Sefer ha-Iyyun* is a collection of speculations on the 32 paths of wisdom, a number obviously derived from the *Sefer Yezirah*'s letters and sefirot.[3]

In the hands of the earliest Kabbalists, however, the sefirot passed from their original identities as simply powers based in mathematics to the idea of their being ten specific aspects of God, as God's Divinity emanates into the World. This was the way that the Kabbalists of Provence, such as R. Avraham Ben David, the RaBaD (or "Raivid" in Eastern European *patois*), understood them, as well as his son, Isaac the Blind. Their ideas seem to have crossed into Spain and been inherited by the kabbalists Ezra and Azriel of Gerona, and by the brothers Isaac and Jacob Cohen, who added powerful teachings regarding the powers of the demonic forces to the earlier understandings.

Another work, whose origins are similarly shrouded in mystery, was known as the book of Brightness, or the *Bahir*. This work, which is clearly only a torso of its original self, combines elements from many of the great mystery religions, including Zoroastrianism, providing a possible link back through the Dark Ages to the original Kabbalah of the Merkavah mystics and their Babylonian descendants.[4]

The *Bahir* contributed a few elements to the mix of what would eventually become the norms of Kabbalah. First, it placed its teachings in the mouths of a mysterious group of Rabbis, such as Rav Ruhamai and others, who drifted in and out of Talmudic history. Another aspect of the *Bahir* was an interest in the Divine presence of God, the famous image of the *Shekhinah*, of which more will be said later. The *Bahir* also expressed an interest in certain powers, which could certainly be interpreted as those of the sefirot. Finally, the *Bahir* discusses the reincarnation of the soul; an idea that would continue to haunt kabbalistic thought and influence the behavior of kabbalists for the next thousand years.

KABBALAH VERSUS PHILOSOPHY

Kabbalah also emerged from the shadows, goaded into the open air through the debates of Jewish philosophers and the kabbalists. Jewish philosophy, which dominated the thought of Jews in the Islamic world, eventually came to allow no metaphysical explanations for things, especially in the thought of Maimonides, the primary Jewish philosopher of the Middle Ages. The premise of Jewish philosophy was, broadly, rationalism, and the attempt to justify Jewish practice within the fields of logic and demonstrable phenomena in present existence. Kabbalists maintained an antipathy to this way of thinking in the thought of its prime exemplar, Maimonides. These discussions were exemplified by the exegetical debates of such figures of the philosophical theologians such as Maimonides and Abraham Ibn Ezra, versus anti-rationalistic kabbalists such as Naḥmanides and other nemeses of rational thought, up to R. Naḥman of Breslav in the early modern period. Naḥmanides was one of the first Rabbis to speak publicly of a different dimension of knowledge, calling this way of understanding the "True Path" (*Derekh ha-Emet*).

Naḥmanides' commentary on the Bible was among the most widely distributed Medieval Jewish texts, and even today it can be found in most traditional Jewish homes, housed in the compendium of Bible commentaries known as *Mikraot Gedolot*. Naḥmanides personally believed that kabbalistic ideas were to be reserved for the elite. Nonetheless, he viewed the spread of philosophical rationales for Jewish observance to be so dangerous to the continuation of Jewish religious practice that he decided to speak openly of kabbalistic ideas in order to combat the spread of philosophy. Eventually, rabbinic opinion swung to his side. In 1391, Spanish Jewry began to suffer the cycle of persecutions that would eventually result in the Expulsion of 1492. In the course of those events, the rabbinic establishment noted that Jews who had embraced Maimonidean rationalism, in which the miẓvot were viewed as means to some other end, often converted to Christianity in order to avoid execution by the Spanish Inquisition. Jews who were influenced by Kabbalah, on the other hand, commonly martyred themselves rather than convert. At that point, Kabbalah became the favored theology of the mass of the Jewish community.

THE *ZOHAR*

Toward the end of the thirteenth century, kabbalists became intrigued by the appearance, section by section and manuscript by manuscript, of a work first known as the "Midrash of R. Shimon bar Yoḥai." The texts that were coming to light shared some literary qualities that—to the kabbalists of their time—were proof of their authenticity. They described the activities of a group of kabbalists in second-century Israel, wandering the hills of the northern Galilee and having visions and adventures. The accounts were written in an approximation of Palestinian Aramaic, the language of such works

Figure 2.2 Traditional portrait of Shimon bar Yoḥai.

as the Jerusalem Talmud and the Bible translations of R. Yonatan ben Uzziel (I have seen the same Aramaic in an amulet preserved in the archaeological museum in the Golan Heights settlement Kazrin). For two hundred years, kabbalists collected fragments of this work, until they had the magisterial collections that saw print in the sixteenth century which consist of nearly a thousand pages of dense Aramaic text.

They called this work the *Zohar*, the book of emanation. This name came about as a result of a number of meditations, in the book itself, that deal with the emanation of God's power out of the upper worlds. The *Zohar* as it came to be constituted from its emergence in 1294 to its publication in the middle of the sixteenth century is, in literary and spiritual terms, a rich and enthralling work. There is no comparison between the *Zohar* and the works of Kabbalah that preceded its emergence. Like the Talmud, the student may probe its inner mysteries or swim around in its shallow end, delighting in the romantic tales of the adventures of Rabbi Shimon and his comrades. The strength of the *Zohar* lay in its perceived authenticity, which operated in two ways. On one hand, it purported to be the inner tradition, the reason for being, of the Judaism of the second century. Its heroes were heroes of the great Jewish legal works, the Mishnah and the Talmud. Yet the *Zohar* seemed to include many of the ideas of the early Kabbalah: the doctrine of the sefirot from the Provencal and Geronese kabbalists, views of heaven and the Divine Palaces that resembled the teachings of the Merkavah mystics, or rather an attempt to write a Merkavah-style text. Stylistically, the work was dominated by the romantic image of Shimon bar Yoḥai and his comrades, wandering the Galilee like Zen monks, encountering strange characters and drifting from this world to the upper worlds with every movement.

The literary style and language of the *Zohar* are unique. Although the *Zohar*'s central pretense is that it is a Tannaitic midrash, its rambling, lengthy form and idiosyncratic Aramaic are unlike any other rabbinic creation. The *Zohar* is not a single work, but a collection of some two-dozen separate compositions. Most scholars of Kabbalah, such as Gershom Scholem, Isaiah Tishby and Yehudah Liebes have posited a process of literary development that can be charted within the confusion of the *Zohar*'s structure.[5] If one collects the texts with an eye to their inner development one can see that there are some initial, tentative passages, called, like the earliest rabbinical writings, "Mishnahs and Toseftas." Building on the ideas in those early writings, there emerge Hebrew narrative accounts of a mysterious group of Rabbis from the Talmudic period, including the Rav Ruḥamai who figured in the *Bahir*. *Midrash ha-Ne'elam*, which Scholem and Tishby considered the earliest material, presents the idea of communities of mystic Rabbis. In later compositions, the *mise en scène* became more detailed, while the theosophical nature became more pronounced, so that the strongest literary compositions were those in which the mystical ideas were most clearly and daringly formulated. According to this "documentary hypothesis," the mysticism of the *Zohar* developed from a system based in philosophy to one based in theosophy. At a certain point, the heroic figure of Rabbi Shimon bar Yoḥai emerges and sort of hijacks the action, and then dominates the majority of the work, much like the role of the Buddha in the Buddhist Sutras.

The main section of the *Zohar*, which runs to more than a thousand pages in the original, concludes with sequences in which R. Shimon bar Yoḥai and his comrades die, in mystical ecstasy, as they are describing the deepest secrets of God, and there are sad, elegiac passages describing the aftermath of Rabbi Shimon's death and the reflections of the comrades on his personality. These culminating texts of the *Zohar* are the *Idrot*, which describe convocations in which several of the participants reveal anthropomorphic visions of the Godhead and perish.

All is not lost, however, as Rabbi Shimon reemerges, either in heaven or in the cave where he had hidden from the Romans in dialogue with the Shekhinah herself, Elijah the prophet, Moses (known as the "Faithful Shepherd" or *Ra'aya Meheimna* in Aramaic) and even God. These later writings are *Tiqqunei ha-Zohar* ("aspects of the *Zohar*") and *Ra'aya Meheimna* and comprise some of the most dense and difficult reading in the entire *Zohar* literature. The dialogues recorded in *Ra'aya Meheimna* and the *Tiqqunim* include references to, among others, the prophet Elijah, Moses, the incarnate *Shekhinah*, and God. There are references to the specific lore of the *Zohar*: to personages such as the legendary Rabbi Cruspedai, to the events of the *Idrot*, and to the revelation of the *Zohar*. The author clearly intended to continue the romantic tradition of the *Zohar* and other contemporary works from thirteenth-century Christian Spain.

Figure 2.3 The entrance to Shimon bar Yoḥai's Cave, Peki'in.

The *Ra'aya Meheimna* is composed in the form of a "book of commandments" (*sefer miẓvot*). Such "books of miẓvot" were a popular genre of medieval Jewish writing. Books of commandments were produced by such seminal figures as Maimonides, Naḥmanides and Menaḥem Recanati. They commonly listed the commandments in the Torah and divulged their inner nature. In accordance with the conventions of this genre, every section of the *Ra'aya Meheimna* is centered on a particular commandment. The "faithful shepherd," Moses, is exhorted by the members of the celestial academy to explain the mystical nature of the commandments, particularly, in the extant sections, the commandments regarding the sacrificial cult. This text has a more coherent literary structure than the rambling, associative *Tiqqunim*.

There are many different theories as to the composition of the *Zohar*. The Safed kabbalists ended to believe that the entire work had been written down some five hundred years after the fact, based on notes left by Rabbi Shimon's son. The great Kabbalah scholar of the twentieth century, Gershom Scholem, attributed the book to the thirteenth-century kabbalist Moshe de Leon, of Guadalajara, Spain, and this idea dominated scholarship in the last century.

The image of Moshe de Leon "writing" the *Zohar* conjures up the image of a Byronic genius spewing out *Leaves of Grass*, *Finnegan's Wake* or *Childe Harold's Pilgrimage*, because once one posits a single author to the work, one calls to mind the romantic model of the turbulent creative genius. In fact, if the *Zohar* did emerge from de Leon's study, it was in his role as at best an ancillary figure, recording the notes of a circle of kabbalists that remains shrouded in mystery. The circle may have included Todros Abulafia or his son, Yosef, as well as Yosef of Hamadan, Yosef Gikatilla, Yosef Angelet and other figures arguably stronger and more influential than de Leon. The *Zohar* is described as a "book" by the author of the last stratum, the compositions *Tiqqunei ha-Zohar* and *Ra'aya Meheimna*, and the circle of the anonymous "elder" described in a recent study by Elliot Wolfson.[6] However, the *Zohar* "book" remained a snowballing collection of random homilies collected by aficionados for the first hundred years or so of its development. The studies of Wolfson, Boaz Huss, Yehudah Liebes, Ronit Meroz, Daniel Abrams and Avraham Elkayam have all served to blur the identity of the *Zohar* as a single composition by a single author, or even a single book.[7] The single authorship of the *Zohar* was a guiding principle of the academic study of Kabbalah until the aforementioned scholars argued for the possibility of multiple authors and levels of composition.

Lately, led by Professors Yehudah Liebes and Ronit Meroz, a view has emerged that attributes the *Zohar* to a series of authors, evolving over a century and a half, reflecting the activities of kabbalists in Spain and possibly including some materials from ancient times. It is certainly hard to escape the gut feeling that the enormous, dense *midrashim* that make up the *Zohar* must have been developed by more than one obscure personality. This latter view may come to be the standard understanding as more analysis is applied to the book and as more early manuscripts come to light.

ABULAFIA

The *Zohar* was not the only source of kabbalistic activity in the early Middle Ages. Another Mediterranean peripatetic, a young scholar and Maimonides expert named Abraham Abulafia was active from the Middle East to Italy.[8] Abulafia disdained the mythos and symbolism of the more widespread "theosophical" Kabbalah, developing a dense theory of sacred names, and a meditative strategy to go along with it. Abulafia was a traveling teacher who excelled in teaching Maimonides' *Guide for the Perplexed*. Abulafia seemed to have been influenced by Sufi and even yogic meditation techniques. He devised a mystical practice, directed toward the attainment of prophecy itself. Technically, the Abulafian form of practice emphasized the contemplation of various sacred names of God, many of which went back to ancient times. This time, contemporary with the initial compilation of the *Zohar*, saw a brief theoretical flowering of a Jewish meditative ethic, between the teachings of Abulafia, Yehudah Albotini's *Sulam ha-Aliyah* and some remarks of the thirteenth-century kabbalist Isaac of Acre.[9]

Abulafian teachings are unique in the annals of directive contemplation in a kabbalistic context in that they involve breath, body position and the linking of noetic textual materials with embodied spiritual practice in order to achieve a spiritual result. Moreover, Abulafian teachings are mystical in the classical academic sense, as they posit experience as the reward or the practitioner. The

guarantee, for example, in Abulafia's practice was that an experience of transcendent light would occur as a result of letter-combination and *hitbodedut*. Hence, Idel avers that all of these prescriptions
for kabbalistic practice in these works do comprise a "living kabbalistic tradition."[10]

As Idel has demonstrated, the Abulafian mystics, such as
the author of *Shushan Sodot* believed that *hitbodedut* meant
a kind of concentration, literally the special concentration
required by the kabbalist in order to combine letters in the
prayer formulae.

Another trend among this small circle is the emergence of the
notion of *hishtavut*, or equanimity. Clearly in this post-Abulafian,
theosophical pocket in the Middle East, people were addressing
the interplay of *hitbodedut, hishtavut* and *devekut*. Yitzchak de-
Min Akko, who of course is linked to the identification of the
Zohar's authorship with Moshe de Leon, was also a recipient
of Abulafian traditions (his cosmopolitanism may have been a
benefit of living in a port city!). He seems to be an early source of
the use of this term, quality of self-abnegation and detachment
that would become a distinguishing characteristic of Hasidism.
Yitzchak de-min Akko used the term *hitbodedut* to refer to spiritual activity, as opposed to the seclusion implied by the verb
poresh. He viewed these techniques as a path to the acquisition
of the "active intellect."[11] Hence his teachings also involve the
evolution of philosophical concepts into the realm of the meditative. The term occurs in Yosef Caro's *Maggid Meisharim*, as well
as being found in Yehudah Albotini's *Sulam ha-Aliyah*, which
was composed in Jerusalem by 1509.

Shem Tov Ibn Gaon, in *Baddei ha-Aron*, also discusses *hitbodedut* as the inward turn to self-discovery. By the time the term has
come to Egypt in the earlier part of the sixteenth century, R. David
ibn Zimra had begun to associate the practice of the *urim ve-tu-
mim*, the prophetic device mounted to the breastplate of the High
Priest, with *hitbodedut*. Even Moshe Cordovero's commentary on
the *Zohar*'s famous composition *Sabba de-Mishpatim* speaks of the
secret of the letters.[12] For Eliahu de Vidas, *hitbodedut* is a source
of "uncovering the supernal source of material being."[13] So, by the
time of its adaptation by Nahman of Breslav, the concept of *hitbodedut* had well morphed into something beyond the mere act of letter
manipulation.

By the time of Abulafia, however, theosophical kabbalists had made *Halakhah*, or the practice of Jewish law, the instrument of religious experience. Kabbalists believed that the practice of the *miẓvot* was the path to both perception of deeper knowledge of the interplay of the Divine and secular worlds. Jewish law was also the venue for achieving positive results in present existence. This preference for *Halakhah* as the instrument of Kabbalah grew from the nature of the *Zohar* literature and the practice that derived from it, which called for the interactive relationship of the law, the deepening perception of reality brought on by its study and the possibility of affecting reality through religious practices or their neglect. Hence, the meditative techniques of Abulafia passed into obscurity until the modern period.

The *Zohar* took about two centuries to be compiled, through the terrible decline of the Spanish Jewish community. Although the first texts began to appear at the end of the thirteenth century, the process of collecting and editing them continued into the late 1500s. At the same time, kabbalistic speculation spread through the Jewish world, East and West. In 1391, the formal persecution of the Jews of Spain commenced, and the rabbinical authorities of Iberia noted an interesting phenomenon, namely, the devotees of rationalist philosophy, such as the ideas of Maimonides and others, were succumbing to the threat of the inquisition and the *auto da fe* with frequent conversions. The devotees of Kabbalah, on the other hand, were accepting martyrdom far more readily, secure in the knowledge that a reward awaited them in the next world. Because it ensured proper behavior under such extenuating circumstances, Kabbalah gained the approval of the rabbinical authorities and it became the official and normative underlying premise of most Judaism until modernity.

SAFED

After the upheaval of the Spanish Expulsion, the Jewish world rearranged itself. Poland and the Ottoman Empire opened themselves up to the refugees of the Expulsion and the Jewish community reconstituted itself in different ways. For some of the remnants of the Jewish community of Spain, the romanticism and messianic pathos of the *Zohar*'s teaching galvanized Jewish mystics from disparate locations. Passing through Salonika as the portal to the

Ottoman world, they scattered through the empire, and a portion of them gathered in the northern Galilee.

Our picture of Jewish life in the Galilee emerges slowly from the mists of obscurity. In 1272, the Jewish traveler Petaḥiah of Regensburg reported seeing Jews gathering at Hillel and Shammai at Mt Meron, in the Northern Galilee to pray for rain. At the same time, the Jews of the northern Galilee reported that Shimon bar Yoḥai's study room was at Meron, and eventually the graves of Rabbi Shimon and his son Eliezer were located on Mt Meron's lower slope. The *Zohar*'s *Idra Rabbah* reports that the townspeople of Meron vied for the honor of burying Rabbi Shimon there (*Zohar* III 144a). The presence of the grave was confirmed by Isaac Luria, who had a vision of Shimon bar Yoḥai at the gravesite. The presence of Shimon bar Yoḥai's grave was a catalyst for medieval settlement in the neighboring town on the opposite mountaintop, Safed.

The Galilee was the *mise en scène* of the *Zohar*. The circle depicted in the *Zohar* wander the mysterious and oblique gullies and passes of the upper Galilee, and uncover great esoteric secrets from the most humble people. This life of mystical quest struck the imagination of the Jewish communities of Europe and the Middle East. Kabbalists of the sixteenth century came there to replicate the events described in the *Zohar* and to continue its mythos. This projection of the *Zohar*'s lore was to transform the spiritual image of the region. The efflorescence of thought and spirituality was so great that in the Jewish popular mind, the golden age of Safed Kabbalah is a sacred memory, significant in general Jewish history. The Safed Renaissance also is the first stage of certain aspects of modernity, such as Jewish settlement in the land of Israel, the eros and charisma of community and social movements, an interest in Messianism and the larger processes of history. These qualities, which come to define Judaism in modern life, certainly begin to coalesce in the Safed Renaissance.

The seething intellectual environment of Safed was stoked by the traditions brought into that Galilee hill town by refugee scholars from throughout the Jewish world. Pietists such as Solomon Alkabeẓ, Rabbi Moses Cordovero, and most of all, Rabbi Isaac Luria created a new mythos of the Jewish mystic as a knight of the Kabbalah, questing for enlightenment and battling the forces of evil and disunity. Each Kabbalistic hero left his mark, physically on the streets of Safed, as the synagogues to which they withdrew for prayer and contemplation await the visitor around every corner and in every alley of the town. In Safed, a community of inspired visionaries and scholars developed the contours of contemporary Judaism.

The Safed kabbalists continued to speculate on the soul's nature. The graves, dolmens and Byzantine ruins signified the lost world and past glories of the *Zohar* and its *mise en scène*. The kabbalists made walking pilgrimages to gravesites, and Isaac Luria, in particular, could identify the souls of the righteous hovering over the grave. For these mystics, the environs of Safed contained a whole society of the dead, hovering over the shrines and tombs of the upper Galilee.

CORDOVERO AND LURIA

In the Safed Renaissance, Moshe Cordovero was the dominant figure, both socially and in the prolific distribution of his writings. Cordovero synthesized a unified approach to the various traditions that had filtered into Safed, by drawing upon the *Zohar*, the teachings of Abraham Abulafia and other traditions, combining them into a vast, baroque system. He collected all of the strains of Kabbalah floating around the Diaspora and synthesized them into one system. This method dovetailed with other approaches to Jewish lore, such as the activities of Cordovero's associate Yosef Caro and his codifications of Jewish law through his commentaries on the legal codes of Maimonides and the Tur and his own law code the *Shulkhan Arukh*, which became the standard for Jewish communities and remains so to this day. Cordovero's method was similarly voluminous and is the foundation of many forms of popular Kabbalah.

Cordovero's most important works include *Pardes Rimmonim* (the Orchard of Pomegranates), which he composed at the age of 27, his *Zohar* commentary *Or Yaqar*, a commentary to the prayer book, *Tefillah le-Moshe*, a popular work, *Or Ne'erav*, a book of ethics, *Tomer Devorah* and his last speculative work, *Elimah Rabbati*. He had a great influence on the composition of such works as Eliahu de Vidas' *Reishit Ḥokhmah* (The Beginning of Wisdom), Isaiah ha-Levi Horowitz' widely circulated *Shnei Luḥot ha-Brit* (The Two Tablets of the Law) and the works of Abraham Galante. More tellingly, Cordovero drew into his circle and under his influence two major figures in subsequent Jewish intellectual history,

Moshe Alsheikh, the biblical exegete and Yosef Caro, the major arbiter of Jewish Law up to the modern period.

Moshe Cordovero and his teacher, Shlomo Alkabez, sought inspiration wandering through Safed and its environs, stopping at gravesites and sites that were increasingly coming to be associated with specific events in the *Zohar*. These ramblings, or *gerushim* (literally "exiles"), were a conscious imitation of the wanderings of the *Zohar*'s protagonists. This romantic relationship to the very topography of Safed also set a certain tone, the idea that there was an inner meaning to be gained from simply being in the land of Israel and recovering the spirituality inherent in the very soil and its history. This sensibility survived into modernity in the various forms of Zionism.

Isaac Luria, the *AR"I* (Acronym for *Adoneynu* ["Our Master"] Rabbi Isaac), was the most important mystic of the renaissance and modern period.[14] His system of Kabbalah took on the force of revealed religion to his followers, as they believed it to have originated with a direct communication from Elijah the prophet. Despite its quiet beginnings, within 30 years Luria's teaching had become central among the mystics of the land of Israel, and within 50 years it was to become the single most powerful influence in Kabbalah.

Luria was born in Jerusalem but left, as a child after the death of his father. His mother moved the family to Egypt, where Luria encountered the *Zohar*, probably from a former secret Jew, or *converso*, from Spain. Upon receiving the *Zohar* he devoted a number of years to mastering its mysteries. Over the course of his short life, Luria developed a particular understanding of the *Zohar* that amounted to a whole new form of Kabbalah. He moved to Safed, at the age of 34, to study with Cordovero, who died soon after. Luria continued to teach a small group of disciples and made a great impression on his circle, though he died barely two years after his arrival in Safed. His life story, particularly as addressed in such enthusiastic works as *Shivhei ha-AR"I* and *Toldot ha-AR"I*, provided a legendary context for his theoretical teachings. A cult of personality, modeled on the *Zohar*'s veneration of Shimon bar Yohai, was carried over into Luria's circle and from there to the movements that accompanied the heretical messianism of Shabbatai Zevi and the sages of Polish Hasidism.

The Lurianic writings, which today comprise at least 20 volumes when purveyed by the Kabbalah Learning Centre, took shape over several generations, at the hands of a number of authors and editors led by Ḥayyim Vital. Vital wrote with loquacious ease. His presentations of the Lurianic system were combined and successively reedited to make up what is commonly referred to as *Kitvei ha-AR"I*, the Lurianic canon. In the first 200 years after Luria's death, only two compositions from the canon were formally published, while hundreds of manuscripts circulated, unofficially, in dozens of formats. Many of the texts were not printed and available in Europe until the nineteenth century. This caused the circulation of many secondary and tertiary recensions and summaries of the Lurianic doctrine. As the "Lurianic writings" evolved there is a growing sense of psychological dread that is evident in them. Gershom Scholem interpreted this sense of catastrophe and dread as a response to the expulsion of the Jews from Spain in 1492. Luria's worldview was nothing less than "a mystical interpretation of Exile and redemption, or even as a great myth of Exile. Its substance reflects the deepest religious feelings of the Jews of that age."[15] However, these qualities may have been primarily the provenance of the later redactors and not the feelings of Luria himself.

It remains a matter of debate whether the most significant figure of the Safed renaissance was Cordovero or his student, Isaac Luria. While Luria seems to have triumphed as Kabbalah emerged into history, the teachings of Cordovero remained important in the development of kabbalistic scholasticism and Hasidism. The Lurianic worldview, with its imagery of a broken, fragmented world, was, for the kabbalists, in constant tension with Cordovero's more positivistic monotheistic understanding.

JERUSALEM

After Luria's death, the Safed community began a period of decline. A plague in 1742 and an earthquake in 1759 accelerated this process. By that time, the Ottomans pacified the Jerusalem area and were able to open the city to development, and the Old City of Jerusalem became a great center of kabbalistic activity. Jerusalem truly came into its own as a kabbalistic center in the eighteenth century, with the founding of a number of kabbalistic academies. The Yemenite Kabbalist R. Shalom Shar'abi came to dominate Yeshiva Beit El, just across from Naḥmanides' synagogue. Beit El was devoted to mystical prayer, taking the words of the Prayer book and recombining them, vocalizing them, pondering the vibrations of the sounds of the letters, spending hours entering the inner meaning of Jewish prayer. The members of the Beit El Yeshivah signed spiritual contracts, binding themselves together in this world and in the world to come. A Moroccan kabbalist, R. Ḥayyim Ibn Attar, built a synagogue, preserved to this day, in the room where Isaac Luria was born. He composed a commentary to the Torah, *Or ha-Ḥayyim*, and his fame spread to Eastern Europe, so that the early sages of the Hasidic movement sought out his circle of kabbalists. Later, groups of ḥasidim from Eastern Europe began to fill the old city and swell the scope of kabbalistic activity there.

SEFARDIM, NORTH AFRICANS AND *EDOT HA-MIZRAḤ*

To this day, the main source of kabbalistic activity, writings and lore is the non-Ashkenazic community of Israel and the Diaspora. In speaking of this community, it is incorrect to use the blanket expression "sefardim," a term that literally means "Spanish." Some elements of the community did, indeed, originate in the refugees of the Spanish Expulsion of the fifteenth century. However, the North African, Middle Eastern and Balkan communities are distinct from each other in many ways, not least in their predilections regarding Kabbalah. The North African communities retained a strong emotional connection to the *Zohar*, which dovetailed with a powerful set of folk traditions, often shared with their Arabic host cultures. For example, the Jews of Draa, in the Atlas Mountains of Morocco, maintained that the *Zohar* was brought to their community in antiquity, shortly after its composition and that, moreover, significant portions of it were lost while fording a stream on the way. From there, according to this tradition, the *Zohar* was distributed throughout the Jewish world, but from the Draa valley. This proprietary relationship to the *Zohar* remained in the Moroccan community, along with a rich tradition of folk practices to rival the devotional qualities of the peasant communities of the Pale of Settlement. The North African Jews venerated the *Zohar* and only came later to the innovations of Isaac Luria's teachings.

By contrast, the kabbalists of the Middle East, comprising Jerusalem, Aleppo, Baghdad, Yemen and points between, developed an advanced interest in Lurianic theory. The students of Jerusalem's Beit El School, led by Shalom Shar'abi, developed a dense linguistic theory of the Lurianic system.[16] This theory was accompanied by a complex practice of kabbalistic prayer, which came to be the dominant element in Middle Eastern Kabbalah. As the Ottoman Empire further consolidated its rule over the Middle East, so the political influence of the Beit El school grew. Beit El kabbalists came to control the Chief Rabbinate of Jerusalem and were thus able to raise funds for the community in the Diaspora, with government sanction. As a result, their complex theory came to be considered the ultimate expression of Kabbalah, particularly by nonpractitioners.

HASIDISM

In terms of sheer numbers, historical significance and social influence, the most widespread and visible incarnation of Kabbalah from the beginning of modernity to the present has been Hasidism. Hasidim are the most visible exemplars of Jewish orthodoxy, and their presence has come to pervade much of the inhabited world. In its brief history, Hasidism has been a religious phenomenon, a popular experiment in mysticism and a social force in Judaism.

Hasidism began its ascent during a period of decline of the old social order in Eastern Europe. The founder of the movement, R. Israel, the "Ba'al Shem Tov," or "good master of the Name" (also known by his acronym, the *Besh"t*) was a wandering preacher and exorcist who moved through Eastern Europe in the wake of the abolishment of the council of the four lands. In his wanderings through the Ukraine and Poland, the Ba'al Shem Tov won over many groups of kabbalists who were operating in obscurity in the wake of the calamitous fall of the Shabbatean movement. The spiritual emphases of these groups dovetailed with the Ba'al Shem Tov's interest: the use of the Lurianic order of the prayer service, special strictures in the area of ritual slaughter and particular interest in ritual purity and the experience of ritual immersion for men. The Ba'al Shem Tov brought a new tone to this society. He was specifically against the asceticism of these groups, substituting a strong emotional aspect and a concern with what can only be called, in contemporary parlance, "spirituality." The Ba'al Shem Tov left few writings, but his recorded remarks reiterate this concern with a religious life suffused with qualities of awe and wonder and a strong psychological awareness. These qualities have continued to bewitch contemporary Judaism in the years since the Ba'al Shem Tov's death in 1760. As with other religious movements, Hasidism may be understood as a classic situation in which the teachings of a charismatic progenitor are interpreted by his students. These secondary and tertiary figures then develop a movement around the original teachings of the founding master, who, customarily, leaves few writings of his own.

The Ba'al Shem Tov's original circle evolved into a religious, mystical and social movement. Among the Ba'al Shem Tov's disciples were rabbis, scholars and, in the case of R. Dov Bear, the "Maggid" of Mezeritch, itinerant preachers. Ya'akov Yosef of Polnoye was the earliest disciple of the Besh"t and wrote the first Hasidic book, *Toldot Ya'akov Yosef.* The Maggid and his students distilled the concerns of the Hasidic movement into a few basic areas. These include the central importance of *devekut*, or "cleaving" to God, as a basic religious attitude. In light of the hasid's relationship with God being primary in his life, he confronts the vicissitudes of life with an attitude of *hishtavut*, or equanimity, a value that had entered into Jewish spirituality during the Jewish encounter with Sufism some five centuries earlier. The Maggid also systematized the Ba'al Shem Tov's paradoxical relationship to asceticism and sensuality. The hasid is primarily concerned with living his life of devekut through the medium of joy in the physical world (*avodah she-be-gashmiut*, worship through the material), yet this celebration of the physical is always balanced by a worldview that transcends present reality and looks into the world of the infinite (*hafshatat ha-gashmiut*, the "casting off" of the material).

In spreading, the Hasidic movement took advantage of the opening of new economic activities for Jews. These served to undermine the Yeshivah-based meritocracy, in which promising young men were bred for lives of penury and study, the better to obtain eventual betrothal to the daughters of the upper classes. Accordingly, by 1772, the ḥasidim were first excommunicated in Vilna, by the leading sage of the time, Elijah, the "Gaon" or sage, of Vilna. The ḥasidim and the *Mitnagdim* (literally "opponents") fought tooth and nail for the better part of the next century, until they made a wary alliance to face their common enemies in the world of the Jewish enlightenment, the forces of Socialism, Zionism and Reform. By the mid-nineteenth century the movement, which had been progressive in its time, had become altogether reactionary.

LINEAGES

As the Hasidic movement grew, it divided itself into a series of lineages or "houses," which were both geographical and ideological. The Maggid of Mezeritch passed on his teachings to a range of students who then spread across Congress Poland, the Ukraine and into White Russia. R. Aaron of Karlin took the movement into the hostile territory of Lithuania, and Menachem Mendel of Vitebsk anchored the community of White Russia, along with R. Schneur Zalman of Liadi who originated the Chabad movement there in the far eastern range of the Pale of Settlement.

Even as the movement grew, the seeds of its decline were nascent in the development of its teachings. Following the death of R. Schneur Zalman of Liadi, a power struggle over his succession ensued. In the course of installing his son, R. Dov Ber, as the new leader of his Hasidic "house," the value of dynasticism for its own sake was introduced into Hasidic social thinking. At the same time, in Galicia, R. Elimelekh of Lizenskh began to preach the doctrine of the primacy of the Tzaddik, or charismatic Hasidic *Rebbe* (the familiar term for Rabbi in Eastern European parlance). A generation later, a descendant of the Maggid, R. Israel of Rhyshin, moved his court to Sadigora in Austro-Hungary and instituted a value of princely opulence as concomitant with the Rebbe's lifestyle. Hence, by midcentury, the Hasidic movement had evolved into an interconnected series of dynastic families of charismatic miracle workers, receiving obeisance from the general population in areas in which they were dominant.

Even as the movement grew, the seeds of its decline were being sown. The battle for succession in the wake of the death of R. Schneur Zalman of Liadi, the progenitor of what would become the Chabad movement, led to the valuing of dynasticism, in that the successors to Hasidic Rebbes were usually their own children, hardly a prescription for maintaining dynamic leadership. The ascent of R. Elimelekh of Lizenskh in Western Galicia also brought about the embrace of the cult of the Tzaddik as vicarious experiencer of

Judaism. This nontheoretical view led to whole areas being dominated by the franchise of a single family, such as the domination of a corner of Western Galicia by Rebbes of the Halberstam family. The mix of dynasticism, charisma, miracle working and the pursuit of wealth inevitably contributed to the decline of the movement.

Against this tendency to decline, certain individuals and lineages pushed back in an effort to retain or evolve the original spark of the Ba'al Shem Tov's teachings. One significant strain dominated the Lublin region of Trans-Carpathia. The Seer of Lublin, so-called because of his ability to discern the inner souls of his ḥasidim, founded a line in which the pursuit of pure and untrammeled spirituality dominated the enterprise, running through his students R. Simḥah Bunim of Psishke and the R. Ya'akov Yizḥak of Psishke, the "Holy Yid (Jew)." All of these Rabbis were united in a concern to resist the decline of the movement into empty posturing and the corruption of miracle working and "zaddikism." Their efforts culminated in the controversial R Menachem Mendel of Kotzk, whose response to the Hasidic world's decline was to sequester himself in his room for the better part of 19 years. Following the death of the Kotzker Rebbe, Rabbi Yitzchak Meir Alter, the Kotzker Rebbe's brother-in-law and his closest disciple, took steps to bring Hasidism into the mainstream of religious orthodoxy, instituting reforms in prayer times, Talmud study and other arbiters of religious normality. Another student of the Kotzker, R. Mordechai Lainer of Izbiz, flirted with forms of religious utopianism and existential relativism. Throughout the history of late Hasidism, certain gifted theologians have managed to effect compelling interpretations of the form, such as R. Kalonimus Kalman Shapira, the Piazezner. Beyond his martyrdom in the Warsaw Ghetto, he left an enduring body of work that includes the bare bones of a meditative system. Hence, the movement remains a platform for compelling theology and religious innovation, and serves as a portal for new developments in contemporary Judaism.

MISNAGDIM

The best phenomenological understanding of the opposition to Hasidism lies in Alan Nadler's work *Faith of the Mithnagdim*.[17] As portrayed by Nadler, opposition to Hasidism really served to verify much of the movement's original self-image: if ḥasidim were sensual, misnagdim were ascetic. Hasidism taught the virtue of unconditional joy, whereas *hisnagdus* was morose. More broadly, Hasidism counseled an embrace of life, while *hisnagdus* advocated for "the sweet bliss of death." Nonetheless, Lithuanian scholastics had their own paragons of kabbalistic endeavor: R. Elijah Kramer, the "Gaon of Vilna," his student R. Yitzhak Eizik Haver Wildmann, and, perhaps most tellingly, R. Shlomo bar Heikel Eliashiv, the author of the work *Leshem Sheva ve-Ohalamah*, an auto-didact whose abilities came through his access to texts, as opposed to transmission from an earlier master. This sanctification of textual study became the last redoubt of *hisnagdus*, and was laid out as an ethical principle by R. Hayyim of Volozhin in his *Nefesh ha-Hayyim*. Eventually, the misnagdim washed their hands of Kabbalah as well. According to their basic ascetic impulse, the basic message of Kabbalah, that one could know the metaphysical underpinnings of things, became thought of as a kind of gratification. Misnagdim preferred to deny themselves of the knowledge of "the secret meaning of things," so that the exemplar of the Lithuanian Yeshivah tradition, R. Yisrael Salanter, could take pride in the fact that his library included not a single kabbalistic work. The world of the Yeshivot sought solace in the Jewish ethical tradition, the short works of ethical instruction, or *mussar*, culled from every stage of Jewish intellectual history.

As hasidim and misnagdim united to face their common enemies, Hasidism became "anti-modern," resulting in the social conservatism that is apparent in the contemporary Hasidic community. As Jews began to modernize in the enlightenment periods of the nineteenth century, Hasidism appointed itself the guardian of the Orthodox faith, so that Hasidism became fundamentalist in nature.

BUILDING BLOCKS

The movements that have been discussed here form the building blocks of the present schools of Kabbalah. Gershom Scholem famously referred to them as the "Major Trends" of Kabbalah, and they are still the components, historically, of what Kabbalah is. The teachings of some of these circles dissolved into the body politic of the Jewish community and exerted an influence on mainstream, exoteric Judaism. As will be discussed in the last chapter, the twentieth century saw tremendous changes in the Jewish demographic, so that the structure of the population at the end of the century could never have been predicted at its beginning. At the same time, Kabbalah has burst the bonds of religious orthodoxy, and there are, as we speak, new schools and circles forming that are social mutations of what has come before. Contemporary Kabbalah embodies a paradox, in that schools of thought that were conservative by definition have now become part of open, postmodern society. Although addressing the historical development of these various movements and circles is necessary, the essence of Kabbalah is in the teachings, which similarly evolved across history into their present state.

CHAPTER 3

KABBALISTIC METAPHYSICS

EMANATION

The basic teaching of Kabbalah is that God emanates Godliness into the phenomenal world, from the realm of the Divine to the physical reality of everyday life.

This Godliness flows into the world as a form of Divine energy. The task of the kabbalist is to receive and direct that energy. The flow of Divine energy into the world eventually came to be called *Azilut*, a word that was in use when the Kabbalah reemerged in Europe in the twelfth century. The flow of Azilut was compared to a world soul, inhabiting the physical world like the soul in the body, like the transference of a flame, in a way that cannot be located or quantified.[1]

This flow of Divine energy was portrayed in many ways by the kabbalists. The most popular and recognized system was that of ten successive stages of God's emanation into the world. These stages are called the *sefirot*, the Divine spheres or emanations. God is infinite and the individual can never experience God directly, but the sefirot are the intermediate elements that sentient beings do experience, to which they can relate and from which they can derive meaning.

According to the most mainstream Kabbalah, the flow of Divine energy through the sefirot creates many signs and symbols which can be interpreted and understood by those who are versed in kabbalistic ideas. Hence, there are many metaphors and symbols for the way that reality flows into the world through the sefirot. The sefirot may be compared to lights flowing out from God's throne in Heaven, to God's chariot and the angels that journey up and down

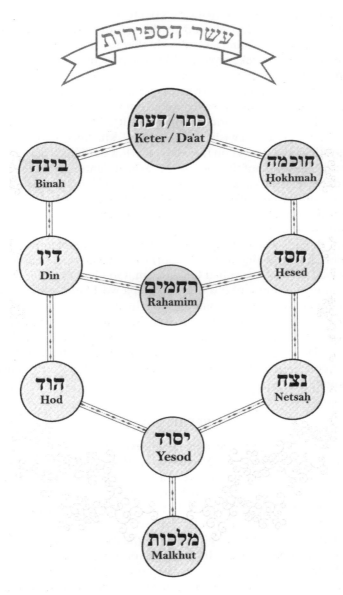

Figure 3.1 The traditional map of the sefirot.

the ladder of creation, and to a series of chambers in a multileveled palace. The relationship of God to the sefirot may also be compared to that of a wick and a candle,[2] in that the flame floats diaphanously above the wick, separated by a gap of pure energy. In all these portrayals, the constant is that here is a perfect divine realm, wholly abstract and separate from phenomenal reality.

The idea of emanation also derived from a trend of thought that influenced the ancient world in late antiquity. Most of the mystics of the West—Greek, Jewish, Christian and Muslim—constructed their mystical worldviews on the basis of a flow of divine energy into the world. The father of this view was the third-century Alexandrian philosopher Plotinus and his school was called Neoplatonism. The teachings of Plotinus are to be found among many early Christian and Muslim mystical writings, including the circles that produced the kabbalistic classic, the *Zohar*.

The Kabbalah also reflected the opposite of the Neoplatonic view, an impulse that saw the world as cut off from the Divine. According to this view, which was called Gnosticism, God had essentially left the building and humankind was living in a world of darkness and pain. Gnosticism was a second great influence on the thinking of the ancient world. In the portrayal of the sefirot, both elements, the optimism of Neoplatonism and the pessimism of Gnosticism, can be found. However, the idea that God had departed the world, the Gnostic conception of a world wholly evil, was a step that Judaism never took.

SEFIROT

The eventual system that became normative for Kabbalah was that God's divine energy emanates into the world through the medium of the sefirot. The sefirot were realms or levels of existence. They first appear in the mysterious little work, *Sefer Yeẓirah*, or book of creation, composed sometime in late antiquity, between the third and the sixth centuries CE. *Sefer Yeẓirah* is a brief pamphlet, no more than 1,600 words long, that nonetheless exerted extraordinary influence for the next thousand years. Written in the concise style of the Mishnah, it describes the process of the world's creation, which comes about, in agreement with the Biblical account, through the power of God's speech. The actual metaphysical process is derived from the 22 letters of the Hebrew alphabet (the component elements, after all, of God's speech) and then from the ten sefirot. Although the *Sefer Yezirah* mentions that the sefirot were the energies that created existence, it did not hold forth on exactly what the sefirot were in their essence. In fact, according to the reasoning in the *Sefer Yezirah*, the sefirot could have been nothing more than the ten integers of the base ten systems.

The idea of each *sefirah* consisting of a certain power or aspect of God came with the reemergence of the Kabbalah in the twelfth century in Western Europe. Kabbalists began to speculate on the essential power contained in each of the ten sefirot. Eventually, these powers were linked with symbolic system, in which every sefirah was an aspect of God that could also be symbolized by dozens of euphemisms and associations. Hence, each of the sefirot spun off a host of subsidiary associations and meanings. The contemplative experience of the kabbalist became the perception of the underlying meaning of present experience, based on the symbols that came up in the kabbalist's experience, from his or her study, religious practice or simply the experience of walking through life. Life became a text, to be interpreted symbolically, according to the language of the sefirot. Hence, understanding the sefirot is a key to understanding the relationship of the infinite God and the material universe; how the perfection of God could radiate into the imperfection of present existence.

As well as being a map of the workings of the Divine, and the structure of the Universe, the sefirot are mirrored in the human soul. Hence, human beings resemble the sefirot isomorphically, and each sefirah can be mapped on the human body. For example, just as there is a sexual energy in the individual, the realm of the sefirah called Yesod, so there is sexual energy in the Divine. In this way, the sefirotic system may be best compared to the system of chakras in Tantrism. Buried in the lore of Kabbalah are hints of nascent meditative practices that incorporate the sefirot in ways that resemble Tantric meditation, although a thorough comparative study is yet to be written. Certainly, vast numbers of Jewish religious practices were reconceived as ways to unify the relationship of the sefirot through the physical act of the *mizvot*.

MALKHUT, YESOD, NEZAH AND HOD:
THE SEFIROT OF THE NEFESH

In order to understand the sefirot and their interrelationship, one should begin "at the bottom," or at least with the most prosaic realm of existence, at the level of the sefirah *Malkhut*. Malkhut comprises the simple fact of existence. All things in the created world, animate and inanimate, share this dimension of existence. To exist in Malkhut is simply to be, and in this way, even inanimate things are infused with a degree of being part of the existence that emanates from God. This would explain the kabbalistic systems that posited reincarnation into inanimate objects, for instance.

The sefirah immediately above Malkhut is referred to as *Yesod*, or "foundation." Yesod is the quality of sexual reproduction—only creations that can reproduce have the quality of Yesod, as the ability to reproduce oneself is granted to sentient beings, but denied to inanimate objects. So, something without the ability to reproduce, such as a rock, would not have attained the second level in the sefirotic hierarchy, namely Yesod. In terms of the human body, just as all of the limbs seem to unite in the act of sexual reproduction, so Yesod is the point of conjunction for the powers of all of the upper sefirot, as they unify with Malkhut. Like all of the intermediate sefirot, it is sometimes viewed as subsumed into the power of *Tiferet*, which is the aggregate of the middle six sefirot. Yesod is often subsumed to the aggregate of the upper six sefirot and described as part of the power of Tiferet.

Above the realm of pure existence, as exemplified by Malkhut, and the added aspect of sexuality, as embodied in Yesod, are two parallel aspects of physical existence. These are *Hod*, "grandeur," and *Nezah*, which is best translated, albeit clumsily, as "everlastingness." Hod refers to the physical scope of a sentient being's existence, while Nezah refers to how long they will live. Hod is generally placed on the right of the sefirotic tree and Nezah is on the left.

The bottom four sefirot are often grouped together at the bottom of the sefirotic tree. Considered together, they make up the sum total of aspects of existence in the physical world. Malkhut defines the simple fact of existence, while Yesod exemplifies the greater complexity of sexual life. Finally, existence is defined by physical complexity and existence across linear time, the realm of Nezah and Yesod. In the human soul, in the larger structure of the Universe and in the dynamics of the Divine realm, these are referred to as the *Nefesh*, the aspect of the soul that governs physical existence.

ḤESED, GEVURAH AND TIFERET:
THE SEFIROT OF THE RUAḤ

The lowest four sefirot address the aspects of pure physical existence. The second set of sefirot govern the emotions, and are made up of the three sefirot *Ḥesed, Din* and *Raḥamim*. These sefirot govern the emotions. Ḥesed ("lovingkindness; also *Gedulah*, "greatness") represents the spirit of pure lovingkindness, while Din ("judgment" also *Gevurah*, "heroism") is the realm of judging and withdrawal.

As well as being the quality of lovingkindness, Ḥesed is also a spirit of pure giving, to the extent that any interaction, even to the point of violence, is also a form of Ḥesed. Din is literally judgment, which also consists of a sort of withdrawal or disengagement. As a Divine quality it refers to God's stern behavior to the world and the Jews. These might seem to be trials and punishments but, in the larger scheme of things, they are only outcomes of what, justifiably, according to Divine justice, ought to happen. Judgment, then, is really what happens when God withdraws to let things take their course. The world only operates through a combination of Ḥesed and Din. If, in one's personal life, one wanted to be an entity of pure lovingkindness, one would only end up as a slave, always subject to the needs of others. If, on the other hand, one withdrew into a world governed by Din, one's behavior would be altogether imploded, to the point of autism. The negative aspects of the emotions also arise from Din, particularly when unmodified by its opposite, Ḥesed. Among these qualities are rage, vengeance and judgment.

The middle way between the two extremes is called *Raḥamim*, "mercy" which is more often considered a force above and beyond the mere combination of Ḥesed and Din, namely the grand sefirah *Tiferet*. Tiferet is also the term used for the aggregate power of the six middle sefirot, Ḥesed, Din, Raḥamim, Neẓaḥ, Hod and Yesod. Together they form an entity that is usually also called Tiferet. It is no accident that the six sefirot of Tiferet are symbolized by the sixth Hebrew letter, *Vav*, which is also an implied phallic symbol, as Tiferet is often portrayed as the phallic male, in union with the receptive feminine spirit of Malkhut, the Shekhinah.

BIBLICAL PARADIGMS

Before we complete the map of the ten sefirot, it would be timely to discuss some of the symbolic language that applies particularly to the lower sefirot. All of the sefirot were subject to symbolization, but no system of symbols was more widespread than associating the sefirot with different biblical paradigms. If certain figures from the Bible were associated with given sefirot, then one could read the Bible as a code for the interaction of the sefirot, based on the way that the actions and life of each figure exemplified the power and qualities of their given sefirot.

For example, the paradigm of lovingkindness, or Ḥesed, is Abraham. He was always giving of himself. He leapt up to host the angels who came to visit him after his circumcision, he pleaded for God's mercy on Sodom and Gomorrah, he even gave his wife away to other men on two occasions, the incidents of Pharaoh and Avimelekh. He obediently followed God's command to bring his

Names of the S'firot	Their Function	Name of God	Vowels	Human Feature	Letter	Feature of the Tabernacle
"Keter" Crown	Complete and total mercy, sometimes without merit.	AHYH	Qamaẓ	Skull and breath	א Alef	Cherubs
"Ḥokhmah" Wisdom	Great mercy, also sometimes without merit, but not like "keter"	YH	Pataḥ	Right brain	מ Mem	Ark Covering
"Binah" Understanding	Mercy, also without merit like above, and from it judgements emerge.	YHVH	Zeirei	Left brain	ש Shin	Ark
"Ḥesed" Grace	Complete lovingkindness to whomever deserves	El	Segol	Right arm and hand	ב Bet	Menorah
"Gevurah" Strength	Complete judgement to whomever is owed	Elohim	Shva	Left arm and hand	ג Gimmel	Table
"Tiferet" Glory	Moderate mercy	YHVH	Ḥolam	Torso	ד Dalet	Alter of Gold (incense)
"Nezaḥ" Eternity	Temperate lovingkindness and what resembles bad is only for the purpose of good.	YHVH Zevaot	Hiriq	Right thigh and leg	כ Kaf	Wash Basin
"Hod" Splendor	Temperate judgement and what resembles good is actually for the purpose of bad.	Elohim Zevaot	Shuruq	Left thigh and leg	פ Pei	Pedestal
"Yesod" Essence	The function halfway between "Nezaḥ" and "Hod"	Shadai El Ḥai	M'lafum	*Membrum Virile*	ר Reish	Sacrificial Altar
"Malkhut" Sovereignty	His Providence and Sovereignty to reveal, and to bring His Divine Presence to the world.	Adonai	-	Crown of the *Membrum Virile*	ת Tav	The courtyard and wings

Figure 3.2 Sefirotic Coefficients 1, from *Kelalei Hatchalat ha-Ḥokhmah*, Aaron Meyer Altshuler.

only son as a sacrifice on Mt Moriah. So Abraham is always a paradigm of lovingkindness and self-abnegation.

Isaac, on the other hand, is the paradigm of judgment. Repeatedly he assesses a situation and does not interact with it. So it is that, on the way to Mt Moriah, he asks his father, "Here is the fire and the knife, but where is the lamb for the sacrifice?" He is given the unsatisfying answer that "God will provide the ram." At the end of his life, old and blind, when Jacob presents himself to steal Esau's blessing, he exclaims, "the hands are the hands of Esau but the voice is the voice of Jacob," and yet proceeds to give the blessing to the imposter. In every situation, Isaac does not respond to what he knows. He continues walking with his father and he gives the blessing to Jacob in spite of the discrepancy. This is the essential emotional quality of Din. Isaac is detached from what he knows, like a judge who doesn't argue the case before but sits on the side passively listening, and then dispassionately rendering the verdict.

An important point, when dealing with the paradigmatic or archetypal role of the patriarchs, is that each one's spouse is in fact a complement for their sefirotic identity. Therefore, just as Abraham is the paradigm of Ḥesed, so Sarah is the paradigm of Din. She personifies the quality of judgment. When she hears Abraham discussing her having a child with the angels, she laughs bitterly and says, "How can I have a child when my husband is so old?" When Abraham palms her off as his sister to Pharoah and Avimelekh, she goes along without protest or interaction. According to a tradition in the Midrash, when she hears that Abraham has taken Isaac up to the mountain to be sacrificed, she dies immediately of a broken heart, not being able to imagine any divine intervention or mercy. Hence, Sarah is clearly the paradigm of Din. Rebeccah, Isaac's spouse, is the paradigm of Ḥesed, just as Isaac is the paradigm of Din. In every situation, she is outgoing and interactive. At the well, when she is first spotted by Eliezer, she is peripatetic; running to and fro, washing his feet, watering the camels; she is like a giving spring of Ḥesed herself. Similarly, as she prepares to help Jacob steal the blessing from Esau, she slaughters the goats, skins them and prepares them as a meal. In every way she is an energetic font of activity as opposed to Isaac's imploded Din. It is this quality of complementarity that leads to depictions in which the sefirot are juxtaposed against one another, compared, in one section of the *Zohar*, to cups balancing on a scale.

The middle way between the extreme of Din and Ḥesed is the middle path of Raḥamim or Tiferet and that sefirah is linked to Jacob. His life is the hardest and most complex and he is least easy to characterize. Jacob's life is punctuated by upheavals and dilemmas: his deceptions of Isaac, Esau and Lavan, the stormy history of his polygamous family, the pain of the loss of his son Joseph and the death of Rachel. These events, and the ambiguous way that Jacob confronts them, are the vicissitudes of life for more people. We do not live according to the absolutes of Ḥesed and Din but somewhere in between.

As Jacob is more complex, so his spousal relationships are more complex. Rachel, his apparent true love and erotic ideal, is the paradigm of Malkhut. In the book of Jeremiah (31.15), she is portrayed as mourning for her children as they are led away into captivity. Yet Leah, the despised first wife, is indicative, in Kabbalah, of something higher, for she is the paradigm of Binah, the next sefirah up, which is a transformative, intuitive feminine wisdom. Therefore, Jacob's relationship with Leah is not without meaning, but that meaning is tucked away in the higher realms of the sefirotic tree.

The four lower sefirot of the cosmic Nefesh also have paradigmatic identities. Aaron, as the original high priest, represents the sefirah Hod, as there is no earthly grandeur, in the Jewish context, greater than the Temple and its cult. It is an article of faith in Judaism that prophecy peaked with Moses, based on the last few verses of Deuteronomy, which state "There was never again a prophet like Moses." Hence, Moses is the paradigm of the sefirah Neẓaḥ, the quality of everlastingness. Joseph, because of his great forbearance in the attempted seduction by his master's wife is considered the paradigm of Yesod, for sexual energy is a mute force that must be conquered and channeled. Finally, King David, the once and future king, is the central paradigm of Malkhut, as his descendant will be the King Messiah.

These paradigmatic relationships enter the liturgy of practiced Judaism on the holiday of Sukkot when, over the course of the seven days of the holiday, each one of the "seven shepherds" are invited into the Sukkah for one of the festive meals. This ceremony, the inviting of the "guests," invokes the role that the observance of the holiday has in shoring up the dimensions of existence. Every one of the days of Sukkot "repairs" one of the lower sefirot, until the autumn holiday season climaxes with the rejoicing of the Law on its final day.

THE SHEKHINAH, A PRIMARY KABBALISTIC SYMBOL

The most common and widespread kabbalistic symbol is that of the Shekhinah, which is the main association of the sefirah Malkhut. The Shekhinah bears the largest number of representations and symbols in classical Kabbalah. She is also the symbol that has to the greatest extent crossed over into normative Judaism. The development of the idea may be traced in linear history, archetypal psychology and as the resolution of the ongoing problem of the nature of an abstracted God's function in the world; immanently. How did it come to be that normative Judaism accepted what, in other cultures, could only be referred to as the "Goddess archetype?"

Originally, the Shekhinah was thought of as simply part of God, the aspect of God that literally "dwelt" in the First and Second Temples in Jerusalem, in the innermost part of the Temple that was known as the Holy of Holies. With the destruction of the Temple, that presence, the "indwelling," or *shekhinah*, went into exile. From that point on, the Shekhinah was invoked by the Rabbis as being a spectral presence of Divine immanence. When ten Jews prayed together, when three recited the grace after meals, when two people studied together or when even one man stood enrobed in his prayer shawl and tefillin, the Shekhinah was seen as resting upon him.

The Jews of the Second Temple Period referred to the Shekhinah constantly, and these references were always rendered in the feminine terms of the word itself. This constant reference to the Shekhinah, which is always modified, declined and conjugated in the feminine form, led to her being conceived as a female presence. This impulse, in turn, led to the Shekhinah's association with all of the images of suffering femininity in the Hebrew Bible: the childless widow of Jeremiah's Lamentations; Rachel dying in childbirth; Ariel, the ruined city of Jerusalem in the book of Isaiah (29.1). Gradually, in the public mind, the Shekhinah became a woman, a feminine aspect of God. Finally, the later midrashim began to refer to her as separate from God, God's consort, His celestial bride and wife.

As God's consort, the Shekhinah drifts in and out of union with God. Their unification came to be seen as the time that divine energy suffuses the world, while their separation was seen as the deathly, Gnostic alienation of the Diaspora experience. The *Bahir*, the first "kabbalistic" text, wedded the immanent notion of God's presence to four female images: the bride, the princess, the Shekhinah and

Names of the S'firot	The Six Directions	Rewards	Astronomy	Days of the Week	On the Human Head	Biblical Wildernesses	Combination of YH"V	Types of Metal
"Hesed" Grace	South	Wisdom	Moon	Sunday	Right eye	Etam	YV"H	Silver
"Gevurah" Strength	North	Wealth	Mars	Monday	Right Ear	Shur	HV"Y	Gold
"Tiferet" Glory	East	Progeny	Sun	Tuesday	Right Nostril	Sin	VY"H	Copper
"Nezah" Eternity	Up	Life	Venus	Wednesday	Left Eye	Paran	YH"V	Tin
"Hod" Splendor	Down	Power	Star	Thursday	Left Ear	Zin	HY"V	Lead
"Yesod" Essence	West	Peace	Saturn	Friday	Left Nostril	Kadmut	VH"Y	Mercury
"Malkhut" Sovereignty	The Inner Temple	Grace	Jupiter	Shabbat	Mouth	Sinai	-	Iron

Figure 3.3 Sefirotic Coefficients 2, from *Kelalei Hatchalat ha-Hokhmah*, Aaron Meyer Altshuler.

the mother. Secondarily, a number of archetypal Freudian or mystic images were also equated with the Shekhinah. Among them the field, sea, land, date, stone, and others, form the essential rhetorical basis of the *Zohar*'s symbolism. In the earliest kabbalistic writings, the Shekhinah is symbolized by various feminine images in the phenomenal world: the hazelnut, pomegranate, dove, well, cave, moon, the rose and all other archetypal symbols of femininity.

The *Zohar*, the writings of Yosef Gikatilla and other sources located the Shekhinah in the functions of the sefirah of Malkhut. This led to the bequeathing or sharing of a number of qualities between the sefirah itself and its symbolic representations. Based on its representation in the Shekhinah, Malkhut has at least four aspects. It is changing and transient, like the Rose, which changes from Red and White. In this way, the Shekhinah is unstable, not set in any one place, requiring a unifying act to gain stability. In order to stabilize itself, the Shekhinah or Malkhut must be unified with the upper sefirot; hence the aim of religious practice is to unify the Shekhinah with the upper realms. In the same way, it is a terrible error to isolate the Shekhinah, as it leads to the gnostic error of "cutting the shoots." Simultaneously, the isolation of the Shekhinah apart from other elements of the Divine is an act of gnostic dualism, the transgression of Elisha Ben Abuyah in the classic account of the four who entered the Pardes. On the other hand, the act of unification is the object of much kabbalistic practice, which is to say much conventional Jewish religious practice, interpreted according to the Kabbalah.

The Shekhinah also has a potential for evil. The problem of evil is resolved, in the sefirotic system, structured as being an aspect of the image of the "Tree of Knowledge of good and evil." This creates a possibility of devouring, Kali-like element of the Shekhinah, as well as a possible struggle between the divine and the demonic within the Shekhinah. There are traditions that Malkhut has its upper roots in Din, and that its harsh "shadow side" derives from those roots in Din.

While the *Bahir*'s paradigm for the relationship of God and the Shekhinah was the paradigm of the father and the daughter, the *Zohar* emphasized the sexual union of the divine and the corporeal. More than any other sefirah, depictions of the Shekhinah conform to the idea of a Divine archetype. Exegetically, the reader of the divine text could see Shekhinah in any invocation of nature, femininity or simply the immanent presence of God. There are, therefore, more symbols for the Shekhinah than for any other of the sefirot. The entire phenomenal world is full of symbols of Malkhut.

Nonetheless, the experience of Malkhut is also fundamentally empty. She is essentially a receptacle for influences from above. Later understandings of the Shekhinah referred to her as Nukvah, namely "the indentation." Other, strong traditions refer to her as merely the "crown" (*atarah*) on the engendering phallus of the upper sefirot.

ḤOKHMAH, BINAH AND DA'AT

The highest sefirot that may be grouped together as being analogous to the highest levels of the soul, namely the *Neshamah*. While *Ḥesed*, *Din* and *Raḥamim* compose the psychological function of the universe, the sefirot *Ḥokhmah*, *Binah* and *Da'at* (acronym: ḤaBaD), by contrast, compose the highest levels of Divine intellect.

Ḥokhmah ("wisdom") is empirical wisdom; the accumulation of facts and figures, the ideas that can be demonstrated by experience. It is often portrayed as the Divine seed that is nurtured in the engendering womb of the feminine *sefirah*, *Binah* ("intuition"). Ḥokhmah is empirical wisdom, the accumulation of facts and figures, the ideas that can be proven and the principles that are demonstrable from experience. It is on the right side of the sefirotic tree, analogous to Ḥesed, because it is ultimately bestowed from without. It is often portrayed as the Divine seed, or Pistis, that is nurtured in the engendering Womb of the feminine sefirah Binah, which is analogous to the Greek Sophia. It is often linked to the beginnings of things, as, "the beginning of wisdom is the fear of the Lord" (Proverbs 1.7). In the Aramaic translations of the Bible, the first word, *Bereishit* (commonly "In the Beginning") is usually translated "in Ḥokhmah."

Binah is intuitive wisdom. It is the knowledge of how things interact, without a prior assessment of their natures. Because of this intuitive quality, it is also a feminine archetype. All images of the womb are understood as being symbols of Binah. In many creation narratives, the sefirot are portrayed as being born out of the womb of Binah. Binah is often considered an older mentor to the *Shekhinah*.

Da'at ("Knowledge") is the highest attainment of wisdom, the union of *Hokhmah* and *Binah*. It is therefore, the highest human attainment. Sitting at the apex of human spiritual attainment, it is also the *Malkhut* of God, the root and base of the beginning of the Divine reality, a system of sefirot whose nature is seen as being beyond human comprehension. The earliest kabbalists said that the fact that the theological nature of Da'at is not described in the Bible or Talmud is nothing more than proof of its transcendent nature.[3]

When the highest sefirot are grouped together, they form the highest level of the soul, namely the *Neshamah*. As Hesed, Din and Rahamim govern the psychological functions of the individual and the attendant World Soul, so the sefirot Hokhmah, Binah and Da'at (acronym: HaBaD) compose the highest levels of human consciousness. The Neshamah is portrayed by many, including the theorists of Chabad Hasidism, to be a part of the Divine, bequeathed from above. Upon an individual's death, the Neshamah will be gathered up and reabsorbed into the Divine.

DA'AT AND KETER

The idea of the sefirot could not remain just as it was; the idea, when queried by the essential tenets of Judaism, bred contradictions that had to be resolved. The construction of Da'at as both the highest level of human attainment and, simultaneously, the Malkhut of God, led to a theological problem, which was resolved by an early generation of kabbalists. The first adjustment of the sefirotic system came about as a result of a theological problem with the nature of Da'at. According to the essential teaching of the sefirot, just as Malkhut is the ground of all sentient existence, so Da'at, the highest level of the sefirot, is the ground of God's existence. It is the ground of God's existence as God, even as it is the highest achievement of the human consciousness. That being the case, there is a theological problem. God, by definition according to Jewish theology, should be infinite, abstract and unbounded by limitation. Human beings, by definition, are limited and concrete, and their minds are limited as well, so if one argues that Da'at is the point at which God overlaps into human consciousness, then one is limiting God. By locating God in the human mind, which is necessarily limited, one has committed an act of idolatry, by confining the idea of God, in any way. Hence, God cannot be in Da'at. So, early in the development of the doctrine of the sefirot, a distinction was made between Da'at, as the sefirah that is the highest attainment of human consciousness, and *Keter*, which is a parallel sefirah that is the beginning of the purely divine realm of God. Da'at and Keter are often used interchangeably in discussions of the sefirot, but, when examined closely, they refer to two different, parallel realms: Da'at, the sefirah as it exists on the human level, and Keter, the aspect of the same sefirah when considered on the Divine level. Most often, Keter refers to the most ineffable, unreachable aspect of Da'at.

Another way that the kabbalists addressed this problem was to conceive a negative theology with speculations about a void, or emptiness, sitting at the apex of the sefirotic tree. This void, which was called *Ayin*, shared the qualities of other voids in other religious traditions, a religious phenomenon known as *apophasis*.[4] The relationship of Ayin to the rest of the created world came over time to share qualities with other theories of the void in other religions. In many spiritual systems, the void, which is reserved for the most ineffable, unapproachable dimensions of existence, becomes, over time, a place that can be accessed by the adept. Two examples are the Christian mystics who spoke of attaining the "Cloud of Unknowing," or the endless speculations of Buddhists, particularly of the Madhyamaka school.

AZMUT AND KELIM

As kabbalistic doctrines began to spread in the early phases of the movement, a problem arose, mainly as the result of the widespread acceptance of Maimonides' conception of an abstracted and unlimited God. That problem was: are the sefirot actually God, or is God ultimately separate from the sefirot? If the latter is the case, does God pour divinity into the sefirot, as if they are instruments or vessels of Godly energy and flow? The first point of view, that the sefirot were essential to God and actually *part* of God, was called the doctrine of *azmut*, or "essence." The idea that the sefirot were vessels for God, into which God poured Divinity, and that God remained essentially abstracted and separate from the sefirot, was called *kelim*, or "vessels." In Jewish theological terms, the idea of kelim was certainly preferable, as it backed away from characterizing God in physical terms by separating God from the essence of the sefirot. The early kabbalists, in general, followed the tradition of aẓmut, up to and including the main sections of the *Zohar*. The later strata of the *Zohar*, the works known as the *Tiqqunim* and *Ra'aya Meheimna*, however, followed the understanding of kelim, that the sefirot were vessels for the Divine flow. Although some subsequent kabbalists remained believers in the doctrine off aẓmut, the influential Safed kabbalist Moshe Cordovero adhered to the notion of kelim, or vessels, and this became normative in Safed. With widespread subscription to the doctrine that the sefirot were vessels of God, the Safed kabbalists were prepared for Isaac Luria's notion of the breaking of those vessels.

The *Zohar* contains many apparently contradictory traditions, and readers of the *Zohar* had a hard time trying to sort them out and synthesize one, consistent metaphysical system. One idea that merged over the course of the *Zohar*'s reception was that every sefirah has within it a set of ten inner sefirot, so that there are sefirot within sefirot. The notion of the inner sefirot was first posited by the early kabbalists of Provence and Gerona, but exegetes of the *Zohar* eagerly brought it to the fore, in order to reconcile variant traditions inside the vast *Zohar* literature.[5] This tradition became normative in Safed, at the hands of Moshe Cordovero. It also became part of one of the most popular kabbalistic rites, namely that of counting the Omer, the intermediate days between Passover and Shavuot, which will be discussed in a subsequent chapter.

THE FOUR WORLDS

Tension over the Jewish idea of the abstraction of God versus the symbolic and mythic aspect of the doctrine of the sefirot led to another spin on the nature of the sefirotic system. The doctrine of the Four Worlds of creation posited at least three sefirotic systems, overlapping on one another, with a highest system above the other three which was not subject to sefirotic portrayals, corresponding to the wholly abstracted God posited by Maimonides and the other Jewish philosophers. This series of four systems was called the system of the worlds of creation, three sefirotic systems that sit one atop the other, with a fourth system that cannot be portrayed in terms of the sefirot.

The names of the worlds are taken from the principal verbs used in the Creation accounts of Genesis. The lowest level, consonant with the most prosaic reality, is the world of action, *'Assiyah*. Above

Names of the S'firot	Their Functions	Countenances	Feature in the Name YHVH	Milluyim	In the Torah	In the Soul
"Keter" Crown	Incredible mercy	"Arikh Anpin" Patient One	Point of the Yod	Name 72	Trope	"Yeḥidah" Essence
"Hokhmah" Wisdom	Great mercy	"Abba" Father	Yod	Name 72	Trope	"Ḥayah" Life
"Binah" Understanding	Mercy, and from it judgements emerge	"Ima" Mother	Hei	Name 63	Vowels	"Neshamah" Breath
The 6 Sefirot of Hesed, Gevurah, Tiferet, Nezah, Hod, and Yesod	Function of the law in merit	"Zeir Anpin" Impatient One	Vav	Name 45	Crowns	"Ruaḥ" Spirit
"Malkhut" Sovereignty	Righteous judgement	"Nukva" Female	Hei	Name 52	Letters	"Nefesh" Physical Existence

Figure 3.4 Sefirotic Coefficients 3, from *Kelalei Hatchalat ha-Ḥokhmah*, Aaron Meyer Altshuler.

the world of action is the phenomenal world, the world of formation, *Yeẓirah.* Above the world of formation is the world of pure
creation, *Briah.* The highest is the world of abstracted and inacces-
sible divinity, as posited by Maimonides, the world of *Aẓilut.*

The doctrine of the four worlds is hinted at in early Kabbalah,
and the term "worlds" was used as a euphemism of the sefirot in a
number of early sources as well as the main sections of the *Zohar.*
The normative conception of the four worlds emerged in a number
of sources that began to circulate in the fourteenth century, such
as the later strata of the *Zohar,* the sections called *Tiqqunim* and
Ra'aya Meheimna, as well as a short contemporary work known
as the *Mesekhet Aẓilut.*[6] Kabbalists embraced the doctrine of the
four worlds because it served to help reconcile contradictions in the
Zohar. If one text contradicted another, the interpretation would
be that the first text referred to reality in the world of, say, Beriah,
while the second described events in the realm of Yeẓirah. The doctrine of the four worlds was also applied to the laws of prayer, in a
fashion that will be discussed elsewhere in this study.

POPULAR KABBALAH

The doctrines described in the preceding chapter found their way
into the mainstream of Jewish belief and practice and remained
normative from the thirteenth century to early modernity. Practices
based on the doctrines of the sefirot, worlds and the mythos of the
Shekhinah are standard, from the rites of Hasidism to the liberal
movements of Western Judaism. They were eclipsed by rationalist
thought in Western Europe and the Americas, but have resurged in
recent years, in various venues.

These ideas gelled as normative Jewish practice in the catalyst
of the Safed renaissance, where a number of central figures in
Renaissance-era Judaism came to rest, as it were in the Galilee
hill-town of Safed. As stated in an earlier chapter, one impetus
to the development of Safed as a spiritual center was the revelation of the *Zohar.* This led to the desire, on the part of the Safed
kabbalists, to recover the practices of Rabbi Shimon bar Yoḥai and
his circle. Safed was home to pivotal synthesizers of the Kabbalah,
such as Moshe Cordovero, as well as influential biblical exegetes,
such as Moshe Alsheikh and those operating in his style of homi-
letics. Ethicists such as Eliahu de Vidas and Moshe Ibn Makhir

were in close proximity to the central halakhic authority for the post-expulsion age, R. Yosef Caro, author of the code of Jewish law (the *Shulkhan Arukh*), as well as a number of sweeping commentaries on earlier codes such as Maimonides' *Mishneh Torah* and the *Tur*. Caro's aim was to standardize and make regular the nature of Jewish practice from Persia to the New World. His presence lent tremendous credibility and authority to the interpretation of the law that underlay the Safed kabbalah, namely that the law was no more than a way to regulate the actions and interactions of the sefirot across the panoply of the worlds of creation. The association of all of these forces in the international Jewish community gave the Safed Kabbalah the muscle of central influence in the Jewish world in all of its quadrants: North Africa, Western Europe, Eastern Europe and the Middle East.

Certain understandings define this general kabbalistic spirituality. The shared ideas of the Safed Kabbalah were that Divinity flows into the world and can be channeled, through the medium of the sefirot. Moreover, when the world was created, certain catastrophes occurred which are still in effect today. The world requires the religious practice of pious Jews, expressed through a grave and rigid adherence to Jewish law, to sustain it in its present sinful state. The Torah, in its written and interpreted form, is a living entity of the Divine, emanated into the world through the medium of the sefirot. These principles, which will be unpacked in subsequent chapters, form the basis of kabbalistic Judaism.

The religious experience of this worldview was one of dynamism and enmeshment. The kabbalist was enmeshed in his experience, his mind literally given over to multiple levels of consciousness. There was the sacred text that lay before the kabbalist, the symbols of which merged with symbols of the phenomenal world. At the same time, there were the demands of Jewish law, its strictures and mizvot. The season according to the Jewish calendar also skewed the interplay of Divine forces. The kabbalist employed a contemplative consciousness, reading reality through these interlocking groups of symbols, enmeshed in multiple levels of consciousness, in what Jung called "The Symbolic Life." At the same time, the process of the opening of the consciousness was, as Elliot Wolfson has characterized it, a dynamic process of always uncovering, a constant unfolding of the revelation of the inner meaning of things, that never ends or comes to a final, ultimate revelation.[7] This view derived from the reading of the whole *Zohar* as a sacred text on par with the Bible and the Talmud. The doyen of such a view, in Safed, was Moshe Cordovero, who read the *Zohar* through the prism of the later compositions, *Tiqqunei ha-Zohar* and *Ra'aya Meheimna*. Scholars refer to these understandings as "Cordoverean" Kabbalah[8] and they represent a mainstream of popular opinion. They are, arguably, the central Kabbalah of popular Judaism, the trunk of the beliefs of the Safed kabbalists, the dominant view of Hasidism and the characteristic form of much North African Kabbalah. This kabbalistic Judaism was popular and widely understood and accepted in the Jewish population. Elsewhere I have referred to these understandings as kabbalistic "common religion" or civil religion and they remain normative to this day in great swaths of the contemporary Jewish community. For the avant-garde and the elites of the community, however, these ideas were liable to be supplanted by the conclusions of Isaac Luria, which would move far beyond the premises of this basic Kabbalah.

CHAPTER 4

LURIANIC KABBALAH

The ideas presented up to this point make up the most widespread and practiced kabbalistic beliefs among the broadest swath of classical Judaism. From the point of view of the kabbalists, these doctrines are most often associated with Moshe Cordovero and his school. He was a socially dominant figure in Safed, and the majority of the community swore fealty to his ideas. He was also the teacher, briefly, of his successor, Isaac Luria, who brought another interpretation to the metaphysics of the *Zohar*, one that, among the cognoscenti, would come to supplant that of Cordovero. This deeper understanding, which is often cited but not widely understood, introduces a whole new mythos into the ideas of the Kabbalah.

The basic difference between Cordovero's Kabbalah and Isaac Luria's interpretation lies in the nature of the *Zohar* itself. The *Zohar* is a vast collection of writings, some two thousand pages of closely spaced Aramaic. The main sections differ from the earlier and later strata in their Aramaic dialect as well as their theological ideas. The earliest strata, the "Mishnahs," "Toseftas" and the section called "The Hidden Midrash" (*Midrash ha-Ne'elam*) seem to comprise an early, somewhat unformed aspect of the doctrine. The main sections are concerned with the interplay of the sefirot, while the penultimate sections of the *Zohar*, the *Idrot*, present a new set of imagery altogether. The works *Tiqqunei ha-Zohar* and *Ra'aya Meheimna* bring in a number of ideas that do not appear elsewhere in the *Zohar*, such as the doctrine of the four worlds of Creation.

In making sense of the *Zohar*, Cordovero chose to emphasize the interplay of the sefirot as vessels for the divine flow, along with the doctrines of the four worlds. That is to say, he emphasized the conclusions of *Tiqqunei ha-Zohar* and *Ra'aya Meheimna*, seeing them as the culminating texts of the *Zohar*. At the same time, in combining the contradictory passages in the vast corpus of the *Zohar*, Cordovero described an increasingly complex sefirotic tree. The four worlds Aẓilut, Briah, Yeẓirah and 'Assiyah each included ten sefirot, with an additional ten sefirot in each of the original ones. Across the many volumes of Cordovero's voluminous writings, there were palaces above, palaces below, demonic realms, errant souls and kelippot, all arranged in a minutely detailed infrastructure drawn from the various accounts presented in the *Zohar*.

Luria was moved by a different aspect of the *Zohar* literature. His system owed much to two separate traditions in the *Zohar*: the Creation traditions that form one of the kernels of the Zoharic traditions and, especially, a group of texts known as the *Idrot*. A contemporary scholar, Rabbi Martin Cohen, has surmised that Luria's interest in the *Idrot* may have arisen in the crevices of his own psyche. The circumstances of his life are well known. Having lost his father as a child, Luria's mother moved the family from Jerusalem to Egypt, where they came under the protection of a wealthy uncle, to whose daughter Luria was betrothed at the age of 12. Accordingly, Luria based his system of Kabbalah predominantly on the *Idrot*, which concern themselves with the tale of a celestial family, which Luria saw as rent asunder by catastrophe. The key to this projection of Luria's own psychological trauma lay in his reading of the *Idrot*. Acting as armchair psychologists, from a vantage point of nearly five centuries on, one could say that Luria saw the doctrine of his own family's trials in the relationship of the cosmic family.

THE IDROT

The *Idrot* make up a special genre of writing in the *Zohar*. The word *idra* means "threshing floor," and the texts themselves describe meetings called by Shimon bar Yoḥai with his circle, in which they gather at a threshing floor to share their ultimate visions of God. In the two major texts, the *Idra Rabbah*, or "great Idra" and the *Idra Zuta* ("lesser Idra"), important members of the circle die in the course of describing the moment of conjunction of the higher and earthly planes of existence. In the *Idra Zuta*, which is customarily placed at the end of the last volume of the *Zohar*, Shimon bar Yoḥai passes away with his son Rabbi Eliezer. Hence, for anyone reading

Figure 4.1 The traditional site of the Idra, Ein Zeitun, Galilee.

the *Zohar* as mere literature, the *Idrot* were already "flagged" as particularly powerful texts.

Another compelling aspect of the *Idrot* is that they present an entirely new symbolic system, connected to the system of the sefirot and the Worlds but still different and distinct. This was the doctrine of the "countenances" (Hebrew: *parẓufim*). The countenances comprise a celestial divine family. At the apex of the cosmic structure is the Patriarch, who existed, was named, variously *Arikh Anpin* ("the patient one"), *'Attika Kadishah* ("the ancient Holy One") and, after Daniel 7.22, *'Attik Yomin*, the "Ancient of Days."[1] 'Attik Yomin has a flowing mane and beard, the "hairs" of which are conduits for divine energy onto his son, Zeir Anpin (literally the "quick face," or "impatient one"). Zeir Anpin's consort, *Nukvah*, represented the *Shekhinah*, although she lacked the bold assertiveness of the Shekhinah and seemed to be a mere receptacle for the Divine flow of energy from above. These three countenances, *'Attik Yomin*, *Zeir* and *Nukvah*, make up the system presented in the *Idra Rabbah*. The *Idra Zuta* presents two more countenances, *Abba* and *Imma* (literally "father" and "mother"), figures who, in the hierarchy, were positioned between *Arikh Anpin* and *Zeir Anpin*.

Of these figures, Zeir Anpin is the most compelling. Standing midway between the highest level of the Divine and the earthly world represented by Nukvah, or the Shekhinah, he commands the duality of life. He has two eyes, seeing the good and the evil in the world and two nostrils. One nostril bequeaths life giving breath, while the other dispenses the flared nostril of divine anger. Into the two chambers of his brain flow the combined pleas and accusations of the people Israel. Zeir functions as an intercessor between the phenomenal world and the transcendent world, much like the role played by the Demiurge in classical Gnostic literature.[2] It is little wonder that, in the Sabbath hymns composed by Isaac Luria, he saw himself as Zeir Anpin and rendered the hymn in the first person! In his system, Zeir Anpin, the child of Abba and Imma, is continually reborn and endowed with consciousness by his parents. This process of the birthing of Zeir is the real aim of Lurianic Kabbalah.

This strange and somewhat dark vision of a celestial royal family presented a dilemma to the Safed kabbalists. Where did it fit in the narrative of the sefirot and worlds that was already the popular discourse of the kabbalists? Moshe Cordovero made the decision that the doctrine of the countenances was simply another way of referring to the interaction of the sefirot. Nukvah, of course, was comparable to Malkhut. Zeir Anpin was a way of referring to the aggregate power of the middle sefirot that the *Zohar* called Tiferet, namely the aggregate of Ḥesed, Din, Raḥamim, Neẓaḥ, Hod and Yesod. 'Attika Kadishah stands for the aggregate of Ḥokhmah, Binah and Da'at. Hence, the parẓufim and the sefirot and the sefirot were analogs of each other—different ways to describe the same system. This, in fact, was the intention of many transitional texts in the Zohar that speak of the countenances in exactly this way. For example, in one of the most widespread influences of the *Zohar* onto popular Jewish practice, the Sabbath meals were portrayed as representing one of the three major countenances.[3] The *Zohar* concluded that the Friday night meal represented the Shekhinah, the Sabbath day meal represented Arikh Anpin and the third meal stood for Zeir Anpin. Clearly, the countenances were considered "bundles" of the sefirot at that transitional moment, even though their portrayal in the *Idrot* would be much more complex. Otherwise, the complexity of the presentation of the countenances in the *Idrot* presented a problem for the Safed kabbalists, one that was strikingly resolved by Isaac Luria.

LURIA'S UNDERSTANDING OF THE COUNTENANCES

Isaac Luria read the *Idrot* in a different way than his predecessors. Cordovero and his students saw the countenances presented in the *Idrot* as a gloss, or reworking of the sefirotic system. Luria saw them as representing a new system altogether. Luria did not believe that the sefirot were the center of mystical reality any longer. They were merely a theoretical system that was no longer in operation. They had been replaced by the interaction of the parẓufim. The object of mystical practice was to unify this celestial family, which was suffering various crises. This, of course, was very compatible with his own biography, which seems to indicate that he may have greatly yearned for a family made whole.[4]

Luria portrayed the countenances as beset by a number of crises that came about in the course of the world's creation. As a result of the breaking of the vessels of creation, which will be discussed presently, Abba and Imma, while being consorts, could no longer "embrace" directly, but were compelled to turn their backs to each other to fend off threats from without. In this "back to back" embrace, Abba and Imma could not attend to the nurturing of their child, Zeir Anpin. Consequently, a concern of Lurianic Kabbalah became the turning of Abba and Imma to a face-to-face embrace, that they might better conceive Zeir Anpin, their child, and then nourish him with their shared flow of consciousness, which Luria calls *moḥin*. Hence, the aim of Lurianic Kabbalah, and the focus of the thousands of pages of "Lurianic writings," is the reconciliation of this divine family. The breaking of the vessels, and the "fixing" (Hebrew: *tiqqun*) of the sundered cosmos is a side issue, albeit one with its own development and history.

Another aspect of Luria's teaching is his adoption of the theory of the worlds of creation. As has been stated, this theory is not in the main sections of the *Zohar*, but comes from the last sections and other works composed in the early fourteenth century. One of the tasks of all kabbalists who worked with the *Zohar* was to portray

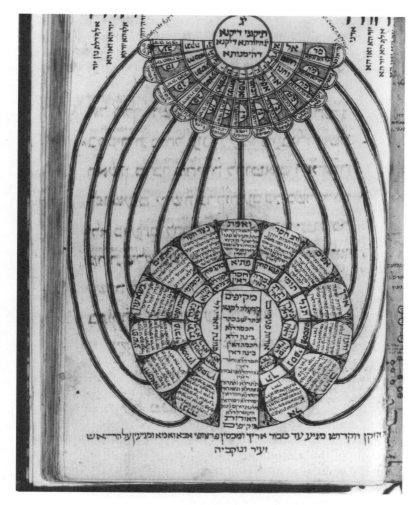

Figure 4.2 The Beard of Zeir Anpin (Jewish Theological Seminary library, manuscript Mic. 4599, f. 345; used by permission).

the mechanics of the earlier parts of the *Zohar* in terms of this later doctrine of the worlds. For Luria, the creation of the worlds was conceived as a series of successive sefirotic structures derived from a single source, like the globules of pure crystal that are inflated by a glass blower, or the nesting cylinders of a telescope or antenna.

The worlds, in the process of their creations, move in and out of each other in an almost phallic tumescence. Luria also assigned aspects of the kabbalistic structure to the worlds of creation. For instance, the Palaces and Divine throne room discussed in the main parts of the *Zohar* were assigned, by Luria, to the second world, Briah, an assignment that would resonate in his understanding of prayer, as will be addressed in a subsequent chapter.[5]

THE CREATION OF THE WORLD

A more widely known aspect of Lurianic teaching is his doctrine of the "breaking of the vessels" of creation (Hebrew: *shevirat ha-kelim* or *shevirah*). Although this idea is much bandied about in intellectual circles, it is not widely understood. At the same time, scholarly portrayals of Kabbalah give weight to this tradition. The narrative of the breaking of the vessels was based on some of the most widespread and compelling ideas in the *Zohar*. In order to understand this tradition, and its true role in general Kabbalah, one has to go back to its origins. One reason that the breaking of the vessels gained such credence as a tradition is that it derived from some very old and very central ideas in Kabbalah.

The AR"I built the tradition of the breaking of the vessels on the basis of the ideas that had already appeared in the *Zohar* and elsewhere; he did not conjure the idea out of thin air. The *Zohar* itself has a very specific creation tradition, which is repeated many times in the course of that work and even appears on many kabbalistic amulets. The purpose of the *Zohar*'s creation tradition is to describe how the "something" of the World and present existence came out of the "nothingness" of reality prior to the World's creation. The main account is first cited on page one of the first edition of the *Zohar*. The *Zohar*, then, as its publishers and most redactors originally conceived it,[6] begins this way:

> In the Beginning of the King's decree (*be-reish hormanuta de-Malkah*), the concentrated spark (buẓinah de-kardinuta) engraved engravings in the supernal luster (*tehiru ilaah*), so that there emerged from within the concealed of the concealed, the beginning of the infinite, a vaporous mass fixed in a ring; not white, black, red or green, or any color at all. When the measure extended, it produced colors shining within. Within the spark

Figure 4.3 The Void, according to the Lurianic System.

there gushed a spring from which the colors were formed below. The concealed of the concealed, the mystery of the Infinite, broke and did not break through its aura. It was not known at all, until, from the force of its penetration, one high and hidden point shone, the supernal concealed one. Beyond this point nothing is known at all. Therefore it is called *reishit*, the first command of all.[7]

This text, which is repeated a number of times throughout the *Zohar*, describes the moment that the real, phenomenal world begins to emerge out of the abstraction that is God. Above the phenomenal world is the nothingness; the indescribable void that is God's ground of being. Into this void comes the prism-like "dark, hardened spark" which engraves, literally, the guidelines of reality. After the space is created in the primordial aether, colors splay out through the hardened spark like light through a prism.

Figure 4.4 The Face of Zeir Anpin.

This text is a recurring theme in the *Zohar* and is rewritten in a number of versions and compositions. One of these, *Kav ha-Middah* (literally "the plumb line") portrays the processes of the "hardened spark" in a slightly different way. In this and other versions of the story the "dark, hardened spark" is described as a plumb line, with which God the architect measures out the contours of the created universe.[8] These later glosses introduced new elements and contained many obscurities and inconsistencies that had to be reconciled through interpretation. The later interpretations also reflected extraneous developments in Kabbalistic thought for which these creation texts provided a rationale. So it was that the idea of the created world entering a void, hewed out and potentially devoid of holiness, was the existential basis of kabbalistic contemplative circles as early as the thirteenth century.

THE FALL AND THE DOCTRINE OF
DIVINE CATASTROPHE

Another component of the Lurianic doctrine was taken from the *Zohar*'s motif of the Fall in the Garden of Eden as the fundamental catastrophe in human existence. This point of view should be contrasted with that of conventional Judaism, for which the Garden of Eden account of Genesis 2.4–3.24 has very little influence on subsequent Jewish practice and theology. The events of the Garden of Eden make little difference in Jewish life or practice. Classical Judaism has no doctrine of original sin, unlike Christianity, which derives its doctrine of original sin from the account of Eve and the serpent.[9] The *Zohar*, on the other hand, *does* have a strong doctrine of the Fall. Adam, the primordial man, was party to a catastrophe that spun the Universe off its axis. This understanding of the Fall is not necessarily antithetical to Judaism but it is somewhat foreign, reflecting as do so many Zoharic traditions, a very particular selection of midrashic sources. It also may reflect the kabbalists' exposure to Gnostic materials coming from groups that were active during the birth of the early Kabbalah, from the Manichaenism of late antiquity to the Catharism, and other esoteric traditions that were present at the recrudescence of Kabbalah in the early thirteenth century.[10]

The *Zohar*'s doctrine of the Fall exemplifies its understandings of the relationship between the Torah, time and sacred history. According to the *Zohar*, the Bible does not describe events that have already happened, but rather describes things that are happening in the present as well. So in every generation, the Flood is still occurring, the Jewish people are leaving Egypt and wandering in the desert and the Jews are, necessarily, in the process of receiving the Law. Reincarnation (Hebrew: *gilgul*), to the extent that a given school of kabbalistic thought believed in it, created a dynamic situation in which the tensions and rivalries of those previous generations continue into contemporary history. Biblical figures confront one another again, renewed through reincarnation, by which all the lineages from the Garden of Eden to the present are among humankind.

The latter sections of the *Zohar* emphasize that the Fall in the Garden of Eden began a chain of catastrophes that continue to unfold, creating and reinforcing the fallen condition of existence. From the Talmud to the *Zohar*, there are common themes of seduction, the power of evil and the role of the demonic in present existence. A number of classical Rabbinic sources describe the seduction and defilement of Eve by the serpent. One Talmudic tradition portrays the serpent as having implanted *zohama* (impurity) in Eve.[11] This tradition recurs throughout theosophical kabbalah.[12] The defilement of Eve implants a demonic strain in the primordial genealogies, as well as creating what the great Jungian psychologist Erich Neumann called the "elementary negative archetype of the feminine."[13] Hence, present reality is an admixture of good and evil. It is the kabbalist's task to attain the former and overcome or eliminate the latter.

Among the authors of the *Zohar*, there was dissension regarding the level at which the Fall occurred in the hierarchy of the sefirot.[14] Did the catastrophe of the Fall only occur at the level of Malkhut, or did the rupture in the cosmos brought about by Adam's sin go all the way into the highest realms of Hokhmah, Binah and Da'at? The *Zohar* sees the nature of contemporary experience as coming from a series of catastrophes. The first of these catastrophes was the Fall, the second was the Flood and the third was the sin of the Golden Calf. Each of these catastrophes created *kelippot*, or obstructions, which required rectification, a process known as *tiqqun*. For the *Zohar*, this rupture, Adam's mixing of the "darkness" into the purity of the higher sefirot sets in play the chaotic struggle of the holy and the demonic, a central part of the worldview of the *Tiqqunim* and *Ra'aya Meheimna*. All of these ideas are present in the *Zohar*; Isaac Luria did not coin them in response to the Spanish Expulsion.

The Fall also brought an ongoing presence of demonic forces, among them Samael, the head of the demons, who serves, at the best of times as God's "hit man" in the lower worlds. His consort Lillit is the queen of the demons and *doyenne* of crib death and nocturnal emission. The initial generations of covenantal history are devoted to an attempt to correct the fallen state of humankind through the refinement of the Jewish nation's genealogical line. At the same time, the nations that surround the people Israel are made up of the residue of the refining process, implying that the gentile nations contain, genetically, traces of the demonic.

The serpent is an agent of the sefirah of Din, but he is also an agent of all chaos and upheaval. The seduction of Eve brought about defilement in the sefirah Malkhut, caused by the miscegenation of the serpent and Eve. The *Zohar* describes the *kelippah*, a husk or obstruction, as the metaphor for Din. In this way, the mizvah of circumcision, which strips the *kelippah*—in this case, the foreskin—away from the infant, is therefore linked to the sexual sin of the serpent and Eve.[15]

Lurianic Kabbalah came to emphasize the autonomy of the forces of evil. These forces are personified in the *kelippot*, which in this case are the shells of the vessels that were left following the shattering.[16] In the simplest terms, these broken shards form the pockets of Din in which evil originates. In developing the doctrine of the kelippot, Lurianic kabbalists exploited a literary distinction between the *Idrot* and the main sections of the *Zohar*. In the main sections, the sefirah Din is most often associated with an incarnate aspect of Divine judgment. In the *Idrot*, however, the generally negative image of Din as portrayed in the sefirotic system is replaced by the *dinnim* (the plural of *din*), a demonic pantheon. These diffuse "dinnim" are simply evil, with their origins in a theory of Divine waste and detritus. This is opposed to the *Zohar*'s less dualistic view that evil is simply the concentration of Divine judgment.[17]

Another component of the Lurianic creation myth lies in the *Zohar*'s tradition that, prior to the construction of the present world, God built many other worlds and destroyed them (Hebrew: *boneh 'olamot u-maharivan*), a tradition that emerged in the classical midrash.[18] Still later traditions would interpret the seemingly random lists of past kingdoms in the book of Genesis as referring to such destroyed worlds. As Luria himself put it:

The first worlds died, because they were made without a tiqqun but the craftsman, Keter Elyon, Attika Kadisha, the wondrous craftsman, came and set forth the male and the female and these sparks were purified and gave way.[19]

Finally, the *Zohar* includes a number of interpretations of a biblical passage referring to the "death of the Kings of Edom" which were interpreted as supports for the Lurianic system.[20] For Luria, the idea of the prior, destroyed worlds was telegraphed by this passage relating to the sons of Esau, the vanished "Kings of Edom." The passage itself is dense and enigmatic:

> These are the Kings who reigned in the Land of Edom before any king ruled over the Israelites. Bela the son of Beor reigned in Edom, the name of his city was Dinhabah . . . Yovav . . . Husham . . . Hadah . . . Samlah . . . Saul of Reḥovot on the river . . . Ba'al Ḥanan son of Akhbor . . . And when Ba'al Ḥanan son of Akhbor died, Hadar succeeded him as king; the name of his city was Pau and his wife's name was Mehitabel daughter of Matred, daughter of Mei-Zahav. (Gen. 36.31–9)

The Kings of Edom portrayed in the passage were, for Luria, an allegory to the lost worlds of prehistory. Each of the "Kings of Edom" is a metaphor for a prior, destroyed world.[21] The *Idrot* and its related text the *Sifra de-Ẓeniuta*, or "hidden book," repeatedly allude to this tradition. These enigmatic allusions preoccupied the Safed commentators who later developed a number of systematic expositions of the "death of the Kings."[22]

Luria developed his kabbalistic doctrine from all of the afore-mentioned ideas: the Divine family of the *Idrot*, the creation of the World in primordial space, the Fall, the "deaths of the Kings of Edom" and the doctrine of four worlds of creation. The anthropomorphic images of God and the Cosmos were essential to his teaching. When all of these factors were combined in equal measure, the sefirotic infrastructure came to be depicted in more and more complex and unstable terms.

ẒIMẒUM AND THE BREAKING OF THE VESSELS

Luria combined the account of the "engraving of reality" in the *Zohar*'s initial creation story with the doctrine of the Worlds, from the later sections of the *Zohar*. The bold innovation in Luria's understanding of those Zoharic traditions was his description of the act that preceded the creation of the worlds. Luria portrayed creation as taking place as an act of Divine thought. In prehistory, the infinite Ein Sof, "filled all the worlds." When God wanted to create the world, He withdrew, in order to hollow out a space. In an image that would haunt much of subsequent Kabbalah, Luria described God's withdrawal or contraction, in order to create the "primordial aether" described in the *Zohar*'s creation traditions, as described above. This withdrawal, an inner contraction in order to create a space of existence, is called *ẓimẓum*. *Buẓina de-kardinuta*, the "hardened spark" is the power of Din that withdraws the light of Ein Sof, the infinity of God. Its engraving action created the first emanated vessels.

God then began to create the worlds of Creation and the sefirot inside of them. Like a glass blower filling molten glass with his breath, God inflated a series of chambers in the universe that hardened and formed the vessels of creation, based on the afore-mentioned doctrine of the vessels of emanation. This space was, nonetheless, not completely empty, for it contained a residue of the Divine light.[23] Each molten vessel hardened, with a bit of the divine light clinging to its structure, as milk would cling to the sides of a glass. This absorbed or adhering light was called the *reshimu*, or residue. The light flooded downwards, and as it withdrew, it created the vessels (*kelim*), which were then refilled with light.[24] The vessels that had been created to contain the Divine light were unequal to the task, "because of the greatness of the light"[25] or, as in the words of Luria's student Yosef Ibn Tabul:

> When the light of the Emanator descended to its location in the vessels, in order that it could rule and complete all the worlds to benefit from its light, to reveal the hidden, then the Keter and the Ḥokhmah and the Binah could bear it, but the seven lower (vessels) shattered. Since they shattered, the light turned above in the first three and fled upwards . . . and made a union above.[26]

These vessels shattered as a result of their inability to withstand the renewed influx of Divine light. Upon the shattering of the vessels, the light divided into two forms, the inner and the surrounding light, so that "whatever the Wisdom could bear was made the inner part and the rest become the surrounding light." This surrounding light was greater than the inner light, for it was not constrained by the vessels that hold it. The inner light, which is less strong, is more fit to be contained in the lower vessels.[27]

Another account in the Lurianic writings portrayed God's role in the creation of the vessels as that of a cosmic potter.[28] In this

version, the *zimzum*, or withdrawal, is followed by the renewed
outpouring of divine light into the vessels. God formed the vessels
with specific thicknesses,[29] making their shell out of Din. The most
meticulous craftsmanship went in to the uppermost vessel, Keter.
The sefirot were emanated as vessels that are in turn flawed by
impurities. As the light descended through the sefirotic structure,
the vessels became more and more crude. The residue (*reshimu*) of
the light remained in the vessels as it passed through the sefirot.
Keter retained the largest amount of light, as it was the strongest
and highest vessel. The lower vessels of Ḥokhmah and Binah, however, could not stand the light. Like a building collapsing from
within and imploding, the structure of the sefirot then descended to
a lower level. The zimzum muddied all the material beneath itself,
creating an unformed mass. The vessels formed ten intermediate
points inside the mass. As the Divine light of Keter moved farther
away, the lower vessels become more and more "darkened."

The effect of zimzum was to realign the whole cosmic order into
lower positions in the structure of the Worlds. The catastrophe of
"death of the Kings of Edom" actually refers to this realignment of
the sefirot. Ḥokhmah and Binah moved out of the world of Azilut,
forming the parzufim of *Abba* and *Imma*. The seven lower sefirot,
upon descending into the world of Briah became the countenances
Zeir Anpin and *Nukvah*. The light began to flow through the reconstructed vessels, which became new conduits for the Divine light
that again emanated out of Keter. Having shattered, the vessels
were reassembled as the countenances.

The first three vessels for the Divine light were the strongest and
they retained the ability to receive the light. The vessels of Keter
were not broken at all. The vessels of Abba and Imma remained
whole from the front but were broken from behind. Only the rear-
most sections (*aḥorayyim*) of the upper three sefirot were broken.
The lower six were not as strong and so they shattered completely.[30]
The seven lower vessels of Zeir and Nukvah are altogether broken,
"forward and back."

Another distinction brought about by the breaking of the vessels
concerned the gender balance of the structure. Luria's earliest writings stressed that in the initial emanation, the Universe was initially
"conceived" and emanated in an unstable or unbalanced way. This
lack of balance caused the seven lower sefirot to be unbalanced by
forces of Din. One of the aspects of Luria's understanding of *tiqqun*,

or Divine repair, was the rebalancing of the structure, with the ten sefirot contained in the five parzufim.[31] In a complementary relationship, Hokhmah would be balanced by Binah, the force of Din would be countered by that of Hesed and Tiferet would be unified with Malkhut. This balance is referred to, euphemistically, as the "weighing on the scale."[32] Without this gender balance, the sefirotic hierarchy could become dangerously unstable.

Part of this task of balancing was attending to the familial relationship of the countenances. As stated earlier, the breaking of the vessels was a great catastrophe which caused the forces of Din, the sefirah of harsh judgment and withdrawal, to break away from their dilute status within each of the other sefirot and concentrate together. These concentrations, in turn, became the malevolent kelippot, or husks of impurity, blocs of malevolence in the cosmic order. According to Luria, This implosion of judgment had interrupted the erotic union of the upper countenances Abba and Imma. Formerly face-to-face, they now stood back-to-back, in order to protect themselves from the Din assaulting them from all sides. As a result of the interrupted union of Abba and Imma, the uppermost countenance, 'Attika Kadishah, could no longer emanate directly onto the lower sefirot. The "kings," that is, the seven lower sefirot, died and dropped beneath the upper world of Azilut. In response to this collapse of the sefirotic structure, the higher sefirot then diminished their light in order that the lower sefirot could better receive it. The entire sefirotic structure moved down a degree, into the second world of Briah, or Creation. The task of the adept became to move the countenances Abba and Imma from their barren "back-to-back" embraces, which must be redirected into fecund, "face-to-face" unions.[33]

Throughout the twenty some-odd volumes of the "Lurianic writings" (which are really the compiled works of several generations of Luria's students) this story is retold in many ways, and through many analogies, in which the same processes are portrayed in terms of different metaphors.[34] Each version invokes different motifs and images from the *Zohar*. Hence, the Lurianic motifs of the "death of the Kings," the back-to-back embrace, the conception (*ibbur*) of the lower countenance Zeir, the *zimzum* and re-emanation of the Divine into the vessels, which then rupture, all describe the same set of phenomena. Subsequent editors, in collecting the various accounts, saw them as separate stages and combined them into an enormous collection of doctrines, the aforementioned *Kitvei ha-AR"I*, or Lurianic writings.

IMPREGNATION

After he settled in Safed, Luria turned his attention to the inner relationship of the Divine family. For the kabbalist, the response to the breaking of the vessels was to turn Abba and Imma into their face-to-face embrace, the better to conceive the child, Zeir Anpin and bring about his coming to consciousness. The goal, or "great tiqqun," which would come about as an aspect of the Messianic Era, would be the reconciling of Abba and Imma which would channel various kinds of Divine flow. The face-to-face union of the parzufim, in the Messianic age, would be characterized by an unobstructed flow of spiritual energy through the astral bodies, from 'Attika Kadishah to Nukvah.

In a poignant metaphor of childhood, the conception of Zeir is equivalent to the conception of the natural world. Zeir Anpin is nursed in the womb of Imma through the stages of his life: impregnation (*ibbur*), suckling, conferring of consciousness (*mohin*) and maturation.[35] The nourishment of Zeir by Abba and Imma takes place through the development of his mohin, which figuratively means "consciousness." The *Idrot* mention the mohin in an unsystematic way, as the "brains" or inner intelligence of the parzufim. Luria portrayed the mohin as the sefirot that underlie and enliven the parzufim. During the conception of Zeir, the mohin unify in various kinds of unions and conjunctions, as in the *mohin de-gadlut* or "greater" mohin, and the *mohin de-katnut*, or "lesser" mohin.[36] Initially, the development of the mohin was known as the "function" (*hanhagah*).[37] Over the course of time, the entire Lurianic system became known as the hanhagah, including all of the various channels of Divine effluence, the sefirot and countenances, as well as such phenomena as the zimzum, shevirah and tiqqun. The thrust of all of these processes was the bringing of the Messianic age. At that time, according to an emerging idea in Lurianic Kabbalah, the mohin would be permitted to flow through all of the countenances, bringing about the production of new souls and, presumably, resurrection of the dead.

Only toward the end of his life did Luria come to his understanding of a broken world, portrayed within the Divine body.

This portrayal of the broken world as an injured body came about after the death of his son, for whom he had messianic expectations. The Divine body was Adam Kadmon, the Primordial Man, who stands at the peak of the Aẓilut, the emanated world. Adam Kadmon contains the sefirot and parẓufim. The *Zohar* had already established that that Adam Kadmon serves as a metaphor for God, the Cosmos, the Torah,[38] and, by association, the Temple and its sacrificial cult.[39] The later strata of the *Zohar* had interpreted the anthropos teachings as forming a response to humankind's present dilemma. Interaction with the Divine is possible through projecting the Divine anthropos onto the human model. Specific rituals begin this transformation and repair the wounded body of the universe.

LURIA'S INNOVATION

To reiterate, Moshe Cordovero emphasized the sefirot and the worlds as the center of his kabbalistic system, while incorporating a vast number of extraneous ideas drawn from the various teachings and texts that had been collected in sixteenth-century Safed. For Luria, however, the image of the parẓufim overwhelmed that of the sefirot as the focus of his teaching. Luria's teaching was initially an attempt to reconcile the sefirotic structure, with the multiple possibilities of the four-worlds doctrine, combined with the mythos of the "hardened spark" occurring within it and the countenances laid across it. Eventually, he could only conclude that the ideal structure had ruptured. The final versions of Luria's own teaching posited the unstable processes of the Divine as taking place in the context of the Divine anthropos, Adam Kadmon and its countenances.[40]

The *Zohar*'s tradition of the death of the Kings of Edom underlay Luria's central existential statement: that the Divine superstructure described in the *Zohar* had in fact collapsed and ruptured. There had been a "breaking of the vessels," which had occurred within the structure of the Primordial Man, Adam Kadmon. God had withdrawn from the phenomenal world, and then refilled the empty world with Divine energy through a series of Cosmic vessels. However, the vessels of holiness ruptured, leaving the world in a state of spiritual chaos. The most widely circulated recensions of Lurianic doctrine began with the ẓimẓum, and then continued

KABBALAH: A GUIDE FOR THE PERPLEXED

the account in terms of outpouring and withdrawal of the Divine essence into the vessels.[41]

Much of Luria's mystique lay in the fact that he actually wrote very few compositions himself, no more than a few pages of commentaries on the *Zohar*. Like Jesus or Lao Tzu, he was an enigmatic figure, who arrived, stated his message and moved on. At the end of the twentieth century, two scholars, Ronit Meroz and Yosef Avivi, launched separate projects to analyze the Lurianic canon. Working separately, they arrived at largely the same opinion, namely that Luria's teaching developed over the course of his short life and was divulged to his disciples in a series of stages. The themes of loss and upheaval reflect his own personal history, and the final elements, namely that of a catastrophe occurring in Adam Kadmon, was only completed following the death of his son, for whom he had messianic aspirations, and prior to his own sudden death.[42]

After his death, Luria's interpretation slowly gained credibility among practitioners of Kabbalah and his model of the broken vessels spread throughout the Jewish world. His reading of the *Zohar* became the most widely disseminated understanding. His influence is ubiquitous in subsequent Kabbalah and Hasidism, particularly the pervasive presence of the ideas of zimzum and the breaking of the vessels.[43] The existential condition of zimzum seized the imaginations of subsequent kabbalists as the "Lurianic writings" were put together, embellished and emerged with greater force among later redactors, particularly in the works of Meir Poppers and Ya'akov Zemakh who, in their recensions, generated much of the messianic Eros and literary pathos identified by Gershom Scholem.[44] The account of zimzum became, for many kabbalists, an account of where they stood in the world, their existential state. To this end, the image of the void in which existence occurred was repeated many times as a motif by subsequent kabbalists. One famous restatement of the tradition is that of Nahman of Breslav in his famous "Torah of the Void":

For the Blessed Holy One, because of His compassion, created the World. For He wanted to reveal his compassion, and if there was no World, to whom could He reveal his compassion? So it was that he created the Creation, from the beginning of the emanation (Azilut) until the central point of the physical world, in order to show His compassion. And when the Blessed God wanted to create the world, there was no place to create it. For everything was Infinite (*Ein Sof*), so he contracted His light to the sides, and from this contraction (*zimzum*) was created a void, and in this void flowed time and space, which is the Creation of the World. And this void was necessary to the creation of the World, for without the Void, there was no space! The zimzum of the void can't be understood or imagined, except in the future. For one must say of it, two opposite things, existence and non-existence. For the void is from the *zimzum*, when God, so to speak, withdrew His Godliness from there, as if there was no God there.[45]

For R. Nahman, the act of zimzum means that God is basically absent from creation, a very un-Hasidic and challenging notion. The voided nature of present reality created a powerful pull in another part of the Eastern European intellectual world. The most influential student of the Gaon of Vilna, Yitzhak Eizik Haver Wildmann, opens his presentation of the entire Lurianic system, *Pithei She'arim*, in this manner:

It is written in the words of the kabbalists, and in the writings of (Luria) that the object of the zimzum was that Man should have free will. Hence there was a place for evil in this world . . . and that Man should be able to choose to cleave to the Good . . . Now the Rav (Luria) revealed the secret of the zimzum through parable and hint . . . So the infinite drove his light to the sides . . . equally, in a circle . . . and the after the light contracted from the place that was left void, this became the place that the worlds were set up.

For the Lithuanian moralist, the most important aspect of the void is that it creates the possibility of Free Will, with its attendant responsibilities. Although they draw different conclusions from this existential possibility, R. Nahman and R. Yizhak Eizik Haver both understand the nature of present existence as being the result of its creation in a void. This void is potentially, in its most radical interpretation, devoid of God's presence. The idea of this context for existence remained pronounced among the Eastern European kabbalists. In the premodern period, in the Ukraine and Lithuania, these theologians were already describing the emptiness of current existence, paving the way for the disaffection, alienation and anomie that were to be described by Kafka and others.

THE SCHOLARLY PERCEPTION OF LURIA

The Lurianic themes of zimzum, the breaking of the vessels and the subsequent need for tiqqun, or repair, had become a compelling theme among European kabbalists from the nineteenth century onward. This emphasis continued in subsequent intellectual theory, as it became a fulcrum of the thought of Gershom Scholem, the major Jewish scholar of the twentieth century and the founder of modern study of Kabbalah. Scholem understood Luria's teaching of the breaking of the vessels as a historical metaphor. The themes of upheaval and catastrophe that Luria described were, according to Scholem, a reaction to the expulsion of the Jewish community from Spain in 1492. In his preeminent work, *Major Trends in Jewish Mysticism*, Scholem made the following presentation of this opinion:

After the Catastrophe of the Spanish Expulsion, which so radically altered the outer aspect of the Kabbalah if not its innermost content, it also became possible to consider the return to the starting point of creation as the means of precipitating the final world catastrophe, which would come to pass when that return had been achieved by many individuals united in a desire for "the End" . . . The Kabbalah of Isaac Luria may be described as a mystical interpretation of Exile and redemption, or even as a great myth of Exile. Its substance reflects the deepest religious feelings of the Jews of that age.[46]

Writing in the years immediately following the Holocaust and the establishment of the State of Israel, Scholem saw Kabbalah as reflecting the Jewish experience in history. Scholem emphasized messianic aspect of Luria's ideas, in which the kabbalist was compelled to act to repair the broken world and thence prepare the way for the Messiah. Scholem saw the recurrence of this paradigm in the ascent of Zionism, a movement that had leapt to prominence with its promise of assuaging the bitter Jewish experience in the twentieth century. Scholem was most impressed by the idea of

Luria responding to history, in this case, the trauma of the Spanish Expulsion in 1492, as opposed to the possibility of Luria as the frightened child, reflecting the sundering of his own family and his flight to Egypt.

In recent years, Moshe Idel has taken issue with a number of Scholem's conclusions regarding the larger sweep of Kabbalah. Scholem had portrayed the concept of zimzum as a novelty of Lurianic Kabbalah. Idel has demonstrated that the idea of zimzum far predated Luria.[47] Building on this discrepancy, Idel has questioned the extent to which the development of mystical movements should be attributed to a mass psychological response:

> Given the absence of Lurianic discussion of the expulsion issue, Scholem's universally-accepted theory regarding the interconnection of the two is in fact only one of the many options that could easily be advanced . . . But Scholem's thesis, or any other like it, places psychology between history and theosophy, and a theory that attempts seriously to connect all three must be carefully proved . . .[48]

Idel's critique of this particular psychological interpretation of mysticism is persuasive. It is plausible to analyze the development of mystical systems, which are so full of psychic contents, as projections of psychological states. Mystical movements may serve as mass responses to national trauma. However tempting it is to interpret mystical social phenomena as responses to specific historical events, it does not ultimately do justice to the religious power and ongoing spiritual validity of such movements. At the same time, it cannot be denied that the Lurianic interpretation of Kabbalah, in its choice of themes from the *Zohar* and other earlier traditions, expressed many themes that would come to be part of modernity, including images of upheaval, destruction, chaos and a sense of God's having abandoned the world. Whether these themes are presented by the kabbalists of early modernity, or their spiritual descendents in the art and philosophy of the twentieth century, it is clear that this tradition extended into modernity and beyond Judaism.

CHAPTER 5

THE SOUL

The belief in a soul that lives on after death is one of the most universal of all religious beliefs. Many religions are structured as they are *because* of their belief in an immortal soul. Many forms of Christianity are centered on the career of the soul and its afterlife. There are many Christians and Muslims who observe their religions because of their concern over the fate of their immortal souls, the rewards of Heaven and the travails of Hell. If all of the peoples of central and southeast Asia were to subscribe to their ancestral religions, then a majority of the people in the World would not only believe in the soul, but also in its reincarnation as one of the given premises of their culture.

Given that belief in the soul is central to so many religions, Judaism's reticence and ambivalence about soul doctrines seems peculiar. It is as if Judaism doesn't care about the afterlife—it doesn't structure its rules for behavior on the eventuality of reward or punishment. Yet Kabbalah did produce, over the course of its history, an increasingly complex and demanding doctrine of the soul. These teachings regarding the soul are among the most resilient aspects of Kabbalah, influencing the folk religion of the masses. References to the soul punctuated the speech of European, American and Middle Eastern Jews of the twentieth century. The behavior of Jews attending the death of a friend or relative is informed by kabbalistic values. Yet, if asked to describe the career of the soul in its afterlife, most Jews would be hard pressed to give a coherent answer.

The reason for this ambivalence lies in the Hebrew Bible. There is very little indication of an afterlife in the Torah or the prophets. The patriarch Jacob, upon hearing of the death of his favorite son Joseph, refuses to be comforted, exclaiming (Gen. 37.35), "No, I will go down mourning to *Sheol* with my son!" The very word *sheol*, meaning "the underworld," expresses this reticence, for it is derived from the Hebrew word *sha-al*, "to ask." In biblical theology the afterlife is itself a question, meant to be unresolved until it is experienced. Much later, Ecclesiastes (3.21) asks, "Who knows if the spirits of animals descend while the spirits of human beings ascend?" The implication is that the events of the afterlife are a mystery not understood by those yet alive.

The Hebrew Bible was so reticent about the subject of the soul that in the time of the Second Temple (some 2,000 years ago), a significant number of Jews declared that people just *die*, and that there is no afterlife at all. These people, known as the *Sadducees*, then proceeded to structure their whole understanding of Judaism around this premise. If there was no afterlife, what was the meaning of life? Why, to live as long as possible, of course! How would one go about living as long as possible? A plain reading of the Torah indicated that God would foreshorten a person's life for the committing of certain sins. The most important life strategy, according to the Sadducees, was to atone for one's random sins as quickly as possible. The one vehicle for this atonement was through bringing sacrifices at the Jerusalem Temple. This is the morality of the biblical Job, whose righteousness is defined by his bringing sacrifices the morning after his children indulge in frivolity at parties, lest they committed any sin the night before (Job 1.4–5). It is not surprising that the Sadducees were themselves the wealthy aristocrats of Jerusalem who maintained close ties to the Temple priesthood and could arrange to have sacrifices brought at will.

There was also something cynical in this view, implying that life could be manipulated and "bought" through the Temple cult. Like the selling of indulgences by the Church in the time of Martin Luther, the mechanistic view of morality was criticized by other groups of the period. One group that particularly objected to the Sadducees' belief in "no afterlife" was the Pharisees, the Rabbis of the Talmud who were the founders of mainstream Judaism. They were generally opposed to the Sadducees' social elitism, teaching a popular, nonliteral form of Judaism that was not based in the Temple cult but in the study of the Torah and in individual prayer and service. In this case, the Sadducees' view was most objectionable because of the problem of evil, of the suffering of the righteous. How could it be that there are righteous saints who suffer in their lives, and wicked people who prosper? No, declared the Pharisees, there *must* be an afterlife that would rectify the injustices of present existence, but what could it be?

In order to identify and provide an afterlife tradition, the Pharisees refined a tradition that had been evolving to that period. This tradition was called the "revival of the dead" (*tehiyat ha-metim*), or, in Christendom, the "resurrection." The tradition declared that at the end of days, upon the coming of the Messiah, the dead would literally rise from their graves and reassemble themselves in Jerusalem. Intimations of this tradition appear in the later books of prophecy in the Hebrew Bible, in works such as Ezekiel (37.1–14) and Daniel (12.2–3). As the Pharisees told the story, the dead would rise on judgment day as all the wicked would be punished. The most severe punishment was to not be resurrected, with an entire chapter of the Talmud (Sanhedrin 10) devoted to the mysteries of who would be denied resurrection. Still, the Pharisees' doctrine of resurrection was still the resurrection of the whole body. It was not until late antiquity that the Pharisees began to think of the body and the soul as being two separate entities. Even the characters in the New Testament did not readily think of a soul/body dichotomy. When Jesus' body disappears from the tomb, and he is seen walking with his disciples, the community assumes that this is the beginning of the messianic age, for the first full-bodily resurrection has occurred.

The Hebrew Bible employs a number of words to express the life force that powers existence. These various names include *nefesh* (Deut. 12.23 and elsewhere), which literally refers to "life," *ruah* (Eccl. 3.21 and elsewhere), which means "spirit" or "wind," *neshamah* (Deut. 20.16 and elsewhere), which derives from the word *nasham*, "to breathe." There is also the term *hayah*, meaning "life (Gen. 1.20 and elsewhere)," and *yehidah* (Pss. 21.22), meaning essence or center. These five terms are used by the Bible to indicate the life force that dwells in people, if not a full-fledged separate entity that most people in the world would call a "soul."

The moment of transition, in which the Pharisees embraced the idea of a soul/body dichotomy, and an accompanying immortal soul, is recorded in the following teaching in the Midrash (Genesis Rabbah 14.9):

> It is called by five names, *Nefesh, Ruah, Neshamah, Hayah* and *Yehidah*. The *Nefesh* is the blood, as it is written *the blood is the nefesh* (Deut. 12.23). *Ruah*, because it ascends and descends,

as it says, *who knows if the ruah of people ascends* (Eccl. 3.21)? *Neshamah* is the countenance, as one would say, "a good countenance." *Hayah*, for all the limbs die and yet (the soul) lives (*hayah*). *Yehidah*, for all of the limbs change and (the soul) remains constant.

With this statement, coming in late antiquity, the Pharisees accepted and appropriated the idea of a distinction between the body and the soul. However, they still thought of the five expressions for "soul" that appear in the Bible as meaning the same entity. For the Rabbis of the Talmud, there was one immortal soul that "rises" to heaven, and is as ubiquitous in the body as the blood and yet outlives the body. It was a short transition to imagine this soul as dwelling in Heaven or sojourning briefly in Hell, concurrently with the "real time" events of the corporeal world.

THE WANDERING SOULS

The idea of a soul/body dichotomy led to two poles of belief as to the nature of the afterlife. One understanding saw the spirits of the dead and their abode as beneficent toward the living. The other opinion reflected and expanded on the horror of the gravesite as the source of death impurity. The Rabbis of the Talmud related the following account of the restless, mischievous souls of the dead (Berachot 18b):

Once a pious man gave a dinar to a pauper on the eve of Rosh ha-Shanah, during the years of drought. His wife berated him, and he went to sleep in the graveyard. There he heard two female spirits talking. "Come, my friend," said one to her companion, "let us wander the World and go behind the celestial curtain and hear what misfortunes will come to the world this year." The second answered, "My friend, I cannot go, for I am buried in a shroud of reeds. But you go, and tell me what you hear." She went and wandered and returned and her friend said, "What did you hear behind the celestial curtain?" She answered, "I heard that whoever plants in the first quarter (of the season) will have his fields destroyed by hail." He went and planted in the second quarter, everyone's crops were smitten and his, not. The following year, he returned (and similarly avoided disaster) . . . His wife asked him, "why are you so prescient, avoiding the disaster that happens to everybody else?" He told her everything. Not long afterward, she got into an argument with the mother of one of the (dead) girls. "Come, and I will show you that your daughter is buried in a shroud of reeds!" she said. The following year the pious man went to lie in the fields. "Come, my friend," said one to her companion, "let us wander the World and go behind the celestial curtain and hear what misfortunes will come to the world this year." "Put these things aside," answered the second "for what has passed between us has become known among the living."

The German ḥasidim, the pietists of the Rhineland, who were active in the initial flowering of early Kabbalah (c. twelfth century), had a great fear of the souls of the dead. This dread is expressed in the widely circulated ethical will of Rabbi Yehudah the Hasid, the leader of the movement. According to that document, the dead were liable to try to lure the living into the netherworld. Therefore, R. Yehudah instructed his community not to kiss their deceased children, grieve excessively or return habitually to the grave. When the dying refer to events or objects that are not in the room, the living are forbidden to acknowledge the reference or accept gifts from the dead in a dream visitation. Were this to happen, the deceased must be confronted at the gravesite, as illustrated in this injunction from the major popular work of the German ḥasidim, *Sefer Ḥasidim*, or "The Book of the Righteous":

> The spirits of the dead wander the world, hoping to hear the Divine decrees. Sometimes they induce the living to join them. If one humors them, then he or one of his family will soon die. Rather one should say to them, "Because of the Blessed Holy One, I refuse to go with you or with another other dead person." The next day he should go out to the graveyard and prostrate himself on that person's grave, saying, "for the sake of the Holy Blessed One who desires life, you and your messengers must desist from following me, my children or any other Jew, for I desire this world and not the other."

For Rabbi Yehudah the Hasid, the dead reacted to any slights or breaches of honor connected with their own burial, and would bring reprisals for them. Graves were not to be left open or unfilled and caskets were not to be stacked on top of one another. The dead of a certain town were apt to take offense if one declined to bury one's kin near them. This horror often translated into the classical superstitions of medieval Europe. Women who were suspected of killing and eating children had to be watched carefully at the time of burial. If their jaws slipped open, their mouths were to be filled with earth lest they rise from the grave to kill more children. Clearly, for the German hasidim, the living were to be protected from the machinations of the dead.

NEFESH, RUAḤ AND NESHAMAH

The mainstream kabbalistic view was that the nefesh, ruaḥ and neshamah were not three names for the same entity, the "soul." Rather, each of them represents a different *aspect* of the soul. This was the position of the first medieval Jewish philosopher, Sa'adiah Gaon (*Beliefs and Opinions* 6.3). Borrowing from the soul theories of Plato, Sa'adiah declared that the nefesh was the physical soul, the ruaḥ was the life of the emotions and the neshamah was the Divine soul, the aspect of God that exists in every perfected human being. This idea persisted in Jewish belief, as some thousand years later, the Hasidic master R. Schneur Zalman of Liadi would boldly proclaim, "The neshamah is a part of God from above, really!" According to the *Zohar* (II 98a), the neshamah does not join with the nefesh and ruaḥ immediately. It is gradually loaded into the individual, beginning with Bar and Bat Miẓvah and continuing to the age of 20.

The *Zohar* also taught that the three aspects of the soul were separate from one another. Such was particularly the case at the moment of death. At that time, the *ruaḥ* and *neshamah* leave the *nefesh* at the gravesite. The *ruaḥ* rises up to the celestial Garden of Eden, a paradise where it passes eternity in the company of the *ẓaddikim*, or righteous saints, who rejoice there on a nightly basis. The *neshamah*, having always been a spark of the Divine that had merely sojourned in the human soul, ascends and is lost within its source in the God, "like a drop of water in the great sea!" The neshamah's absorption into God takes the better part of a year. Jewish tradition maintains that survivors must recite the Kaddish prayer for at least 11 months, in order to expedite the ascent of the neshamah. Synagogues publicly pray for *ilui ha-neshamah*, for the "ascent of the soul." Contrary to the impression of most Jews, the customs of mourning in general were not developed to psychologically comfort the survivors, but rather to aid the soul of the deceased in finding security.

The nefesh is present at the grave, and yet remains in direct contact with its ruaḥ, in the celestial Garden of Eden, and its neshamah, which has reunited with God. Hence, from the circulation of the *Zohar* and forward, Jews naturally began to think of the gravesite as a portal to God, a sacred space for pilgrimage.[1] This understanding is the opposite of that of the German ḥasidim. The latter expressed a dread of the afterlife, while the *Zohar* saw the spirit world as beneficent to the living. The grave of a particular saint is a beneficial site for all people, while the grave of a doting relative has particular power for his or her descendants. In times of emergency, the community goes to the graveyard to beg the ẓaddikim for their intercession. The deceased *nefashot* of the righteous then gather and plead the case of the living with God. Gravesite pilgrimages often climax a period of fasting and personal mortification. These are considered like sacrifices and offerings, preceding the pilgrimage, as the *Zohar* explains (*Zohar* III 71b):

> Israel goes (to the gravesite) bringing only their repentance before God, with fasting and contrite hearts, in order that their holy souls may beseech mercy for them. Therefore we learn that the righteous man, even when he departs from this world, does not really disappear from any world, since he may be found in any of them more than was so in his lifetime.

The dead are almost more alive in death than in life, for they say (*Zohar* II 16a–b), "If not for us, the dead, who intercede before the angel of the grave for the living, the living would not remain alive for even half a day." Pilgrimage to the tomb of the patriarchs in Hebron is the most essential pilgrimage in Kabbalah, as the *Zohar* declares (*Zohar* III 70b):

> When the world requires mercy, the living go and inform the spirits of the ẓaddikim and weep over their graves, in order that soul may cleave to soul, and the souls of the righteous come together and tell the sleepers of Hebron of the pain of the world, then all enter the gates of Paradise. These spirits, who are crowned in

Paradise like celestial angels, join them. They tell the neshamah, who tells the Blessed Holy One, and then God has mercy on the world for all of their sins.

The influential Safed kabbalist, Hayyim Vital, echoed this sentiment, saying: "One should never imagine that the Righteous, on their passing . . . are idle from service. Were it not for the prayers of the dead, the living could not continue living!" The zaddik's nefesh is an active presence at the gravesite, a listening ear ready to relay messages upward to the *ruah* and *neshamah*.

To this day, gravesite shrines exert a pull on Jewish communities, although many Jews cannot say why. Formal kabbalists hold celebrations at the graves of great mystics on the anniversary of their deaths (Yiddish: *yahrtzeit*). The Breslaver hasidim have always seen a pilgrimage to their *rebbe*'s grave, in the Ukrainian town of Uman, as one of their most profound spiritual experiences. With the opening of Eastern Europe, Jewish groups have tramped through the death camps and the ruined graveyards of the cities and villages of the Pale of settlement with an inchoate sense that they ought to be doing so, but without being able to explain why. But the graveyards are a forest of lonely, benevolent souls, and the simple visit is part of their comfort, a consolation that they may be called upon to return.

CONVERSION AND THE NESHAMAH

The idea that gentiles don't have a *neshamah* is the dirty little secret of much kabbalistic belief. When Chabad hasidim approach people on the street with the question, "Are you Jewish?" the implication is, "if you are not Jewish, then we really aren't interested in you in the same way." Of course, there are gentiles with *neshamot* according to all kabbalists. At the very least, the "righteous gentiles" (*hasidei umot ha-olam*), who perform heroic acts of loving kindness, have souls according to most kabbalistic systems. Still, many kabbalists believed that at least some gentiles don't have a neshamah.

One could explain this racist doctrine away by referring to the bad state of relations between Christians and Jews during much of Kabbalah's golden age. Jewish life in the Christian world was a dense series of persecution and expulsions and there was no love lost between both communities most of the time. The intellectuals of the Jewish enlightenment shunned this nonhumanistic aspect of belief in the neshamah. Nonetheless, in recent years the idea has resurfaced in the thought of various kabbalistic Rabbis of settler groups in the West Bank.

The idea that gentiles begin, at least, without a neshamah also gives new meaning and intensity to the experience of conversion. Many Rabbis who do conversions would be hard pressed to know the actual nature of the change that occurs to the convert at the moment of conversion. At present, there is a disparity in conversion, between the laws of conversion established by Jewish tradition and the popular phenomenon as it is observed. In orthodoxy, converts are customarily greeted with suspicion, and the legal instruction to attempt to dissuade them is carried out with gusto. Many orthodox Rabbis seemingly take sadistic pleasure in tormenting would-be converts. And yet, at the end of the process, there is a phenomenon with which all synagogue members are familiar: that the converts are among the most ardent and profound members of the Jewish community. How could an individual pass from being the object of such suspicion to being the object of such respect?

Classical Judaism was vague about the status of the convert. The very terminology for each status is unclear. In the Bible, the convert and the "stranger," or non-Jew, are both referred to as the *ger*, as in (Exodus 23.9): *"you know the soul (nefesh) of the ger, for you were strangers (gerim) in the land of Egypt."* Popular religious assumptions among Jews seemed to maintain a difference between the souls of Jews and gentiles. Certainly, in their theological conflicts, Christianity and Islam did not refer to the nature of the soul, but to the rewards of the afterlife that would be bequeathed to the soul of a believer. In the absence of such guarantees regarding the afterlife, which Judaism famously did not emphasize, they could only offer the existential experience of being a Jew. Yet, if the reward of Judaism was to gain a Jewish soul, the questions remained to be asked: what is the nature of the convert's soul? Is it originally Jewish, or is there a change in the nature of the *neshamah* during the individual's lifetime? Is there a moment in the process of conversion of *becoming*, or is the convert always Jewish in his or her essence?

According to the *Zohar*, the convert's *neshamah* has a different origin than that of other Jews. In the *Zohar*'s cosmic worldview, most *neshamot* are taken from a treasury beneath the Divine Throne. In the celestial Garden of Eden, the *neshamah* is clothed in the *ruaḥ,* which in turn is clothed in the *nefesh.* The *neshamot* of the converts, however, are generated by the sexual liaisons of the righteous in the celestial Garden of Eden.[2]

Another tradition in the *Zohar* slightly contradicts this idea. According to this second tradition, sometimes a mishap occurs in the processes of redemption. Some Jews, upon their deaths, do not have a smooth entrance into the afterlife. Their nefesh and ruaḥ are redeemed, but their neshamah does not manage to escape terrestrial life. It is called a "naked soul," and it begins a career of restless wandering much of the type described by the German ḥasidim, as noted above. The naked soul wanders until it finds a suitable chassis to appropriate for the ascent to heaven. This is the nefesh and ruaḥ of a particularly righteous gentile, arguably the child of a righteous gentile who had been otherwise unrewarded. The Safed kabbalists, particularly the students of Isaac Luria, suggested that conversion might also be the process of a "free" ruaḥ having to undergo a similar process. In this case, the nefesh of a deceased Jew is redeemed while the ruaḥ has to reincarnate in the body of a convert, as described above in the case of a convert.

REINCARNATION

Reincarnation traditions had been circulating among kabbalists from the moment that Kabbalah reemerged in France, Spain and the Rhineland. The first "kabbalistic" book, the *Bahir* (#86, Scholem ed.), speaks of the soul as analogous to a person who, having worn out one garment, simply changes into another. In the same way, the eternal soul is apt to shed one body for another. This idea of reincarnation was called *gilgul* by the kabbalists, and it slowly became an important part of Jewish mysticism.

The main sections of the *Zohar,* however, were very reticent regarding reincarnation. The boldest reincarnation tradition to be found in the main sections of the *Zohar* is in the composition *Sabba de-Mishpatim,* "The old man of the (Torah reading) *Mishpatim*." In this section, an old man, Rabbi Yeiva the elder teaches the kabbalists the inner meaning of the miẓvah of Levirate marriage, the situation in which a man must marry his late brother's childless widow (Exodus 25.1–10). When such a marriage takes place, the Torah teaches that the child born to the grieving widow and the former brother in law is known as the son of the deceased brother,

Figure 5.1 The traditional gravesite of R. Yeiva Sabba, the "Sabba de-Mishpatim," Meron, Galilee (Photo: P. Giller).

and is recognized as the first husband's child in all legal matters. Rabbi Yeiva explains that the child of the second marriage is really the reincarnation of the first husband, with all of the oedipal complications that such an identity would imply.

Besides this teaching, however, the main sections of the *Zohar* do not contain many reincarnation traditions. These would come in the later strata of the *Zohar*, the writings transmitted after the death of Rabbi Shimon bar Yoḥai, in the works *Tiqqunei ha-Zohar* and *Ra'aya Meheimna*. These later sections teach that the soul is reincarnated six times, once for each of the intermediate *sefirot*. The implication of this teaching, which would be fleshed out in the teachings of the Safed kabbalists, is that in every reincarnation a person has to "fix" a certain aspect of his soul. This idea resembles the work of reincarnation in Eastern religions, which is to expunge the particular karma that has attached to one's soul in a past life. According to the kabbalistic version, when this process is completed, the soul undergoes a final liberation as it has a reincarnation at the realm of the Shekhinah, the sefirah Malkhut.

The two main kabbalists of Safed, Moshe Cordovero and Isaac Luria based their understandings of reincarnation on this idea, and their teachings became the normative kabbalistic doctrine of reincarnation. Their main challenge in doing so was that all of the prior traditions of the soul in Kabbalah contradicted one another. The doctrine of reincarnation at the end of time contradicted the concurrent afterlife of the nefesh, ruaḥ and neshamah found in the early sections of the *Zohar*. If the nefesh, ruaḥ and neshamah had set roles and went, upon an individual's death, to finite places, at what point did the process of reincarnation take place?

Moshe Cordovero taught his many students in Safed that it was the neshamah that reincarnated, in order to rectify problems left over from its previous incarnation. According to Cordovero, sinful behavior produces results, which are passed on from incarnation to incarnation. The soul is reincarnated for three reasons: to rectify the effects of sin, to punish the neglect of a particular *miẓvah* or to complete unfinished business with those still living. It descends into the corporeal World to redeem itself through worthy actions. The most essential incarnation of the *neshamah* is the first one, as the *neshamah* does not have a character prior to this first incarnation. If the person has been sinful, then the soul is punished for a while in the underworld, *Gehennom*. Cordovero believed that *gilgul* was nearly universal, although some sinners were never reincarnated. Reincarnation is a privilege, then, for those who have made an honest effort to be good in their lives.

Cordovero seems to have limited the number of reincarnations to ten, parallel to the ten sefirot. Every lifetime would be defined by a different theme, relating to one of the sefirot. For example, there would be a reincarnation for the sefirah Din, in which the soul would have to address its problems with harshness and judgment. There would then be a reincarnation for the sefirah Ḥesed, in which the soul would have to rectify issues of loving kindness. Finally, the last reincarnation would be the one related to *Malkhut*, at which point the neshamah would be free to dissolve into God. Implicit in this doctrine is the idea that the neshamah is itself a blank slate, which undergoes the experiences, related to every sefirah.

Could men reincarnate as women, Jews as Gentiles, human beings as animals, sentient beings as inanimate objects? The kabbalists viewed the neshamah as androgynous, and able to alternate between male and female bodies. Under the influence of earlier authorities, particularly the writings of Yosef of Hamadan, Moshe Cordovero also adopted the view that reincarnation could occur into animals and possibly even plants, which was also the belief of two of Isaac Luria's teachers in Egypt, Yosef ben Shalom Ashkenazi and David Ibn Zimra.

Luria adopted the teachings of his teachers. He explained that human neshamot could reincarnate into lower life forms because, according to his doctrines of *zimzum* and *shevirah*, the world was broken to begin with. Human souls could descend into lower realms of existence in order to gather the broken spark of Divinity that had fallen to the lowest levels of creation. Even eating food in a state of ritual holiness could gather and redeem those sparks. Many dietary laws, according to Luria, are merely devices for redeeming the sparks of the Holy. The ritual slaughter of the animal frees its transmigrated soul. Similarly, Jewish law forbids the fruit of trees less than three years old because the transmigrated souls have not entered it until this time. In reviving this tradition, Luria provided for the repair of this aspect of the cosmos, by teaching that the very act of eating is an act of transformation and transition, an interaction with the living Universe, including the possibility of entering the bodies of animals and vegetation.

A distinction between Cordovero and Luria has to do with the initial, intrinsic identity of the neshamah. Luria emphasized that every soul came from a specific root, each of which is based in one of the great progenitors of the world according to biblical history. Everyone, of course, was descended from Adam and Eve, but then there was the option of being descended from either Cain or Abel, or from the three sons of Noah, Shem, Ham and Yaphet. These first incarnations comprised the "soul roots" that made up the great families of reincarnation. As opposed to Cordovero's strict limitation of the number of reincarnations, Luria did not believe that there were merely ten reincarnations, but innumerable possibilities for reincarnation. Through knowing one's soul root, one could, through prayer, fasting and hypnotic trance, be connected to one's past life incarnations.

Luria and his students practiced what might popularly be called "past life regressions." The past life regression should be understood as an extremely secular act. In contemporary New Age practice, past lives are induced as part of a "waking dream," through which a powerful personal mythology may expressed through the construction of a past life, which has, for its owner, great existential truth. Most people would agree that the symbols of a sleeping dream are really indications of one's subconscious thoughts and desires. However, the images presented in dreams are indirect symbols. The clothing of the dream images is a device to keep a person asleep, less the released images of the subconscious be too troubling. If one is put into a hypnotic state, however, and asked to construct a narrative of a "past" life, one can compose a narrative that will expertly sum up all of one's inner desires and neuroses. Images will not be presented with the extraneous clouding of the "dream censor," because one has entered the hypnotic state voluntarily, without the anxieties of sleep. The "past life" that is recovered will be a convincing existential fable of one's deepest desires, fears and neuroses. Anyone, then, can conduct a past life regressions, and an exceptionally satisfying result may still not necessarily be divinely inspired. In this, and many other ways, Luria used his knowledge of the soul, and particularly the soul root, as a kind of psychological and mystical tool. In the past life regressions that he conducted for his students, Luria provided a form of psychotherapy in which they came to some self-knowledge about their natures and impulses.

Luria made the veneration of the sacred grave an important part of his mystical teaching. Prior to Luria, the living had petitioned the dead with traditional prayer. The pilgrim set out to wake up the sleeping *zaddik* at the gravesite and send him to intercede with the Divine. Luria's method of prostration, or *hishtathut,* consisted of his literally lying prone across the gravestone, with his face at the face of the deceased, so as to align all the levels of his soul with that of the departed *zaddik.* According to Vital: "Whenever he desired to speak with a certain prophet or sage, he would go to his grave and lay himself down upon it, with outstretched arms and feet . . . He would bind his *nefesh, ruah* and *neshamah* to those of the *zaddik* and bring about supernal unification."[3]

Lurianic texts often based themselves on the *Zohar's* vision of whole communities beseeching the righteous in times of crisis:

> Cleaving to the *zaddikim* and prostrating oneself at the gravesite, cleaving spirit (*ruah*) to spirit and soul to soul (*nefesh*) is as described in the *Zohar* (III 70b): when the world is in need of mercy and life they go out and inform the *zaddikim*, weeping on the gravesite of those who it is appropriate to inform, conforming

to their will and cleaving soul to soul, to purify with great purification and to sanctify them with great sanctity and to delight
greatly, to behold the kindness of God, to know that his path
and his actions are illuminated with the light of God's presence.
[The *zaddik*] tells him true things and does not lead him astray,
on the condition that he behaves with holiness and humility and
fear of sin, keeping God's great and terrible name before him
always, to unify the name of the Blessed Holy One always, with
love and fear.[4]

In Luria's world, the living and the dead mingled. He boldly
identified various gravesites with figures from the Bible, Talmud
and *Zohar*. From the hill overlooking Safed, he observed a whole
society of the dead, in the shrines and tombs in the area. He could
recognize the soul of the departed saint hovering over the site.
Sometimes his pronounced opinions were at variance with prevail-
ing traditions. As well as identifying the inhabitant of the gravesite,
Luria was aware of the deceased's fate in the afterlife. Sometimes,
because of some outstanding transgression, the dead transmigrated
into inanimate objects for an unspecified period of limbo.

With his identification of many new gravesites, Luria helped
shape the emerging mythos of the Galilee. Hayyim Vital's son,
Samuel, included most of the sites linked to Luria in chapter 38 of
his *Sha'ar ha-Gilgullim*, which acts as a guide to the tiny communities surrounding Safed: Ein Zeitim, Biriah, Avnit, Akvarah, Gush
Halav and others. Luria even identified Jesus' grave at Ein Zeitim,
off the Safed–Meron road.

Another of Luria's most striking practices was known as the *sod
ha-ibbur*, "the secret of impregnation." This practice was a kind of
shamanism, through which one could also take on the nefesh of a
departed zaddik while still alive. In this ritual, the neshamah of
a departed saint is acquired as a kind of "extra soul." The Safed
kabbalists used their souls as instruments. They bonded with the
souls of the departed, sending them into illuminating trances and
oracular, shamanistic experiences. With their knowledge of their
soul root, the students could go and practice a kind of shamanism, lying by the grave of a dead saint and literally taking on their
nefesh. Since the nefesh of the dead saint remained connected to
their ruah and neshamah, then the kabbalist was literally receiving divine inspiration by acquiring the nefesh of their spiritual

"relative." These practices did not originate in Safed. Rav Moshe Karo, the author of the authoritative code of Jewish Law, was an established clairvoyant and medium. Luria formalized the practice, and it became common among Hasidic adepts and the sages of the Middle Eastern Jewish communities to commune with the souls of the dead and experience ascents of the soul.

CONCLUSION

Kabbalistic doctrines of the soul and its afterlife comprise an amalgam of conflicting traditions. The tradition of resurrection at the end of time contradicts the tradition of the nefesh, ruah and neshamah. The concurrent afterlife of the nefesh, ruah and neshamah contradicts the dynamics of reincarnation. To respond to these contradictions, kabbalists crafted dense theories and systems in order to resolve such issues. The Safed Kabbalists produced complicated works such as Hayyim Vital's "Gate of Reincarnations" and "Book of Reincarnations," as well as the contemporary work "Revelation of the Secret." Luria and his students left many instructions regarding the nature of the soul, "family trees" of the most important reincarnations of different soul roots and directions as to how to practice the "ibbur," or impregnation, the taking on of the nefesh of a departed zaddik.

The influence of astrology was not ignored by the Safed kabbalists. Moshe Cordovero was receptive to the effects of astrology on the course of a life. The astrological signs, as well as the 12 tribes of Israel and the 12 stones on the breastplate of the High Priest of the Jerusalem Temple all reflect 12 aspects of the *neshamah*. Sometimes, up to 12 reincarnations are devoted to the resolution of these 12 qualities and the karmic burdens that they incur. Cordovero located the influence of astrology at the level of the neshamah. His successor, Isaac Luria contradicted this opinion, and argued that astrology was only relevant to the realm of the lowest sefirah, Malkhut. According to Luria, astrology was simply a natural and secular phenomenon, without aspiration to the holier realms of the upper sefirot. Locating astrological influence on the higher levels of the soul would give altogether too much importance to astrology, a body of knowledge that classical Judaism had always deprecated as separate from and inferior to the truth of Kabbalah. The Talmudic dictum *ain mazal le-Yisrael*, "Israel has no mazal" does not mean that the Jewish people have no "luck." It means, rather, that the fate of the Jews in dictated by God alone, who supersedes the vagaries of astrology.

All of these practices fly in the face of the conventional Jewish view, which, from the time of the Bible, was relentlessly agnostic about the afterlife. Kabbalah, being relentlessly concerned with metaphysics, really began their understanding of existence with the life of the soul. The life of the soul was more real than the life of the body. As a consequence of this, present existence became, as in the words of the High Holy Day liturgy, "a passing shadow, like dust in the wind."

All of this was to free the neshamah from reincarnation. Just as Buddhists long to extinguish their karma in the extinction of nirvana, the Safed kabbalists sought to cleanse their neshamot from their own sins and the sins of the neshamah's previous owner. These ideas were animistic, in that they admitted that the most vital part of the development of life is its inner spirit, and that there was conscious life in inanimate objects. The view of the kabbalists could also be called pantheistic, as they portrayed God as being the universe and the universe as a manifestation of God. This point of view was influential on Hasidism; the Ba'al Shem Tov, the founder of the movement can honestly be called an exorcist by profession. Kabbalists, from the *Zohar* to Hasidism, walked through a world of souls in every entity, awaiting liberation.

CHAPTER 6

MYSTICAL PRACTICE AND THE MIŻVOT

There are reasons for miżvot that are not intended to be revealed.
—*Tiqqunei ha-Zohar 130b*

Jewish Mysticism is the sum of the attempts made to put a mystical interpretation on the content of Rabbinical Judaism.

—*Gershom Scholem*[1]

Enthusiasts and students of Kabbalah often ask me to suggest a kabbalistic practice that they could incorporate into their lifestyle. In such cases, I often give what is considered a disappointing answer: that the practice of conventional Judaism, its rituals and stringencies, is the most authentic kabbalistic practice. Jewish law and practice was both the prerequisite and the expression of lived Kabbalah. The classical prescriptions and proscriptions of the legal structure, or *halakhah*, adhered to and were embedded in the mentality of the *Zohar* and all of the mainstream works of the tradition. Hence, the sensibility of Jewish law and lore is enmeshed in kabbalistic practice. It is a prerequisite, for the kabbalist, to avoid prohibited acts and substances. At the same time, the practice and performance of the rites of Judaism is the essential kabbalistic act. Hence, there is no greater prayer tool than the prayer shawl and the tefillin, and no greater catastrophe than violating the kosher laws, or the rules of the Sabbath, or the strictures of chastity.

MAIMONIDES AND NAHMANIDES ON
THE REASONS FOR THE MIZVOT

Kabbalists, like most mystics, were religiously conservative.[2] Anyone looking for the romantic notions of rebellion against authority and release from social and legal boundaries will have a hard time finding such behavior in the annals of Kabbalah. Famous exemplars of freedom and innovation, such as the Ba'al Shem Tov, couched their ecstatic practices in a grave concern for the regulations of the Law. The Ba'al Shem Tov himself enacted new stringencies for ritual slaughter, and made efforts to institute the practice going to the ritual bath and trying to maintain a state of ritual purity for men. The *Zohar* literature is drenched in halakhic thinking and contains at least two "Books of Mizvot" based on Maimonides' counting. There are related works left by Moshe de Leon and others in the circle that are concerned with the analysis of the commandments in terms of their metaphysical implications.[3] This concern with Jewish Law and the commandments continued to the Safed Renaissance, Shabbateanism and Hasidism.

In order to understand kabbalistic practice, it is helpful to review the structure of Jewish law itself. The strictures of the Torah, the first five books of the Bible, were adapted through a thousand years of interpretation by the Rabbis of the Second Temple Period. These, in turn, were interpreted and developed by medieval scholars who were sometimes kabbalists themselves and sometimes their contemporaries. At various times, the kabbalistic world included powerful members of the legal community. This was particularly the case during the Safed revival, when the compiler of the standard code of Jewish law, R. Yosef Caro, studied with Moshe Cordovero. Isaac Luria himself edited a volume of the *Shittah Mekubezet*, a widely distributed anthology of legal analyses. At other times, there was antipathy to the rabbinic establishment, particularly among the German hasidim of the thirteenth century, on the part of the author of *Ra'aya Meheimna* and *Tiqqunei ha-Zohar*[4] and at the inception of Polish Hasidism in the eighteenth and nineteenth centuries.

PHILOSOPHY AND PURITY

The kabbalistic interpretation of Jewish law and practice stressed that every *mizvah* had a metaphysical result. This was in contrast to the view of the philosophical tradition, which viewed invoking metaphysical reasons that could not be demonstrated through analysis as inadmissible.[5] The debate between the two schools was fought out over a number of centuries in the Middle Ages and has resurfaced in modernity among the various sects of Judaism. These two ways of seeing Judaism, the metaphysical and the rational, remain a source of tension in practiced Judaism today, with each approach claiming to be the authentic core of Jewish tradition.

One of the debates that brought Kabbalah "above-ground" in the twelfth century concerned the reasons for the mizvot. The sharpest debates regarding the role of metaphysics in understanding the nature of the mizvot were those of the Andalucian philosopher Moses Maimonides (RaMBa"M) and the Castilian kabbalist Moses Nahmanides (RaMBa"N). Were the mizvot simply "good deeds" for the perfection of the individual, as Maimonides argued, or did mizvot and sins, respectively, trigger Divine and demonic impulses in the world, as Nahmanides and his myriad supporters contended? Kabbalists believed the latter.

There were many areas of contention between Maimonides and Nahmanides, both in the realm of theology and in terms of ritual practice. To bring but one example, the law against sexual contact during the menstrual cycle represents the nature of their disagreement. The Bible's laws of ritual impurity, or *tumah*, express primordial Semitic anxieties, in which impurity was linked to contact with death or infertility. Contact with a corpse, with carrion and vermin, menstruation, venereal discharges and all seminal emissions were viewed as a "kind of death" by virtue of the short-term infertility, in terms of inability to conceive, that they conferred on the individual. In ancient times, a state of impurity prevented a Jew from entering the Jerusalem Temple, eating sanctified food or having conjugal sex.

Maimonides saw ritual impurity as merely a means to an end: That end was the separation and veneration of the Temple Mount. The salient fact of ritual impurity, for Maimonides, was that the person who had suffered that impurity was prevented from participating, directly or vicariously, in the national religion. In his *Guide for the Perplexed* (3.47), Maimonides averred that:

> ... the whole intention with regard to the sanctuary was to affect those who came to it with a feeling of awe and fear ... this being

the intention, the Holy Blessed One forbade the unclean to enter the sanctuary in spite of their being so many types of impurity that one could—with but few exceptions—scarcely find a clean individual.

Maimonides considered ritual impurity as a wholly arbitrary, creaturely phenomenon of human beings. It was not in itself toxic; it was simply a device to render one unfit for entering the Temple area, in order to create a rare sense of privilege and heightened consciousness when one finally did enter that sacred precinct. The associations of ritual impurity remained philosophical constructs and not empirical states.

In contrast to this understanding was the position of Naḥmanides, who often cast himself as the respondent to Maimonides' rationalist positions. At one point in his Torah commentary (itself a widely distributed text, found in most traditional Jewish homes) he endorses the notion of ritual impurity as a palpable force. With regard to the menstrual impurity, Naḥmanides (on Leviticus 18.19) declares that:

(The menstrual blood) is the elixir of death, it will kill any living thing that consumes it . . . and if it remains too long in the pregnant womb the child will be a leper . . . and if a menstruant at the beginning of her flow gazes into an iron mirror, red droplets, like blood, will form on the surface of the mirror.

According to Naḥmanides, women during menstruation are seized and overcome by a palpable malevolent spirit. The menstruant, in turn, conveys palpable pollution. There is nothing figurative or symbolic in his construction of the dark reality of ritual impurity. The palpability of tumah, as expressed in Kabbalah, leads directly to the inherent, independent nature of evil, for if ritual impurity was palpable, its source must be a palpable malevolence.

The same concerns hold true in other expressions of ritual impurity. Later understandings of tumah saw the cycle of purity and impurity as a struggle between the forces of the demonic and the Holy.[6] Classical Kabbalah, following Naḥmanides, came to view tumah as a source of empirical evil. For instance, the later sections of the *Zohar* sometimes referred to a demonic spirit that could be found in wounded [*tref*], prohibited meat. According to this view, the angel of death rises from between the dying beast's horns and this demonic association is personified in the Tannaitic appellations that conflate the torn animal with the case of the "goring bull" that dominates the discussions of civil damages in the Talmud.[7] According to this view, ritual impurity is fetishized. The gentile meat in the marketplace is not merely forbidden but evil. Contact with it, and indeed with all elements of gentile culture, pollutes and defiles the adept, lowering his spiritual attainment. The leprous irruption, the sudden menstrual discharge and the seminal emission are all spiritual catastrophes, reflected in the flesh. Just as ritual impurity is manifestly evil, the "evil inclination" is not a psychological impulse, but an empirical force operating on the individual from without. In all these cases, and with all the theological risks to monotheistic Judaism, ritual impurity is the trace, the effect of these forces of evil.

This is one of the great defining questions in the distinction between the rationalistic Judaism of Western Europe and North America, and the spirituality of Eastern Europe and the Middle East, before the Second World War. The question is also essential as to how tumah was viewed in the time of the Bible. Is ritual impurity "real"? Are people who have contact with the dead, who are afflicted with the biblical leprosy or have suffered menstrual or seminal flows, actually, empirically "polluted" in some way? It is the conceit of the kabbalistic myth that it mirrors the original intent of the Bible, and that Moses and Aaron understood tumah in the same way as Isaac Luria.

Among many moderns, there is a tendency to dismiss the laws of menstrual impurity or leprosy as relics of a savage Judaism far removed from the present. It is a tradition distinguished by bleak fears, in which the impure is synonymous with the dangerous. One of the central questions that separate people who are sincerely involved with Kabbalah from the legions of dilettantes and frauds that currently occupy the field is the question of whether ritual impurity is literal and palpable. One who commits to the metaphysical reality of Kabbalah has little choice but to view the experience of ritual impurity as actual, as opposed to "as if."

THE NATURE OF EVIL

From the composition of the *Zohar* through the premodern periods, the literature of the Kabbalah was committed to countering the mischief brought about by the forces of the demonic. The instruments for this struggle between the forces of good and evil are the mizvot themselves. The positive commandments are protective and restorative, while the commission of prohibited acts strengthens the forces of demonic chaos,[8] for, in the words of Daniel C. Matt, "the demonic is empowered by human sin."[9] Throughout Kabbalah, evil is not merely, as rationally defined, the absence of the good, a kind of super-banality. Many kabbalists believed in a great essential malevolence in the world that caused calamity, death and misfortune. In entering the kabbalistic myth, there must be a moment in which one puts aside all objectivity and embraces the subjective realm, in which neutral phenomena are freighted with significance that goes beyond their plain nature.

The metaphysical understanding of the law led to certain reversals in the kabbalistic sensibility. The medieval rabbis had long wrestled with the question of the relevancy of the mizvot. Sa'adiah Gaon, in the ninth century, famously divided the commandments into rational and traditional categories, to separate those that conformed to natural law from those whose nature was nationalistic or obscure. Maimonides allowed that certain mizvot were commemorative in nature. For instance, the commandments not to fully shave one's head and not to tattoo or cut one's skin were strictures against pagan practices from the time of the Bible. Although these practices might no longer be in effect, or be specifically pagan, the prohibitions were still observed as a remembrance of that earlier time.[10]

In Kabbalah, these identities were reversed. For kabbalists, if a mizvah seemed obscure or irrelevant, then its identity must be wholly metaphysical, and it must be a very important mizvah indeed. Leaving the corners of one's field for the poor is a nice thing, but since the commandment to avoid mixing wool and linen in a garment seems to have no relevance, then it must be a direct interaction with cosmic forces of good and evil, so that a sports jacket with a wool and linen mixture stiffening the collar must be . . . abhorred!

According to this understanding of the Law, the prohibitions act to limit actions that might seem innocuous but are really invested with metaphysical power. In this way, the Kabbalah appropriated sensibilities that may have lost their relevancy and renewed them through the power of taboo and fetish. This process was not reserved for Kabbalah; even Maimonides would preface his presentation of the laws of circumcision with the reminder that "the foreskin is an abomination!"[11] Seemingly, there might be people who did not already know this.

This sensibility led to a valuation of certain miẓvot that seems to approach a fetish. When wandering the neighborhoods of the pious in centers of Jewish, visitors are often bemused by the sheer indulgence of the religious lifestyle. The luxuriant side curls of some Hasidic men, enormous *mezuzot* on the doorposts, expensive *tefillin* worn at prayer, and other examples, point to a phenomenon in which the results of religious practice have become ends in themselves. Folk customs that had long receded from general practice have resurged, such as *kapparot*, the displacement of sins onto a vicarious victim (usually an unlucky chicken) on the eve of the Day of Atonement.

Some changes are the product of traditional Judaism's clash with modernity. The horror of sexual transgression has, in the orthodox community, led to greater boundaries between the sexes. This empirical view of the commandments and their transgression has led to many uncompromising social positions in Israeli society on the part of ultraorthodox, *ḥareidi* society. This is unsurprising, for if there is empirical malevolence in the general transgression of the commandments, then the kabbalist cannot be relativistic about the Law.

THE DEMONIC

Underlying the horror of sin in the classical Kabbalah is the acknowledgment of there being a demonic element in the cosmic order. This demonic element is as old as creation. Lillit, the doyenne of crib death and nocturnal emission, was, according to one somewhat *outré* account,[12] nothing more than Adam's first wife, banished from the Garden of Eden, according to some accounts, because she merely wanted to be an equal partner, as described in the first creation account in the first chapter of Genesis. Lillit and her consort, Samael,[13] lead a corps of demons and malevolent spirits who often function as God's "hit men,"[14] as sociopathic as any Luca Brasi.[15]

Another metaphor for the operations of the demonic in Kabbalah is that of the organs of the body. The sefirotic structure mirrors

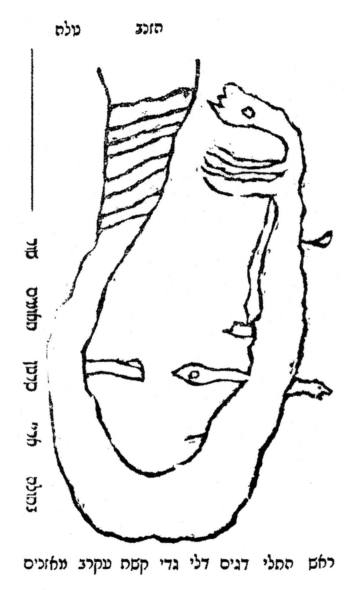

Figure 6.1 "The Serpent in the Universe is like the King on his Throne" (*Sefer Yeẓirah* 6.2), from Eliezer of Worms' Commentary to *Sefer Yeẓirah*.

the human body in many ways, almost like the well-known chakras of Tantrism. Hence, just as the human body has organs that filter impurities and waste, such as the liver, the spleen and its bile, so the Divine structure has comparable aspects that filter the evil of the world.[16] Encountering the forces of the demonic is as possible as encountering any given septic aspect of the phenomenal world.

One of the most controversial aspects of Kabbalistic belief is that certain practices in Judaism are conceived to keep the forces of evil at bay. These miẓvot are "sops" to these demonic forces, such as the spilling of wine at the Passover Seder. According to the *Zohar*, the scapegoat, the bitter waters of the unfaithful wife, the decapitated calf (Deut. 21.1), the straps and the extra threads of hair in the tefillin are also detritus left for demonic forces and "appeasement of the evil eye."[17]

In the kabbalistic mind-set, the world exists in a dichotomized condition of good-and-evil. Worse still is the confusion of these two forces. Hence, the horror of mixing in the halakhah, such as the mixture of wool and linen, or multiple seeds in a field, reinforces the chaos of the phenomenal world. The biblical prohibitions against mixing things, such as seed crops (*kilayim*) wool and linen (*sha'atnez*),[18] and the grafting of fruit trees,[19] are all restrictions on the demonic, according to the *Zohar*. In this regard, Kabbalah carries on the biblical horror of miscegenation. This horror is a reflection of one of the central anxieties of the Torah and its laws, which is the very fertility of the land. The prohibitions of incest and other illicit liaisons are further examples of this illicit mixing.

Elements of this belief in the demonic were among the most tenacious remnants of Kabbalah to survive into the twentieth century. Jewish immigrants to America were likely to tie a red ribbon (widely known as a "red bendel") in the carriages of their infants, decades before the Kabbalah Learning Centre had begun to market the red strings common to the indigenous Jews and Palestinians. The expressions *bli ein ha-ra'* (or Yiddish *kein ayin hara'*) was a widespread imprecation against the evil eye, an idea that expressed anxiety about the propensity for evil to befall the complacent. Jewish life in the medieval Diaspora was remarkable for its tenuousness. A belief in a random and perverse force of evil pervaded the magical thinking of the Jewish street to a greater extent than rationalistic rabbinical leaders have ever liked to acknowledge.

ETHICS AND PIETY

The metaphysical absolutism described above lent itself to the life of piety and asceticism, which was the lifestyle already advocated by the Judaism of the Middle Ages. By contemporary standards, life was bleak and fragile. Jewish existence under the Christians and even the Muslims was governed by the most capricious of whims. The religious life of the Jews took place in a general state of anxiety that was only amplified by the idea that the miẓvot themselves had an empirical power to affect one's fate. According to this worldview, sin triggered catastrophic consequences in the struggle between good and evil, while miẓvot and virtuous behavior rebuilt and restored the cosmic order. Committing transgressions led to the individual's being overwhelmed by fate, while the faithful performance of the miẓvot provided the only hope of walking a clear path through life. In this spirit, the *Zohar* literature continued and reinforced the grave pietism of medieval Judaism.

In these ways, the kabbalistic worldview was patently otherworldly. The aim of religious life was best realized by the cultivation of a saintly lifestyle. One might aspire to the life of a *ḥasid*, or pietist, which in its pure form resembled the pursuit of individual saintliness through the fear of sin. One might also observe from afar, the behavior of the ẓaddik, the leader who is distinguished in his spiritual attainments. In either case, attainment of a higher spiritual level was reserved for those who pursued the religious life bounded by the halakhah and the extra-halakhic demands of a religious piety that went beyond the letter of the law.[20]

As a result of this worldview, the *Zohar* is riddled with guarantees of the rewards for a life of piety. This is particularly evident in the later strata, the *Tiqqunim* and *Ra'aya Meheimna*, with their model of the *maskil*, or enlightened sage.[21] Accordingly, the righteous are subject to the vicissitudes of fate, but they are never forsaken, and they patiently await their eventual redemption. The righteous must display forbearance with regard to the ascent of the wicked,[22] for in the struggle between good and evil, the righteous saint, or ẓaddik, will ultimately be triumphant. The day of final judgment will be a time to settle scores, at which point the righteous will be redeemed.

As in all classical Jewish theology, the Messiah sits in the throne room of the lower Garden of Eden, waiting to redeem Israel. Upon his advent, the vicissitudes of the exile will all be resolved. The *Zohar* adopts the full script of historical possibilities attending the Messiah's coming. Two Messiahs, the fallen Messiah son of Joseph and the triumphant Messiah son of David, will come to redeem Israel, amid the full range of cataclysmic wars and temptations detailed in the Apocrypha and the Aggadic traditions. Messianic tension pervades the Kabbalah and the various historical movements that attended it.[23]

In social terms, this meant a probity that shunned, with horror, the coarse and forbidden speech of the street. Tale bearing, lies and obscenity were impossible to reconcile with the behavior of a pious kabbalist. With regard to the emotional needs of the kabbalists, anger is viewed, from the *Zohar* to the Safed renaissance, as the central spiritual impediment. Arrogance is not far behind as a social ill, and antithetical to the value of humility and self-abnegation.[24]

The opposite of these impediments, *ḥasidut*, the quality of simple piety, is the domain of Abraham, paradigm of *Ḥesed*, or lovingkindness. The miẓvot are the natural instrument of this piety. Preoccupation with the Torah makes one wise and pious, while repentance and action bring one to union with the Shekhinah, particularly the transformative aspect of the Shekhinah that is part of the sefirah of Binah, symbolized by the Latinate term *Matronita*. Beyond the demands of the law, certain pietistic behaviors will also serve as protection for the righteous, such as studying the Torah at night, which is a practice already specified by the rabbinic literature that is reinforced in the *Zohar* and its attendant literature.[25]

The absolute identity of the ḥasid or ẓaddik also, conversely, dictates absolute identities of the Jewish community's social "other." To that end, gentile culture, as a whole, is viewed as the antithesis of the Good. It is forbidden to teach Kabbalah to gentiles.[26] According to the *Zohar*, Israel and the gentiles are under the control of different Divine names.[27] The Safed kabbalists' understandings of Jewish/gentile relations reflect the brutal legacy of the recent Spanish Expulsion. Cordovero portrayed the nations of the world as *kelipot*, empty shells or husks that surround the kernel of Holiness. These demonic forces are under the control of the Divine, particularly the *sefirah Tiferet*. Following the teachings of the philosopher Yehudah ha-Levi, the land of Israel and the people Israel are purifying entities, while anyone who lives in the Diaspora is automatically at a lower spiritual level.[28] The same is true of the unlearned, who occupy a particularly benighted social class in the kabbalists' worldview, being characterized as having a propensity for sexual offenses, brazenness to teachers, bloodshed and falsehood.[29] A rabbinic aphorism that the *Zohar* likes to repeat is, "The ignoramus is a reptile, and his wife is vermin, and of his daughter it is written, 'Cursed be the one who lies with a beast (Deut. 27.21).' "[30]

In both the *Zohar* and the *Tiqqunim*, there are references to the corrupting and demonic nature of intercourse with a menstruous woman, a maidservant, a gentile woman or a prostitute (respectively *Niddah, Shifhah, Goyah, Zonah*; acronym *Nashgaz*). The vehemence of these references goes far beyond the degree of mere halakhic or philosophical value structures. They reflect the influence of the Toledano reforms of 1280–81, in which the Castilian community, under the leadership of Todros Abulafia imposed social restrictions designed to combat the excesses of Jewish slave owners with their gentile maidservants. This attribution of the archetypal qualities of the demonic to these four examples of forbidden intercourse indicates the kabbalistic support for these ethical reforms.[31]

LAW AND GENDER

For the kabbalists, sex and gender comprised a direct relationship to the metaphysical world. Sexual union is the metaphor for the union of the Heavenly and Earthly planes of existence, through the unity of sefirot such as Tiferet and Malkhut or Hokhmah and Binah. Because of the dangers of transgression in the realm of sexuality, however, the subject is also suffused with anxiety and dread. Hence, while the central metaphor of Kabbalah is erotic, kabbalists are not sexy. They view sexuality as profound and utterly compelling, but they do not take it lightly. With all of the extolling of marriage as a state, it is hard to avoid the idea that the kabbalists also saw it as the resolution of a problem, namely the problem of human sexuality, which is fraught with potential transgression. To that end, the *Zohar* is intensely erotic, yet its eroticism is tinged with darkness. The prevalence of erotic metaphor only serves to emphasize a terror of its illicitness.[32]

As has been explained previously, the sefirotic system runs on a series of sexual unions and erotic relationships that ebb and flow over time. The events of the cosmos and the astral body are mirrored in the events of human beings and their bodies in present existence. Hence the shifting unions of Ḥokhmah and Binah or Tiferet and Malkhut will emerge in the life of the kabbalist in his or her conjugal relations and the raising of their families. This idea, which is called *isomorphism*, permeates kabbalistic thought and practice. Marriages are necessarily complicated, because unions are, literally, "made in Heaven," according to the Talmud.[33] Yet the dynamics of this complementarity take place across the sefirot, worlds and other metaphysical dynamics, all transposed onto the souls of the couple and their marital dynamics.

The *Zohar* is obsessed with the vicarious romanticism of the life of the Shekhinah and the Holy Blessed One (the *Kadosh, Barukh Hu* or *Tiferet*). The sexual tensions, unions and especially yearnings of the Divine couple sometimes overrule the marital relationships of the kabbalists. The *Zohar* stresses that the kabbalists themselves are the courtiers of the Shekhinah, forever rescuing her from danger and repeatedly escorting her to her wedding feast. Poignantly, in the feudal, "courtly love" mentality of the *Zohar* and its protagonists, happiness and joy were the preserves of the Shekhinah and the Holy Blessed One, and the best that married humans can do is to imitate them. The kabbalistic position is that people are flawed without spouses; life is incomplete and the very structure of the sefirotic flow does not reach them.[34] The married state is the only state of real wholeness. Maintaining a marriage is essential for the upholding of the miẓvot. Married life is the template around which the kabbalist manages his sexual and social continence.[35]

Marriage is also the platform for the conveyance of new souls into the world, a matter of great responsibility. In fact, marriage could be defined as the union of two souls, for the purpose of creating new souls. The union of the husband and the wife's souls, if the match is appropriate, is predestined and their souls are fused and conjoined. The children that they create house new souls. Hence, marital life is a grave and joyous privilege. The way to perfect one's own soul, in order to be worthy of a good soul mate, the better to have a happy marriage, is through the perfection of one's religious practice. Sin, therefore, leads to bad marriages, in which the couple's two souls are combined imperfectly. The wedding itself unifies the earthly couple, but it also unifies the cosmos. It is a widespread practice, to this day, to link the seven blessings over the nuptial couple to the seven lower sefirot.[36] The ring itself symbolizes the original void of the creation of the world, according to the *Zohar*'s creation tradition.[37] The three guarantees to the bride, of livelihood, clothing and sex are provided as rewards for Torah study, the wearing of the prayer shawl and the timely recitation of the Shema'.[38] A good spouse is predestined, while an unsuccessful marriage is a punishment for transgression.

Marital sex had to be loving at all times, as the spirit of the parents during the act of intercourse determines the nature of the children.[39] The most propitious time for sex was Friday, so that the act was paralleled the union of the Holy Blessed One (*Kadosh Barukh Hu*) and the Shekhinah.[40] At that time, sex was particularly wholehearted; the married couple are themselves made part of the unifying cosmic order.[41] This erotic spirit suffuses most kabbalistic literature, as well as the liturgy for the Sabbath evening and the first days of Passover.

UPHEAVALS

As with all matters of religious practice, the religious laws regarding sexuality are, for the kabbalists, the keys to the understanding of what sexuality is. Relationships and other transactions between the genders, such as marriage, divorce and childrearing, are governed by halakhah. The meaning of sexual desire comes in part from the way it is governed in the laws of marriage, menstrual separation, divorce, levirate marriage and widowhood.

The inevitable upheavals of conjugal life, such as divorce and levirate marriage, all derive from the descent of holiness into this fallen world.[42] Levirate marriage, the ancient responsibility for a man to marriage his brother's childless widow (Deut. 25.5–10), was a particularly powerful metaphor in classical Kabbalah. According to the law, a child born in the second marriage, fathered by the former brother-in-law, is formally called the "son" of the first husband. In the section of the *Zohar* known as *Sabba de-Mishpatim*,[43] the theme of levirate marriage is employed as a metaphor for the soul's reincarnation. The unborn child of the first marriage is born in the second union so that the child of the second union is the reincarnation of the first husband. Hence, the *Zohar* sees reincarnation as the very *reason* for levirate marriage, reflecting an idea championed by Todros Abulafia, the patron of the Castilian kabbalists.[44]

The metaphysical underpinnings of levirate marriage are full of tensions and anxieties. The child of the second marriage is destined to be the opponent of the second husband for the love of his mother. The souls of the first and second husband struggle in the wife's womb. The tragic outcome of this struggle is that one spirit must be discarded. This spirit has, in the struggle for hegemony, been overcome and pushed out to wander. Wraithlike, it wanders the world, appearing to people in dream visions and haunting its own gravesite.[45]

Sexual struggle and romantic pathos are not limited to levirate marriage. Any remarriage, whether in a case of levirate marriage, divorce or widowhood, results in the spirits of the former and present husband contending with one another. The *Zohar* points out that "one who marries a widow is like one who sets sail on the sea in strong winds without ropes, not knowing if he will pass in peace or not . . ."[46] The deceased husband's spirit dwells with the widow for the year after his death, leaving only to visit his *nefesh* (presumably at the gravesite). Widows were therefore instructed not to remarry within the first year of the husband's death, for the first husband's presence was likely to come between her and her second husband.[47]

Classical kabbalistic thought considers divorce as another tragic upheaval, a rending in the fabric of reality.[48] The *Zohar* avers that "divorces combine, divorces of this world and divorces of the upper world." When the wife is enjoined, in the Torah's injunction regarding divorce (Deut. 24.1), to "go to another," this "other" is necessarily linked to the otherness of the demonic.

According to the *Zohar* and the Safed Kabbalah, a married couple's sexual life was a symbolic act, their intercourse a parallel to the Divine union. Hence, paradoxically, it was through their own intercourse that they could cleave to the Shekhinah. Forbidden sexual relationship had no such utility, and there evolved a significant system of penitential rituals to atone for premarital sex, sex during the menstrual cycle, adultery and homosexual liaisons. Notably absent from this list was masturbation, and that was because the kabbalists were divided as to whether any act could atone for so heinous an offence, the "blemishing of the covenant." The fantasy inherent in masturbation conjured the demonic Lillit in one of her guises. This was an act of Satanism, no more or less, and so kabbalistic discourse was divided as to whether it could ever be rectified.[49]

Otherwise, the rectification of sexual sins was an important part of the atonement process for the kabbalists of Jerusalem. There has, recently, been a resurgence in public rituals for the atonement for such sexual offenses as masturbation, adultery, homosexual relations and intercourse during the menstrual cycle. These rituals developed during the Safed renaissance, were described in the Lurianic writings and persist to this day. The Beit El kabbalists continue to publicly perform these rites, as evidenced by the public atonement for homosexual relations recorded in the film *Trembling Before G-d*. There is a regular *tiqqun ha-yesod* (prayer for the rectification of sexual sins) held by the Nahar Shalom community, which is usually portrayed as a response to the general debasement of modern Israeli society. Otherwise, it is really impossible to categorize the kabbalistic view of sexuality in modern terms; it is foreign to the modern sensibility.

PATRIARCHY

The world of Kabbalah, in its classical period, was most often a male preserve, and while kabbalists might have exalted the Shekhinah, their own marital relationships seem to have been ambivalent.[50] Kabbalists "had" to be married; yet their primary allegiance was to the Shekhinah.[51] Moreover, the mystique of Kabbalah drew on the most ancient, recondite patriarchal traditions of Judaism. This truth has been hard to accept for many. The enthusiasm for Kabbalah in the twentieth century often drew on a celebration of the Shekhinah, which often was applied to twentieth-century metaphors of empowerment and liberation. The Kabbalah scholar Elliot Wolfson has qualified the triumphant view of the feminine in Kabbalah, exposed many examples of the subsidiary status of the Shekhinah in much theosophical Kabbalah and identified a number of phallocentric themes. At the time, Wolfson's initial studies were often shouted down as affronts to Jewish progressivism and the erotic freighting of Zionism itself. The Shekhinah had her lobby, but the kabbalistic world remains a man's world, particularly when the mythos of the Shekhinah is applied to the ubiquitous religious law in the sacred texts.[52]

Inherent in the relationship of the various partners in the marital upheavals of levirate marriage, widowhood and divorce is the wife's subjugation to her husband. The missionary position is a literal metaphor for the relationship of *Tiferet* and *Malkhut*, and so, in the act of procreation, the husband is considered the *mashpi'a*, the "one who influences."[53] This dark partriarchality is echoed by Ḥayyim Vital, who repeatedly asserted "you have no (man) who takes a wife and has intercourse with her who does not leave in her one part of his spirit."[54] Otherwise, the *Zohar*'s view of divorce is patriarchal, in that it is usually the wife's fault.[55] A misogynist horror is expressed toward the woman who marries a succession of husbands (Deut. 24.1–3). Contact with such a woman corrupts her spouses, for her womb is compared to a used vessel, unfit for sacramental purposes.[56] Nonetheless, it is terrible for a husband to neglect his wife sexual needs, and conjugal neglect became a theme in Lurianic Kabbalah.[57]

The bleak view of human relationships that has been thus far presented reflects the medieval milieu that produced the *Zohar* and the Safed Kabbalah. The Hasidic movement that developed in Eastern Europe in the eighteenth century celebrated and idealized the love relationship of marriage, as part of that movement's recognition of the validity of pleasure. Accounts of the Ba'al Shem Tov dwelled on the trust and intimacy of his relationship with his wife. Later, Hasidism would become dynastic, and Hasidic society would scrutinize each partner in the marital relationship. Although we have the impression that arranged marriages were the norm in Eastern Europe, these were often reserved for the rabbinic aristocracy, and among the common folk romantic love remained the norm.[58] Kabbalistic notions of soul union and predestination (expressed in this Yiddish term *bashert*, "assured") and the freighted, cosmic dimensions of achieving a happy married life gained importance as modern notions of free will in determining one's personal future became normative. Today, as ever, young couples ponder the cosmic significance of the choices that they are making, and many is the time that they plaintively ask their Rabbi, "Is this my soul-mate?"

THE SABBATH

The Sabbath (Hebrew: *Shabbat*) served as the most widely known time cycle in classical Jewish practice. Sabbath rest is an act of *imitatio Dei*, "imitation of the Divine," remembering the act of God's rest during the seven days of creation. As the Sabbath was commemorative of God's rest on the seventh day, so the practice of the Sabbath was viewed as a return to a kind of Edenic innocence, particularly in its celebration of the value of pleasure. One doesn't have to be a kabbalist to have this sensibility; it is the case throughout exoteric Judaism.

The nature of the Jewish Sabbath evolved through the interpretations of the Rabbis of the Talmud, as filtered through the sensibilities of the kabbalists. The rabbis were concerned with determining what "rest" was commanded on the Sabbath. This concern led to an atomistic analysis of what "work", or rather "labor," consisted. The rabbis concluded that the activities to be prohibited were those that were employed in the construction of the tabernacle during the desert wandering, as described in the books of Leviticus and Numbers. Food production, building, cloth making, construction and a number of other processes were included in the prohibited actions that comprise the avoidance of work on the Sabbath.

The *Zohar* added another level of drama to this legal structure. The *Zohar* portrayed the Shekhinah as exiled from God, during the week, by being blocked from a direct union with the upper sefirot. Put in sefirotic terms, the sefirah Malkhut is blocked from receiving the power of the upper sefirot in the bundle of forces that is called Tiferet. Shabbat is the time when the sefirot are aligned properly, so that there is an unobstructed flow of Divine energy into the world. The main event of the Sabbath is the experience of energy that suffuses the world from the beginning of the day at sunset to the following sunset. Part of this is the descent of the "extra soul" on the Sabbath, a rabbinic idea that gained deeper significance in the *Zohar*.[59]

This separation and reunion of these elements of the Divine portrayed as a sacred wedding. Many times, in the *Zohar*, the Shekhinah is described as a lost princess, separated from her consort. On the Sabbath, she rejoins him and they experience a sexual union, the effects of which suffuse the world with Divine energy. Before this can occur, she has to be "rescued" from the malevolent forces that are obstructing her. This is the work of the kabbalists, who go out to escort her to the bridal canopy, in their role as the *shushvinin*, wedding courtiers. This mythos still reinforces the Friday night ritual of the kabbalists. It became the normative liturgy of Judaism for Friday night, through the addition of extra Psalms and the hymn *Lekha Dodi*.[60]

The lighting of the Sabbath candles was instituted in the Second Temple Period as an ideological statement. At that time, there were ascetic groups who maintained the ideological position that Jews should rigorously abstain from all forms of consumption and interferences with the phenomenal world. Not so, averred the rabbis of the Talmud, one may take advantage of the preparations that one has made for enjoying the evening, among these being the lighting of the Sabbath candles on Friday night, so that they may shine through the evening. The moment of candle lighting became a moment of reflection and contemplation, as the earliest signs of sunset began to show and the entire community detaches from matters of the secular and prepare for the tranquility of the Sabbath. The lighting of the candles was defined, from the Second Temple Period, as a "women's miẓvah" and it has survived as such to this day. So powerful was the effect of this practice that R. Menachem Mendel Schneursen, the last Rabbi of the Chabad movement, made candle lighting a pillar of Chabad outreach, even specifying that girls begin to light from the age of 3.

The Sabbath table is compared, by the Talmud, to the altar in the Jerusalem Temple, but many graphic representations from manuscript prayer books seem to have portrayed it as a Mandala, implying, after a conclusion by Arthur Green in another context, that it functioned as a kind of "Axis Mundi," a world center.[61] At the table, the requisite hymns are recited, depending on the tradition, and after the hand washing two loaves are produced. One loaf is cut prior to the blessing and placed under the second, symbolizing the Shekhinah in her missionary position under Tiferet, the aggregate of the upper six sefirot.

The observance of the Sabbath evolved from the directives of the Talmud and the *Zohar* to their execution by the Safed kabbalists. Any number of times, the *Zohar* would make some remark about what Rabbi Shimon bar Yoḥai and his comrades liked to do. Centuries later, the Safed kabbalists would develop a service or rite that expressed the same idea or practice. For example, the Talmud[62] describes the practice of dressing in white and rising to greet the Sabbath queen. Accordingly, a Safed kabbalist, R. Shlomo ha-Levi Alkabetẓ, wrote a Hymn, "Come my Beloved to Meet the Bride (Hebrew: *Lecha dodi likraat kallah*)." This hymn became liturgically normative for Friday night, along with an entire collection of psalms and hymns that had not been in the liturgy previously but were inserted by the Safed kabbalists and subsequently embraced by the larger Jewish community.

An observance that originates with the *Zohar* concerns the Sabbath meals. At one point, R. Shimon bar Yoḥai is reputed to have sung a series of hymns for each of the three meals of the day.[63] A discussion ensues among the sages as to which countenance (here viewed as a bloc of sefirot) each meal exemplifies and welcomes. The conclusion is that the Friday night meal is a feast in honor of the wedding, and union, of the Shekhinah, in accordance with the theme of the divine wedding. The Sabbath day meal is dedicated to 'Attika Kadishah, the patriarch. The last meal is that of the middle bloc of sefirot, Zeir Anpin, the restless youth who is the center of Divine activity according to the later strata of the *Zohar* and the Lurianic system. The *Zohar* remarks that Rabbi Shimon used to welcome them with the cry "we are setting forth the meal of the Shekhinah, we are setting the meal of Zeir" and so forth. To that end, upon his arrival in Safed, Isaac Luria composed three extensive hymns, one for each meal, that each build on Rabbi Shimon's initial greeting to the countenances.

As the shadows gather, the kabbalists repair to the synagogue for the afternoon and evening prayers, with the third meal between them. The Lurianic hymn for Zeir Anpin is recited, and the kabbalists gather to ward off the forces of malevolence gathering with the departure of the Sabbath in the coming evening. The braided candle of the closing service wards off these malevolent forces and the spice box revives the soul as it loses its extra dimension. Buoyed by a series of hymns and prayers for safety and prosperity, the palpable presence of the Shekhinah departs the community for another week.

LITURGY

It was at this point, the sixteenth century, that texts from the *Zohar* itself began to be incorporated into the prayer book and general liturgy. The liturgical employment of the *Zohar* is widespread today and embedded in many different rituals. Even the liberal rites have preserved the prayer of the angels, *Berikh Shmeih*, in its Torah service, while narratives of the union of the Shekhinah and God are incorporated in the rite of the ḥasidim. Some communities even sang R. Shimon Lavi of Tripoli's panegyric hymn "Bar Yohai" near the Lekhah Dodi hymn, as well as inserting the passage from the *Zohar* regarding the Sabbath union of the "Holy Blessed One" and the Shekhinah on the Sabbath. The Hasidic rite has included extensive readings from the *Zohar* for the Sabbath meals and at various points in the festival services. Other texts find their way, albeit less obtrusively, into the North African and Middle Eastern liturgies. The appearance of texts from the *Zohar* is significant, as the transition of materials into the Jewish liturgy arguably makes these Jewish texts canonical.[64] When the text has reach the level of credibility that it can be chanted, without knowledge of its content, then it can arguably have crossed the line from a mere "sacred text" to "canon."

As mentioned, the Friday night service, with its additional hymns and Psalms, was largely developed by the Safed kabbalists. Up to that time, the Friday evening service was little different from that of a regular evening service, with little break for any additional prayers. Not so in Safed, where a series of Psalms emphasizing the coronation of God were interspersed with the Hymns of the sacred marriage, not least Alkabetz' "Lekha Dodi." Each of the Psalms for the Sabbath Eve was developed in light of its kabbalistic significance, with the possible exception of Psalm 29, which seems to have been in effect liturgically prior to the Safed renaissance. There emerged a widespread practice of including the recitation of the Song of Songs, with its themes of erotic love and yearning, as well as the later Safed kabbalist Elazar Azikri's moaningly erotic *Yedid Nefesh* ("Soul Love") as part of the pre-Sabbath ritual, in order to suffuse the atmosphere with the eros of the Shekhinah's approach. Hasidic practice made official the addition of certain rituals, such as the recitation of Psalm 107 prior to the afternoon service. The longer morning service for the Sabbath and festivals was mandated prior to the development of classical kabbalistic innovation, with the exception of the non-Ashkenazi practice of reciting the Merkavah hymn "the Glory and the Faith" (*ha-Aderet ve-ha-Emunah*) prior to the series "Blessed is He Who Spoke."

SEPARATION

The traditional Sabbath also celebrates the virtue of separation from the secular. The very Hebrew word for "holy," *kadosh*, means, literally, "set aside," so that the sense of the Sabbath as a special preserve was essential to classical kabbalistic understandings of the day. Preparations, such as setting aside one's Shabbat clothes (preferably with themes of white, to indicate the purity of the virginal Shekhinah) and cutting one's hair and fingernails, were transformed from neutral acts of hygiene to forms of purifications, of removing personal "extranea" much as the cosmic extranea would be purged from the universe or the extent of the Sabbath. With the onset of the Hasidic movement and the teachings of its progenitor, the Ba'al Shem Tov, it became widespread for men to immerse in the mikveh, or ritual bath. The Ba'al Shem Tov popularized this act of purification for men.[65] The times for going to the mikveh become, more often than not, the eve of the Sabbath and Festivals. Immersion in the mikveh, for men, had been the practice of adepts, but the Hasidic community popularized this custom. It remains common in the Hasidic community to this day.

The Sabbath is a physical space, with physical boundaries beyond which one could not cross, boundaries of the home, the public thoroughfare and that walled city. On the Sabbath, traditional Jewish communities are marked by physical separation, as the community confines itself to a limited place from out of which one may not carry or even stray. In every instance, the kabbalist was concerned with creating the walled in, private space of the Sabbath, particularly with a meticulous inspection of whatever physical Sabbath boundaries had been put in place for the event of the Sabbath. For the authors of the later sections of the *Zohar*, the private and public domains on the Sabbath signify the realms of the holy and the demonic. The private domain is that of the holy, while the public thoroughfare signifies the profane. This concern with "inner" and "outer" mirrored the physical space in traditional Jewish communities, with their closed boundaries for carrying and their outer boundaries for walking. The Sabbath space also exists temporally, as the Sabbath is "a palace in time," according to Abraham Joshua Heschel, so that besides being a physical sacred space, the Sabbath is a temporal period of sacredness, in which all forms of labor were prohibited and a dynamic of pleasure and contemplation was set out.[66] The Sabbath, being wholly given over to the sacred, had to be separated from the profane in every way.

THE FESTIVALS

A basic premise of classical Kabbalah is that cosmic processes are unfolding over Jewish liturgical time. Among the most important of these cosmic dramas is the kabbalistic mythos of the seasons. In the structure of Jewish law, there are two festival cycles that intertwine and complement one another. One is the repentance cycle, which begins a month before Rosh ha-Shanah, the New Year and continues to Yom Kippur, the Day of Atonement. The other is the cycle of historical and harvest festivals that dot the year, Passover, Shavuot (Pentecost)—the festival of the receiving of the Torah, and Sukkot, the festival that commemorates the wandering in the desert. In Kabbalah, these two cycles have two separate mythic bases, which call for specific responses on the part of the kabbalists.

In Kabbalah, the Jewish holidays are merely the surface events that underlie cosmic struggles and transitions in the life of the Shekhinah. These underlying mythic themes are the true rationale for the exoteric practices of the holidays. For example, the blowing of the ram's horn (*shofar*) on the New Year literally "awakens" a sleeping aspect of divinity, the sleeping power of Tiferet,[67] from its slumber, in order to advocate for the Jewish people. All Jews, not just kabbalists, view these not as a re-enactment but mirror events that are happening in real time in the cosmic realm. The Passover holiday, as well, represents a "flight" from the forces of impurity, which is then followed by a seven-week process of purification, ending with the holiday of *Shavuot*, or Pentecost.

The image of heavenly court is supplanted by another image from the rabbinic period, namely the function of the Jerusalem Temple, which is the overt preoccupation of the liturgy and the legal realm. Hence, the additional service for the Day of Atonement is centered on a rite of identification with the passion of the High Priest in the Temple on that day. During the additional service, every worshipper internalizes the progression of the High Priest through the various stations of his worship. In the same way, the commandments of blowing the *shofar* on Rosh ha-Shanah and bringing the four species of plant life to the synagogue are an importation, into the synagogue, of the Jerusalem rite of antiquity. Clearly, the first business of Kabbalah in all these respects is to imbue the actions themselves, which the Rabbis of the Talmud resolutely considered as conceived "for their own sake," as pointing to larger processes in the Cosmos.

THE ATONEMENT CYCLE

The cycle of atonement is a period of heightened anxiety in the Jewish year. This season, from the beginning of the month of Ellul, continuing through the New Year and culminating on the Day of Atonement (*Yom Kippur*), is a period of Divine judgment. The central image of the repentance cycle, especially its culminating ten days of repentance from Rosh ha-Shanah to Yom Kippur, is the celestial court, in which God judges humankind and, particularly, the Jews. The celestial court is an image that derives from sources in the Bible and the Apocrypha. It convenes to settle the collective and individual fates of humankind for the coming year. The Jewish nation assembles; their conduct is reviewed in the Divine court, at which point a ten-day period of "sentencing," the ten days of repentance, ensues. Finally, on the Day of Atonement, the great gates of heaven close as the Jewish nation assembles outside, wildly singing the praises of the creator. Throughout the ten-day period, the nation avows its faith in God's granting them agricultural prosperity and freedom from pestilence, sickness and the oppression of the gentiles. This mythos, together with the imagery of the Divine court, the Book of Life and the decrees for the year, remains in all Jewish liturgy, in even the most liberal and reductionist movements. By taking part in the cosmic dramas of the season of repentance and the Days of Awe, the act of repentance and the expunging of sin were expressed with a muscular spirituality, fueled by a wailing sense of penitential remorse.

One particularly significant liturgical passage, for kabbalists, was the refrain of the silent devotion for the ten days of repentance: *Remember us for life, King who desires life, and write us in the Book of Life, for your sake, living God*. The kabbalists saw this moment in the synagogue service as the opportunity to dispose off the forces that have accrued to the Jewish people during the year by "offloading" them onto the feminine aspect of God, the *Shekhinah*, or more specifically her incarnation in the Lurianic system as *Nukvah*. The Shekhinah then carries away all of the judgments that would have fallen upon the people Israel, just as the scapegoat of the Temple Period atonement rite was sent into the desert bearing the communal sins.[68] The refrain, *Remember us for life, O King who desires life, and write us in the book of life*, is an explicit reference to the jettisoning of the forces of judgment. The adherent beseeches God to return the people Israel to the condition that they enjoyed before the destruction of the Temple.[69]

Over the course of the ten days between the New Year and the Day of Atonement, the forces of judgment pass though the sefirot and the countenances. Each day of the ten days of repentance is characterized by the aura of *sefirah* or countenance that is being stripped of those forces. The third day of the ten days of atonement is traditionally a fast day, the Fast of Gedaliah. That day is still beset by the forces of judgment but it doesn't have the blowing of the *shofar* to neutralize them, as was the case on the first two days. Hence, that is the day Gedaliah, the Babylonian governor in the First Temple Period, was killed, thereby hastening the destruction of the first Temple.[70] On the Day of Atonement, the five forms of self-affliction that are practiced reflect the function of the sweetening of five "judgments" (*gevurot*), exemplified in the five acts of penance or abstention associated with that day.[71]

THE PILGRIMAGE FESTIVALS

The pilgrimage festivals, Passover, Shavuot (Pentecost) and Sukkot, are simultaneously harvest festivals and commemorations of the Jewish people's wandering in the desert. Because the allotted time of each festival revolves around the number seven, each one is portrayed as having something to do with the lower seven sefirot, implying that they relate to the nature of the phenomenal world.

For example, the Sukkot festival takes place over seven days. One obligation of the holiday is to build a makeshift booth in which to eat and live for the duration of the festival. The other significant mizvah is that of bringing the four species of vegetation, the citron, palm, myrtle and willow, to the synagogue and waving them at select points in the prayer service. Each of these mizvot points to the idea that Sukkot is a *tiqqun*, or repair, of the spiritual aspects of the phenomenal world.

One of the most widespread customs of the festival originates in the *Zohar*,[72] which teaches that on every day of the festival, one of the "guests" should be invited into the Sukkah to celebrate with the family. These "guests," Abraham, Isaac, Jacob, Moses, Aaron Joseph and David, are, of course, the paradigms for each of the lower sefirot, so that every day of the holiday is suffused with the aura of that sefirah's influence. The Sukkah itself, being a cube, stands for the special dimensions of the universe: North, South, East, West, up, down and the very fact of existence itself, which is symbolized by the sefirah Malkhut.

During Sukkot, the waving of the four species of plants is the most important synagogue ritual. Among the Jerusalem kabbalists today, the meditations attending the waving of the palm, myrtle, willow and citron therefore supplant those of other prayers.[73] The four species represent the ten sefirot: the citron is the Shekhinah, as all fruit are paradigms of the feminine. The palm branch symbolizes the expanded form of Tiferet, as it resembles the Hebrew letter *vav* whose numerical coefficient is six, implying the triunity of the middle six sefirot. The myrtle, which is the series of triune structures, symbolizes the sefirot Ḥokhmah, Binah and Da'at. The willow, having no scent of its own and withering very quickly, is included to assuage the forces of the demonic. The four species are waved in six directions during the Hallel service, drawing the flow of Divinity into the phenomenal world. Having undergone the cleansing experience of the atonement cycle, the purpose and effect of the miẓvot of Sukkot is to restore the spirituality of the phenomenal world. In order to do this, the miẓvot of the holiday draw the flow of the Divine into the dimensional, phenomenal world of the lower seven sefirot.

PASSOVER AND COUNTING THE OMER

Passover is different from the aforementioned Sukkot cycle. Instead of seven days, the entire festival is really a cycle taking place over seven weeks, from Passover to Pentecost. This larger cycle is, in classical Kabbalah, linked to the mythos of the Shekhinah and the experience of the Exodus. The *Zohar* taught that the first days of Passover constitute a spiritual redemption that liberates God's earthly presence, the Shekhinah, from the cosmic "Egypt."[74] Since the Passover Seder is only the beginning of the process of redemption, it is haunted by images of unfinished and broken things. These include, for example, the broken maẓah on the Seder table and the diminished order of celebratory Psalms (*Hallel*) during the holiday services.[75]

The night of the Seder is viewed as a burst of lovingkindness. However, as this liberating impulse subsides, the redeemed Shekhinah is thought of as only emerging from her "impurity." The ravages of the Winter travail are seen as the Shekhinah's. As the process of menstrual purification requires seven "clear" days of purification after the menstrual cycle, so the Shekhinah requires seven weeks in order to be presented to her bridegroom for marriage.

The miẓvah of counting of the Omer consists of marking each of the days between the Passover and Shavuot holidays with a special ritual. These days, called the *Omer*, were the days of the gathering of the first wheat in the time of the Jerusalem Temple. The counting of the Omer is a popular kabbalistic ritual that has persisted among Jews who pray according to the orthodox and Hasidic rites.[76] Most Jews simply count off the days every evening, but the kabbalistic understanding linked the act of counting to an underlying spiritual process. These are the 49 days of the Omer, which purify the Shekhinah from what amounts to the defilement of her sojourn in Egypt. She is restored to God at the holiday of Shavuot, at the end of the counting of the Omer, at which point the Torah is given as a wedding gift.[77]

The most widespread kabbalistic meditation for the counting of the Omer links each day of the Omer to a particular confluence of sefirot. The seven lower sefirot transform into seven times seven according to a basic premise of Cordoverean Kabbalah, namely that every one of the *sefirot* has a full complement of *sefirot* within it. Therefore, the 49 days of the Omer are devoted to the repair of any flaws committed in the bottom seven sefirot of each of the lower seven sefirot.

This visualization of this repair of the lower sefirot is the basis of the "semi-popular" view of counting the Omer, the popular devotion that is widely reproduced in most Hasidic prayer books, and has recently been incorporated into the Ashkenazic rite in the Anglo-Saxon *Artscroll* editions. The most widely circulated version of the ritual may be found in a number of popular prayer books as follows:

Master of the Universe, you commanded us through your servant Moses to count the Omer in order to purify ourselves from our kelipot and our impurities, as you have written in our Torah . . . in order to purify the souls of Your people Israel from their impurity. Thus may it be thy will, our God and god of our fathers, that in the merit of the counting of the Omer that I counted today, that it fixed whatever I have blemished in the sefirah _____ in _____ and I will purify and I will be sanctified in the Holiness of Above, and through this will flow a Divine effluence through all the worlds to repair our physical souls (*nafshoteinu*) and spirits (*ruhoteinu*) and highest souls (*nishmoteinu*) from every blemish and to purify us and sanctify us with you highest holiness, *Amen Sela.*

According to this system, each day of the Omer is aligned with a certain combination of the lower seven sefirot with one of its own seven inner sefirot. It seems that this sefirotic counting of the Omer is the intention that Luria himself practiced, according to the new reconstructed version of this rite and the writings of his student Ya'akov Ẓemakh.[78]
Notwithstanding the fact that Luria used the earlier system, the systems of counting the Omer in the "Lurianic Writings" differ from this model in that they do not concern themselves with the system of the sefirot, but rather with the interplay of the countenances, especially the conception, nurturing and maturing of the countenance *Zeir Anpin.* The basic difference in the Lurianic system, across the board, is that rather than tracing the act of repair through the seven lower sefirot, the entire sefirotic system is reviewed during the process, from *Da'at* to *Malkhut*, with the intermediate seven sefirot being collapsed into the amalgam Tiferet, which is synonymous with *Zeir Anpin.* Eventually there came to be, in the mainstream kabbalistic tradition, at least five understandings of the metaphysics of counting the Omer in the intervening weeks between Passover and Shavuot. Four of these traditions are Lurianic and all five largely contradict one another. These discrepancies in the counting of the Omer originate in the vagaries of the Lurianic canon, in which two versions were presented, which were then interpreted differently by subsequent kabbalists.[79]

INTENTION

There are, according to Jewish tradition, 613 commandments in the Torah, which were expanded by the Rabbis into countless strictures and admonitions. There are nearly 2,600 pages of basic text in the Babylonian Talmud, not to mention the Jerusalem Talmud, the various volumes of Midrash and other halakhic writing. All of this material was grist for the mill for the kabbalists. Kabbalah is drenched in the sensibility of these laws and their underlying mentality. One can't extract Kabbalah from that context in pursuit to some false notion of an "essence," separate from what might be, to the modernist, the arcane and archaic structure of the laws.

Therefore the remarks in this chapter have only been of the most general sort, and I can't hope to write comprehensively about the entire influence of kabbalistic thinking in the ritual, sexual and social life of the Jews, or its effect on their eating patterns or family life. Suffice it to say that the images of the law were shuffled into the general mix of symbolism and metaphysical influence, employed as direction signs to a larger plane of reality. Every law or principle was like a flag or buoy, saying, in effect, "beneath this marker lies a deep well of meaning; observe the law and thence open the door to the powerful forces and compelling realities that impel it."

CHAPTER 7

PRAYER

As meditation is to an Eastern religious worldview, so prayer is to Judaism: the human act that expresses the basic statement of what the religion is about. In Eastern religions, meditation separates the believer from the "illusion" of present existence, pointing to the emptiness that lies beneath it. In Judaism, prayer expresses the relationship with God that is at the core of the religion. Prayer defines the theology of Judaism and is the instrument of breakthrough to God. From the Bible on, prayer has always been the way to confront and encounter God.

Prayer has always been intrinsic to Judaism and yet so radically individual that it cannot be fully controlled. It has always been slightly out of reach of religious authority.

The Rabbis of the Talmud did not compose the Jewish liturgy; all that they did was to take preexistent prayer traditions, such as the *Shema'* and the silent devotion, and impose rules on them.

The kabbalists began with the legal identity of the prayers, which they imbued with metaphysical significance, as they did to all categories of Jewish law. The act of reciting the Shema' became a moment in which the kabbalist actually unified God with the phenomenal world, the point of juncture being the kabbalist's mind. The morning prayer service became an ascent through the four worlds of creation to the most infinite heights of the Divine, followed by a wild careening surf down the flow of the Divine effluence or *shefa'*.

Prayer also involved participation in several different types of mythology, from the myth of the lowly supplicant in the halls of the Divine palace to the myth of the questing hero, who has come to provoke a response from the Divine. This meaning applied to extemporaneous "heroic" prayer in times of crisis, particularly for the Jewish community, but the kabbalistic understanding brought this sensibility to mundane, rote liturgical recitation as well. Every kabbalist was an intercessor for the Jewish people, with God, at a time of crisis, and the crises, to this day, have never stopped.

Like the rhythms of the Jewish year, the ritual of Jewish prayer is based in the unfolding of time, measured over the course of the day, week, month and year. This secular time is merely a reflection

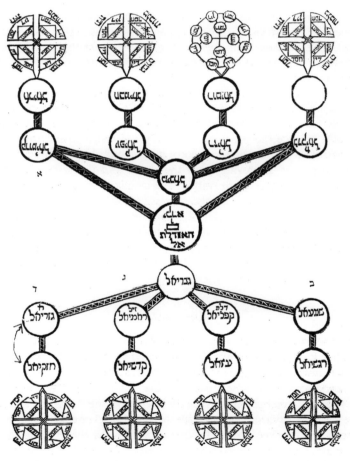

Figure 7.1 Sefirotic energy as it pours into the Tabernacle, from Avraham Azulai's *Or ha-Ḥammah.*

of events occurring in the realm of God over the same time periods. God's time, the interplay of forces in Heaven and the underworld, is merely reflected in liturgical prayer. The kabbalistic form of prayer, which understands the processes taking place beneath the surface of present existence, points to the truth of these underlying forces.

At the lowest level of spirituality, some Jewish prayer involves asking God for *things*. Even the daily silent devotion is a laundry list of the people Israel's demands and desires: peace, health, livelihood and the end to the exile. Kabbalists saw this prayer service as a *rite*, not a means to having a good "feeling." In order to spiritualize the process of Jewish prayer, they made it clear that they had no needs at all, and were performing the prayer ritual simply to lock themselves into sync with God, without even the reward of a good *feeling* from the process.

The position of classical Judaism is that petitional prayer was developed to compensate for the loss of the soteric powers of the Temple rite. This is particularly the case in the Days of Awe, which literally replace the passion of the High Priest in the Temple with the petitions of the synagogue congregation.[1] At that time, prayer had the power to elevate both the inner and the outer nature of the cosmic structure, but only at the celebration of the New Year. Since, the destruction of the Temple, however, mere prayer no longer "works" for the purposes that it claims to rectify, namely the fulfillment of the concrete needs of the Jewish people. In the idealized past, the temple rite and petitional prayer were enough to expunge harsh judgment from the world. Today, all that remains of the process is the kabbalistic rite.

KAVVANAH

For most people practicing classical Judaism, the "fuel" for prayer, whether kabbalistic or not, is considered to be the rabbinic notion of *kavvanah*, which literally means "intention" but in the popular parlance might be called the "feeling" of prayer. The very term "kavvanah" emerges out of Jewish law, implying "will" or volition. The idea of kavvanah began with the rabbinical concern with spontaneity and "feeling" in a religious act versus the rote practice of the same act. Certain commandments could not be fulfilled by the act alone, but the act had to be accompanied by the "intention of the heart." The rote performance of a commandment might not fulfill the obligation, while the performance with this intention (Hebrew: *kavvanah*) was seen as the ideal.

This distinction between rote and intended action was particularly sharp with regard to the act of prayer. The Rabbis were highly conscious that the rote recitation of prayer had to be accompanied by an emotional commitment to the prayer's meaning.

In the history of Kabbalah, concern with kavvanah stretches from the early Kabbalah, in Gerona, Provence and the Rhineland, to Hasidic movement of the eighteenth century. A founding figure of early Kabbalah, Azriel of Gerona, portrayed kavvanah as ". . . systematic absorption in the Divine Will and the desire to be united with it."[2] Azriel saw Jewish prayer, in its popular form, as practiced by the entire Jewish community, as a way to confront God and also as a method for enlightenment. Shortly afterward, the German pietists (*ḥasidei Ashkenaz*) of the Rhineland were the first to insist that the text of the prayer book be absolutely consistent, in all of it's minutia, from edition to edition. For the *ḥasidei Ashkenaz*, the prayer book was a sort of formula for gaining access to God's will, as long as prayer was executed according to the absolutely accredited version of the text, executed with precision. The liturgy was sacred canon and could not be altered in any way.

It was at this early juncture that kabbalists began to practice formal prayer intentions, or *kavvanot*. This kabbalistic prayer unifies and links all the worlds in the highest levels of the cosmos, to make the Divine flow, or *shefa'*, descend into the corporeal world. It is, as defined by the contemporary scholar Jonathan Garb, a mysticism of "drawing down." Garb has written that the primary nature of kavvanah, from practically the inception of the term in antiquity, referred to the channeling and harnessing of Divine power. In harnessing kavvanah, the adept may draw down the power from the cosmic realm (hydraulic) or he may provoke Divine expression through the relationship between the cosmic form and the human (isomorphism). Through the empowered consciousness of kavvanah, human and Divine thought connect and intersect, so that the body and mind become platforms for the Divine.[3] According to kabbalistic thought, the real function and meaning of prayer is not to simply profess faith in God and then ask for things, as it would seem from the manifest structure of the Shema' and the silent devotion. In fact, the kabbalistic worldview considered the prayers to be devices to bring about processes that have nothing to do with what the words really say in their plain meaning. The role of kavvanah in prayer, as in other miẓvot, is to draw the Divine effluence and power from above to below, or, in the Lurianic model, to repair and reconcile the elements of a broken, disrupted cosmic structure.

PRAYER AS UNION

Kabbalistic prayer was the part of Kabbalah that came closest to the principle of mystical union as a universal trait of the mystical experience.[4] For kabbalists, if there was ever mystical union with God, then it was manifest in the *miẓvat ha-yiḥud*, the "miẓvah of God's unity," identified by Maimonides as a specific commandment of the Torah, namely the constant knowledge that there is one God.[5] Kabbalah inherited the philosophical idea that the oneness of God led the practitioner to certain spiritual responses. Prayer offered a chance to meditate on God's oneness through an active gesture, the unification, inherent in professing the Jewish creed known as the Shema': "Hear, Oh Israel, the Lord our God, the Lord is one!" This profession, by definition had to be heartfelt, as the *Zohar* states "If one comes to unify the holy name and did not intend it in his heart . . . his prayer is cast out and evil is decreed on it."[6] This idea was reiterated by the remark of Isaiah ha-Levi Horowitz:

> The true unification is the root of the religion and faith, of which Torah commands us in the verse "Hear O Israel, the Lord Our God the Lord is One." The inner truth of this tradition is to link and unify the emanation, which is the Divine. These are the powers that are gathered in the special Name, in One. The term *Shema'* ("Hear") implies gathering and assembly . . . The essence is that one must link and unify the branches to the root. Hence one must unify with intention and with thought purified from any other impulse, so as not to make any rupture or separation.[7]

Prayer is often understood as an act of union, between the petitioner, God and all of humankind or between the individual and the Shekhinah.[8] The goal of many kabbalistic prayers is to bring about the union of God and the world, through the drawing of the Divine energy into the soul of the practitioner.

As is so often the case, prayer is also portrayed as but one more expression of the people Israel's relationship with the Shekhinah.

In the idealized past, when the Jerusalem Temple was standing, the Shekhinah literally dwelt in the center of the shrine, the Holy of Holies. When the Temple was destroyed, the Shekhinah went into exile with the people Israel. It is a given, in Jewish history, that with the destruction of the Temple, Jewish life decentralized and the spirituality became text oriented and "portable." The eighteenth-century Jerusalem kabbalist Shalom Shar'abi portrayed the idea of the kabbalists as having a relationship with the Shekhinah, expressed through prayer, which is as mythic as any given Friday night in Safed:

> The goal of our turning in prayer is to pray and to pour out our souls to the Blessed God, to redeem the Shekhinah from the exile and to break down her prison and to free the prisoners . . . If there is one who is aroused in repentance to break down her prison, the Holy Blessed One will answer and return the Shekhinah to him, for the Shekhinah has been in exile for many days and years.[9]

In seeking to unify the Universe through the practice of mizvot and prayer, one rite that has proven particularly resilient is the *le-shem yihud* prologue, in which a given rite would be preceded by the statement "for the sake of the union of the Holy Blessed One and his Shekhinah, behold I am ready and about to perform the mizvah of _____ as it is written . . ."[10] This ascription still appears in many editions of the prayer book to this day, and acceptance of its metaphysical premises was widespread in Jewish folk religion. Hence, the idea that a given mizvah, or prayer, was really an instrument for bringing together the transcendent God and the earthly Shekhinah.

The Lurianic system also saw prayer as a device to bring about a union of transcendent forces. In the case of Luria's system, however, the union sought was that of the parent figures in the cosmic structure, Abba and Imma. The purpose of prayer in the Lurianic system was to bring about the harmonious and untroubled union of Abba and Imma, thereby causing the conception and nurturing of Zeir Anpin, the central countenance that was of central importance in the Lurianic system. The goal of all Lurianic theurgy is to turn the members of this troubled family toward each other, thus effecting "face-to-face" union and thence to repair the broken and sundered universe portrayed in the Lurianic myth. This is also the goal of prayer with the mystical intentions, to effect unions among these familial elements of the cosmic structure. From the onset of the development of Lurianic practice, certain prayers were specified as facilitating specific unions and embraces. The recitation of central prayers, such as the Shema' prayer, the reader's repetition of the silent devotion and prostrations[11] during the silent prayer were also important in reconciling the countenances Zeir and Nukvah, and bringing about their union.[12]

DEVEKUT AND THOUGHT

Another theme in kabbalistic prayer is that of *devekut* or "cleaving" to God. Devekut has its origins in the biblical adjuration to "cleave to Him (Deut. 11.22)." This "cleaving" is a constant theme in kabbalistic thought from early Kabbalah to Hasidism. In its eventual form in Polish Hasidism, it would consist of a personal experience of closeness to God. In later Hasidism, devekut expanded to a general theme, becoming a kind of "walking meditation" applied to all religious practice and not just prayer.

The instrument of devekut is the kabbalist's thought itself. "Thought" (Hebrew: *maḥshavah*) is the substance that fuels the union of the individual and the Divine. For example, the achieving of devekut thrust the kabbalist's thought to the realm of the Divine. The kabbalist's mind and thought would become receptacles for the flow of Divine energy. Similarly, Ezra and Azriel of Gerona convey the power of thought as a channeling of Divine flow:

Thought expands and rises to its place of origin . . . For the (one undergoing devekut) thought is the source and blessing and endless flow and from this emanation and adhering of thought, words are increased and multiply, and from the joy they are revealed to him, and thus was the extension of prophecy, when the prophet would concentrate and direct his heart and adhere his thought above. According to his adherence the prophet would see and know what is going to happen.[13]

Azriel of Gerona's understanding sees thought as a muscular instrument for "channeling" the Divine flow and its positive effects. In subsequent Kabbalah, the directed thought was directed to penetrate the various metaphysical systems presented by classical Kabbalah.

This directed thought, which originates in the kabbalist's mind at the time of prayer, penetrated the sefirot, the successive worlds of existence, and the celestial Palaces with their attendant angels. Kabbalists therefore saw the structure of the liturgy, the progression of the service and the prayer book text, as a code for the interaction of the sefirot.

This leads to a number of trends in the history of kabbalistic prayer. One is the boisterous emotionalism of Hasidism, which may be encountered in that movement's many contemporary outposts. The other is silent, a mind-only ritual. This developed in the aforementioned teaching of Azriel and the thought of Isaac the Blind, and presumably survived within the Jewish communities of medieval Western Europe. We assume that in every corner of the Diaspora, there were those who paid special attention to the recitation and begin to introduce the use of sacred names and other kavvanot with regard to the discipline of their minds. This practice reached an early efflorescence in the teachings of Abraham Abulafia. Today, it is the stock-in-trade of the venerated Beit El school of Jerusalem, Aleppo and Baghdad.

In all of these systems, the intention, namely, the contents of the mind, was never uttered. This is not actually unusual as Jewish practice. Throughout the world, Jews read the traditional name YHVH and yet don't pronounce the name, saying, rather, "Adonai." In this case as well, the contents of the kavvanah remain in the mind and are never sounded out.

THE ASCENT THROUGH THE WORLDS

Across a certain swath of the Jewish community, the one that runs from the Hasidic world to the Jewish Renewal community, one finds the rite of "four-worlds prayer."[14] The premise of this kind of prayer is that during the morning service, an individual's prayer and/or soul ascends through the four "worlds" of existence, as described earlier.[15] Sometimes the individual's prayer is portrayed as rising, loosed liked a slingshot into the upper worlds, while in other accounts it is the adherent's soul that rises in visionary experience.[16] In the end, the distinction hardly matters, for, eventually, the prayer was the soul and the soul was the prayer.

The four-worlds rite is based on the structure of the Morning Prayer service, which is comprised of four sections, each divided from the others by a "kaddish" prayer. According to the mythos of the four-worlds prayer service, these sections of the morning service are really chambers in a series of Divine Palaces, an image that has its origins in the earliest reaches of the Merkavah tradition and biblical prophecy. Each of the celestial palaces is a stage in the levels of Divine emanation, which correspond with successive stages of the prayer service. The soul ascends through the stages of emanation, through the successive worlds of creation, peaking at the silent devotion, and then descending.[17]

The service begins with the morning blessings, which accompany the morning routines of waking, washing and preparing for the day. These morning blessings on the first actions of the day, as well as the commemorative recitation of biblical and rabbinic verses regarding sacrifices, traverse the world of 'Assiyah. The following section consists of the recitation of Psalms, bracketed by a blessing before and after this recitation. These morning Psalms lead the adherent through world of Yezirah,[18] which in turn ends with the recitation of the Song at the Sea.[19] The third section is the recitation of the Shema' prayer, the essential credo of Judaism, which is also introduced and followed by extended blessings. The Shema', and its blessings, signal the entrance into the world of Briah, and the Divine palaces (*Heikhalot*). The 18 blessings of the silent prayer, or Amidah, follow the Shema'. The silent prayer is accompanied on most weekday mornings by a confession of sins, akin to the language of the Day of Atonement. This recitation of the silent devotion represents the attainment of the highest world, that of Azilut. This moment of confrontation provokes the flow of Divine energy, or shefa' into the phenomenal worlds, a moment of danger, and potentially martyrdom, so that the confession, or *vidui*, must be recited.[20]

It was Isaac Luria himself who associated the prayer service with the four worlds.[21] In doing so, he drew on sections of the *Zohar* known as the Heikhalot, or "Palaces," which seem to be based on the earliest Merkavah writings, as well as having parallels in the early Kabbalah.[22] Luria then adapted the *Zohar*'s understanding of prayer as it related to the Heikhalot and applied it to the tradition of the Worlds in general.

The Heikhalot passages in the *Zohar* are an apparent effort to produce a tradition that resembled the earlier Heikhalot traditions of late antiquity.[23] The second Heikhalot account in the *Zohar* (II 245b) declared that the adherent passes through the palaces during recitation of the blessings before and after the Shema'. The lowest palace is called the *Livnat ha-Sapir* (the star sapphire) and it is associated with the sefirah Yesod. In the liturgy, it is located in the acrostic "Blessed God, great in Mind (*El Barukh Gadol Deah*) and the blessing *Yoẓer Or* (creator of light). The second palace is called the *Eẓem Shamayim* (the center of Heaven) and corresponds to the inner sefirah Hod in the larger sefirah of Malkhut. The third palace is called *Nogah* (glow, Venus) and corresponds to the sefirah of Neẓaḥ, while the fourth palace is *Zekhut* (merit), corresponding to the sefirah Gevurah. The Palace of Love (*ahavah*) is suffused with the aura of the sefirah Ḥesed, and is invoked at the blessing "With great and everlasting love" (*Ahavah Rabbah*). The sixth palace is the palace of will (*Raẓon*), which corresponds to the sefirah *Tiferet*. The seventh palace is called *Kodesh ha-Kedoshim* (Holy of Holies) and corresponds to the sefirah Binah.[24] Luria's predecessor, Moshe Cordovero, had previously located the Palaces in the world of Briah, with a parallel series of seven medurim (dwellings) in the world of Yeẓirah.

According to Luria, the kabbalist must do his part in order to "fix" (*metakken*) the four worlds of Aẓilut, Briah, Yeẓirah and 'Assiyah by cleansing them of contamination. Having cleansed them, it is then possible to unify the world, as they are contaminated by kelipot, the "husks" or the detritus left over from the well-known tradition of the breaking of the vessels.

Another purpose of the four-worlds rite was to redeem the souls of humankind, which are isomorphically connected to the "world soul" and the other hierarchies of the kabbalistic system. In the course of the ascent through the worlds, the adherent's prayer rises and unifies the souls of the righteous that are built into the cosmic structure.[25]

The four-worlds liturgy created a tradition of ascent and descent that was dramatic and compelling. In effect, it was the acting out of a mystical or prophetic revelatory experience. Prayer was more than the fulfillment of certain commandments and the creation of an emotional context for their performance. Prayer was a quest, full of risk and danger. Little wonder, then, that this remained among the most tenacious of kabbalistic rites. It was slow to pass from the structure of Hasidic prayer and has been reinstituted at such venues as the Elat Chayyim center of the Jewish Renewal movement.

LITURGICAL DEVELOPMENT

Four-worlds prayer was among the factors that influenced the development of a new order of prayers, the *Nusakh AR"I* ("version of the AR"I"). This version of the prayers was popularized by the Hasidic movement and is now widely purveyed under the title "Nusakh Sefard," though not to be confused with the prayer practice of North African and Middle Eastern Jews, which is significantly different from either the Ashkenazic rite or Nusakh AR"I. Nusakh AR"I largely resembles the Ashkenazic rite, but with some changes in the order of the prayers, and some textual differences. The changes were dictated by the description of the prayer in the Lurianic writings.

These changes came about because Luria himself was, in Safed, something of a "shul-hopper." He attended Ashkenazic services, in keeping with his European background, yet frequented Middle Eastern or North African services when he wanted to observe certain practices not found in the Ashkenazic rite. The differences will be evident to any one who has ever attended each rite. For example, Luria preferred to recite a full confession in the "supplication" (*taḥanun*) service after the silent devotion, complete with the breast beating that Ashkenazic Jews recognize from the Day of Atonement.[26] In reciting the morning prayers, Luria seemed to place the "Hodu" prayer, the recitation of Chronicles I 15, in the preliminary blessings. In the Ashkenazic rite, it follows the first blessing of the morning psalms (the blessing "Blessed is he who spoke" or Barukh She-Amar) while in the Sefardic rite, it precedes Barukh She-Amar.[27] For Luria, the difference in placement went back to the concerns over the proper order of four-worlds prayer. The transition from the world of 'Assiyah to the world of Yeẓirah took place after the Hodu prayer, so that the "Blessed is He who spoke" blessing should come after Hodu, in order to properly commence the ascent through the world of Yeẓirah.[28] Hence, Luria and his students began the preliminary prayers with Hodu, in accordance with the Sefardic rite.

In order to emulate Luria's practice, one would have to take on a similar amalgamation of Ashkenazic and Sefardic prayer customs. Generally, the structure of the prayers would be rearranged, although the bodies of the texts would largely conform to the Ashkenazic version. From the seventeenth century, kabbalistic scribes began to assemble the alter liturgy in manuscript prayer books. The emergence of the Hasidic movement along with the development of more popular printing methods distributed the new form widely in the Diaspora. Nusakh AR"I eventually became the normative order for Hasidism and, later, the state of Israel.

Eventually, the structure of the prayer book and its special mediations became so complex that manuscript prayer books were developed that encompassed all of the changes and additions. These prayer books were faithfully copied and handed down by the cognoscenti. In many cases, the formulae of the Lurianic kavvanot had grown so complex that they needed to be signaled in a specially marked prayer book that included the sacred names and intentions that a given system saw as underlying a liturgical text.[29]

Prayer books that drew on Lurianic traditions were generally based on a certain set of sources, from various strata in the Lurianic canon.

HASIDIC PRAYER

The *materiel*, or "stuff" of prayer, according to Hasidism, was the emotional spirit. Hasidic prayer began with an emotive and naïve meditation on the plain liturgical text. In Hasidism, prayer draws on the emotions and may be channeled into all sorts of activity, ecstatic music, dance, drinking or even a concentrated sense of awe and wonder at the nature of the phenomenal world.[30] The quality most often associated with Hasidic prayer has been an experience of simple ecstasy or emotional frenzy, drawing on these various elements to supplement the prayer itself. In order to be in touch with the spiritual, emotive power, ḥasidim were advised to cultivate emotional simplicity and even innocence was also seen as a virtue, so that in one instance, the Ya'akov Yosef of Polnoye advised an adherent to "pray like a day-old infant, from out of a book, as so happened to my teacher (the Besh"t) . . . for when he prayed from a text and cleaved himself to the letters, he attained the World of Assiyah."[31]

Hasidism turned away from the most abstruse complexities of the Lurianic system, arguing that the theological core of Judaism in emotional relationship to God was being lost from the most authentically Jewish act, namely prayer. It turned away, as well, from the most abstruse conclusions of Lurianic Kabbalah toward a theology more rooted in Cordoverean thought and what might be called "the common religion of Safed," a basic metaphysical system rooted in the *Zohar*, the sefirot and their psychological implications.[32]

The early Hasidic movement was begun by kabbalists who were, among other things, practitioners of the aforementioned kavvanot, or "intentions." By the second generation of its existence, however, the Hasidic movement moved broadly to expunge the technical, mechanistic understandings of kavvanah and reinstitute emotional investment in the experience as the central act of prayer. The Ba'al Shem Tov was literally a "master of the good name," indicating that he was a practitioner of sacred names for healing and, presumably, prayer. However, the early Hasidic masters polemicized against the formal Lurianic prayer ritual, which had devolved into the arid contemplation of sacred names, in favor of the emotionalism that would come to characterize Hasidic prayer as we know it. The movement shifted its interest over to devekut, putting aside the technical understanding of kabbalistic theory, and reconnecting to the emotional core of prayer as evinced in traditional Judaism.[33]

One salient element of Hasidic teaching was the emphasis on self-abnegation, or *bittul*. Bittul was considered a theurgic "fixing" or *tiqqun*, at the core of prayer. In the Lurianic system the goal was to immolate one's consciousness in the embraces of the countenances, which were signaled by the sacred names attached to them. The original Hasidic masters were no less concerned with self-abnegation and immolation of their own desires, but they chose to pursue this goal without the apparatus of the prayer meditations implied by the Lurianic theory.[34] The Hasidic masters dispensed with the obscure, esoteric and elitist practice of kavvanot, in order to forge a more accessible, popular practice.

*****

As stated in the beginning of this chapter: in Judaism, the prayer experience fulfills the same role as the noetic, or meditative, or revelatory one in other disciplines, namely as the practice that defines the essence of the religion's given theology. The goal of Jewish prayer is to access the highest levels of the Divine, for purposes of theurgy, and thence affect Divine providence, or put plainly, to beseech God for a positive result. It must follow that the experience of prayer must be "felt" and sincere. But besides that quality of existential sincerity, what should the experience be?

The vast literature of the kabbalistic prayer intentions does not emphasize the nature of the experience. There are, in general, few accounts of the experience of mystical ecstasis in comparison to the myriad accounts left in other traditions, and some of the accounts that we do have remain unexamined. The broadly defined "kavvanah," meaning "will" or "intention," of rabbinic theology evolved into the more narrowly defined "kavvanot," or "Prayer intention formulae," of Kabbalah. In each case, the intentions that might accompany the performance of a miẓvah became far more specific when applied to the act of prayer. It is also challenging to evaluate the effects of kavvanah in the context of prayer. How can one evaluate devekut and technical acuity, when all that is available for this evaluation is the textual record?

The Lurianic prayer system, as practiced by the adepts of late Kabbalah, is a rite, not a meditative process. Therefore, personal sensation is beside the point, because the object of the rite is not the receiving of a noetic experience, but simply, the completion of the rite. The experience of the contemplative is one in which the practitioner enters a realm in which he was no longer motivated by any the liturgy's overt concern with human needs.

The culture of the ḥasidim and their fellow travelers made great strides toward an emotional and theologically rich tradition of kabbalistic prayer, stripping their souls open with a splendid religious emotionalism and psychological richness. They left a rich record of their goals and methodologies. That is how Hasidism can be evaluated as a spiritual movement for, as the scholar of mysticism, Steven Katz, has put it, there are no unmediated religious experiences and that, in interpreting the mystical record, scholars have only the texts before them as witness.[35] The analysis of lost traditions, such as the works of Abraham Abulafia and the circle of the *Zohar*, differs from the study of the practice of Hasidism and the Jerusalem adepts of Beit El, because the latter are being practiced by living communities. These communities believe they are implementing the ideas of their founders authentically. They also maintain an unbroken chain of this tradition, extending from its earliest practitioners, who took their mandate as biblical, to the present acolytes of the tradition.

The person standing next to the scholar in a synagogue may be in a state of mystical ecstasy, but the scholar cannot enter his mind to see, and modern practitioners may, or in fact probably will be hostile to questions from the academic sector. For example, in one prayer circle in Jerusalem, I noticed a man standing outside the main synagogue on the balcony. During his prayer, he would sob, despondently during the silent devotion. The researches of Moshe Idel and Eitan Fishbane have addressed the role of weeping in classical kabbalistic practice, so I was intrigued at encountering this experience in the field.[36] Upon investigation, I determined that the young man in question was felt by all to be mentally unbalanced, a social pariah, and was verbally abused by the other kabbalists. He certainly came from outside the community and may, in fact, have been influenced by Idel's articles. If such a "freak" enters the community and recovers practices described in academic writings and then practices them in the community, is this practice "authentic?" Or, then again, is all prayer necessarily authentic, when it comes from the unmediated, inchoate cry of the heart?

CHAPTER 8

THE QUESTION OF MEDITATION

The quest for a "Jewish" form of meditation is freighted with the yearnings of the contemporary generation. Since the late 1960s, schools of yoga and meditation have spread throughout the world, attracting many people enthralled with the spiritual turn of the culture. Some contemporary Jews have found meditation to be a profound spiritual experience, which they, in turn, want to reconcile with their faith commitment to Judaism. Such people have a visceral desire to practice meditation and are willing to synthesize a Jewish meditation form, yet in their heart of hearts they believe that there *must* be an "authentic" meditation tradition. Accordingly, they have a natural inclination to believe that this meditative practice ought to be "kabbalistic," as Kabbalah and meditation have been popularly assumed to be the core "spiritual" experiences in Judaism.

In calling something "meditative," let it be defined in terms of the sitting meditation favored by adepts in yogic, Taoist and Buddhist traditions, in which the practice and effects are remarkably similar across a broad range of time and cultural differences. Yogic meditative practices were adapted from Vedic religion to Buddhism. In turn, they crossed to China where they were couched in Taoist terms. So if one is to speak broadly of the development of Eastern traditions from Hinduism to Buddhism, from India to China, people knew meditation when they saw it and recast it in their own terms. And similarly, people who like to meditate know meditation when they see it.[1]

This desire for a Jewish meditation system, and the impulse to seek it in Kabbalah, is natural, according to the understandings of

mysticism organized by Steven Katz.[2] Meditative prayer *ought* to
arise from Kabbalah, if, as Katz stipulates, mysticism represents
the expression of a religion at its greatest intensity. Kabbalah sees
itself as the most intense form of Judaism, and prayer is the quin-
tessentially Jewish religious act. According to this line of reasoning, kabbalistic prayer ought to be the quintessence of the Jewish
mystical experience, as meditation is the realization of the Eastern
experience. These people seek the meditative element in kabbalistic
prayer based on its salience in other religious cultures.

In the liturgy and practice of Lurianic prayer intentions, the
adherents recite the name "Adonai" while contemplating the inner
mysteries of the name YHVH and its various permutations. One
might expect that the words so contemplated become a silent mantra, the body silently resonating to the energy of a given vocalization.
The scholar of religions, in search of cross-cultural phenomena,
might ask whether the practice of kabbalistic prayer intentions is a
"meditative" system of practice and is it, therefore, the great, lost
meditation practice of Kabbalah.

KABBALISTIC PARALLELS

Certainly there are reasonable parallels to meditative, contemplative or at least "conscious" behavior in the kabbalistic milieu. Let
us reiterate that human *thought* is the instrument of kabbalistic
prayer, in which "cleaving of thought" (*devekut ha-maḥshavah*) in
the act of union with God. This is opposed to the *actual* absorption
of the self into God, the *unio mystica* that serves as one of the mark-
ers by which scholars recognize "mysticism." The idea that thought
could ascend linked the experience of kabbalistic prayer to classical
prophecy. This association with prophecy, in which the prophetic
mind is the vessel of the revelation experience, is pronounced in
such works as Ḥayyim Vital's *Sha'arei Kedushah*.[3] There were explo-
rations of this notion of unity that spilled over from Sufi practices,
which themselves seemingly absorbed yogic influences on the bor-
ders of India and Persia.

These elements of spiritualization comprise the main hand-
holds for those wishing to recover a "meditative" tradition from
Kabbalah and/or Hasidism. However, they differ from Eastern
models in terms of a basic paradigm: They are largely transitive in
nature, presupposing contact, across the bounds of space and time,

with an "other," or monotheistic deity. Their goal in beseeching this "other" is to gain some form of power.[4] This may or may not include the apophasis of the meditation experience, or even the quest for the void that sits at the apex of the sefirotic hierarchy, the "cloud of unknowing" in Christian parlance.[5]

In examining kabbalistic prayer, it is perhaps useful to divide the instances between those that advocated and sought an *experience* from prayer and those that did not. For instance, it is characteristic of Polish Hasidism, which is nothing if not a movement devoted to contemplative experience, to posit an experience or noetic sense that comes from prayer. In the kabbalistic school of Beit El, which is widely regarded, from within and without, as the quintessential kabbalistic practice and the final evolution of Lurianic theory, the cultivation of a personal feeling or the achieving of a mystical state were not goals of the practice. Directives about achieving ecstasy or cleaving are largely absent from the literature. Rather, prayer with mystical intentions was a transitive experience, directed at the object(s) of prayer. In Beit El, prayer is a *rite*, not a meditative process. Therefore, personal sensation is beside the point. The object of the rite is not a noetic experience, that is to say, something that one can learn. The object is, simply, the completion of the rite. In much other kabbalistic prayer, the contemplative's experience is to enter a realm in which he was no longer motivated by the liturgy's overt concern with human needs. Although the expectation of "meaning" or "experience" in prayer is by no means un-Jewish, it is the overt concern of these kinds of Jewish prayer that are kabbalistic.

The association of meditation with Kabbalah in the popular mind is largely the result of the circulation of the works of the late Aryeh Kaplan, who came to meditation from the Hasidism of the Breslav school, which contained within it a practice of contemplative withdrawal that the Breslavers call *hisbodedus*. In pursuing a connection between this Hasidic practice of seclusion and contemporary notions of meditation, Kaplan cited many pivotal texts discussed in this chapter. Unfortunately, he also presented any number of hagiographical and etiological fantasies regarding the evolution of Jewish practice. In many ways, his writing presaged the hagiographies presented in the Jewish fundamentalism of the later twentieth century.[6]

Another presentation of Jewish meditation is the work of Mark Verman, whose scholarly presentation differs from Kaplan's etiological reconstruction. Verman offers a synthesis of disparate strains in Jewish spirituality, in which all contemplative experience is offered as a possible instrument that may be called meditative.[7] In the same way that Steven Katz is willing to declare all intensified religious experience potentially mystical, Verman points to all mindful, contemplative religious activity, both within and outside the purview of the Halakhah, as meditative. Verman defines as meditative anything that acts to "increase an individual's understanding and experience of the Divine." Hence, any activity that bridges the chasm that Verman describes between the individual and God is, of needs, "meditative," be it the whole tradition of Hasidic naturalism, from Naḥman of Breslav to the mystic and martyr Hillel Zeitlin."[8] Verman engages in broad synthesis, drawing on wildly disparate figures: from the mysterious "early pietists" of the Talmud, Josephus' view of the theraputae, the Sufi-loving medieval circles of Baḥya Ibn Paquda and Avraham Maimonides,[9] all the way to the group around the kabbalist Max Theon and his contemporaries in prewar Paris. Still, contemplative practice is not necessarily meditative, for those who do like to sit.

ABULAFIA, HIS CIRCLE AND HIS ADVOCATES

An ethic of Jewish meditation is certainly found at the nexus of a number of medieval schools of thought. These include the prophetic kabbalist Abraham Abulafia, the aforementioned Sufi acolytes, Yehudah Albotini's *Sulam ha-Aliyah* and some remarks of the thirteenth-century kabbalist Isaac of Acre, at which point the preoccupations of classical Kabbalah took another turn.[10] With regard to Abulafia, his limited and rather insular career has enlivened the study of Kabbalah since Gershom Scholem introduced him back into the discourse.[11] Abulafian teachings are unique in the annals of directive contemplation in a kabbalistic context in that they involve breath, body position and the linking of noetic textual materials with embodied spiritual practice in order to achieve an experience of transcendent prophecy. Moreover, Abulafian teachings are mystical in the classical academic sense, as they posit experience as the reward of the practitioner. The guarantee, for example, in Abulafia's practice was that an experience of transcendent light would occur as a result of letter-combination and *hitbodedut*.

Hence, Idel has called Abulafian Kabbalah a "living kabbalistic tradition."[12] Abulafia viewed his techniques as a path to the acquisition of the "active intellect," a philosophical term for the force that intercedes between the phenomenal world and God. Abulafia's teachings bring philosophical concepts into the realm of the contemplative. The prerequisite instrument of Abulafian practice is his interest in the sacred names tradition, which is theologically rather barren of content, in and of itself.

Moshe Idel, Mark Verman and Kaplan saw the core of the contemplative, or, for Kaplan, "meditative" impulse in Kabbalah in the concept of *hitbodedut*, which literally means "seclusion," or "to make oneself alone." As Idel has demonstrated, the Abulafian mystics, such as the author of *Shushan Sodot* believed that hitbodedut meant a kind of concentration, literally the special concentration required by the kabbalist in order to combine letters in the prayer formulae. Isaac of Acre used the term hitbodedut to refer to spiritual activity, as opposed to the seclusion implied by the term *poresh*, which literally means "to withdraw." Shem Tov Ibn Gaon, in *Baddei ha-Aron*, also discusses hitbodedut as the inward turn to self-discovery.[13] Even Moshe Cordovero's commentary on the *Zohar*'s famous composition *Sabba de-Mishpatim* speaks of

> the secret of the letters which are transmuted in his mouth, and the secret of the vocalization signs, and the secret of the hitbodedut brought down to man, as is written in the book *Sha'arei Zedek* by R. Abraham Abulafia author of *Sefer Ḥayyey ha-Olam ha-Ba*.[14]

The Safed kabbalist Eliahu de Vidas portrayed *hitbodedut* as a source of "uncovering the supernal source of material being."[15] So, by the time of its adaptation by Naḥman of Breslav, the concept of *hitbodedut* had well evolved into something beyond the mere act of letter manipulation.

Another trend among this small circle is the emergence of the notion of *hishtavut*, or equanimity. Isaac of Acre, who is linked to the identification of the *Zohar*'s authorship with Moshe de Leon, was also a recipient of Abulafian traditions (his cosmopolitanism may have been a benefit of living in a port city!). He seems to be an early source of the use of this term *hishtavut*, the quality of self-abnegation, detachment or equanimity. The term occurs in Yosef Caro's *Maggid Mesharim* and Yehudah Albotini's *Sulam ha-Aliyah*, and would later become a monolithic concept in Hasidism.[16]

Clearly in this post-Abulafian, theosophical pocket in the Middle East, people were addressing the interplay of *hitbodedut, hishtavut* and *devekut*, withdrawal, equanimity and cleaving to God. On the face of it, there could be few better recipes for the development of a contemplative practice than these! At the same time, however, theosophical kabbalists had made the observance of the Law and miẓvot the instrument of religious experience, as opposed to sacred names and meditative techniques. The Provence and Gerona kabbalists of the thirteenth century had comprised many *Rishonim*, that is, primordial halakhic authorities, while the German pietists seemed to have a connection to the heirs of Rashi, the *Ba'alei ha-Tosafot*.[17] All of these spiritual communities believed that the practice of the miẓvot was the path to both perception of deeper noesis and the achievement of soteric effects. This preference for Halakhah as the instrument of Kabbalah grew from the nature of the *Zohar* literature and the practice which derived from it, which called for the interactive relationship of the law, the deepening perception of reality brought on by its study and the possibility of affecting reality through religious practices or their neglect. This point of view dominated the *Zohar* and saturated the Safed Kabbalah. Prayer and the observance of the commandments was the vehicle of their engaged experience, as opposed to a formless contemplative practice.

MEDITATION AND KABBALAH

Meditation is most essential to a religion when it is the purest expression of that religion's beliefs and essence. The contemplative acts of a given religion are its most essential practices, the truest expressions of a given faith's theology. In Eastern traditions, meditation is the practical realization of the religion's theology. The attempt to qualify the reality of present existence through the pursuit of a thoughtless mind is a realization of the aims of Buddhism as embodied in its earliest teachings. In Zen Buddhism, the moment of meditation sums up the underlying emptiness and nullity of present existence and the futility of the search for sensual pleasure. For Hindus and Buddhists, meditation clarifies the need to cleanse one's soul of the accumulations of karma in order to escape the endless cycle of birth and death that defines existence. Similarly, the rites of Sufism took shape around a theological concept, the *dhikr*, or "remembrance" of the oneness of Allah, a realization of the essence of Islam. Hence, the contemplative acts of a given religion are its most essential practices, the truest expressions of its theology.

Yet the embodiment of the act is largely absent in kabbalistic practice and the practice of kabbalistic prayer is not easily reconciled with meditation as so many Eastern schools defined it. The original practices described in the Jewish source texts were transitive and theurgic; they were acts of dialogue and interaction with the Divine. In the East, to put it broadly, the wages of meditation is meditation. The only thing the Eastern mystic wants to do in meditating is meditate better; the teleology of enlightenment, while present, is far off. There is a parallel in the egolessness of the prayers of the Lithuanian opponents of Hasidism, but again, this is not kabbalistic. If one begins a meditation practice in an Eastern context, all that is promised is meditation, but the practices originally described in the kabbalistic vein are transitive; they were geared to breaking through to a soteric end that, in modernity, is elusive, to say the least.

Western religions differ from the Eastern model in their basic theologies. Instead of an underlying emptiness, God exists at the apex of reality. In Judaism, the prayer experience fulfills the same role as the meditative one in other disciplines, namely as the practice that defines the essence of the religion's given theology. The quintessential Jewish moment is the turning of the individual, such as the biblical Abraham, Moses or Hannah, to God in prayer. There were Jews who, in the course of prayer, devoted themselves to contemplate the oneness, even the emptiness that existed at the apex of God. Yet many of these contemplatives were not even kabbalists. Jewish and Muslim philosophers stressed that this oneness was unlike any other oneness, in that it could not be multiplied or halved but remained a unity. The original meditative act in Judaism was the contemplation of this unity, termed the "Secret of Unity" (*sod-ha-Yichud*) by many kabbalists.

The possible formal resemblances between Zen Buddhism and Hasidism are a separate issue of parallel religious phenomenologies. Historically, each tradition sought to lighten the superstructure of religious hierarchy in its most developed state by carrying the burden of practice rather more lightly than before. However, these resemblances have largely manifested in the aphoristic tradition as purveyed by the reworkings of Martin Buber and D. T. Suzuki in the postwar period.[18] The original literature in both traditions looks a lot less similar than the secondary writings of these modern, academic popularizers.

Contemporary Jews, by assuming that mysticism is the expression of a religion at its greatest intensity, and that Kabbalah is the most intense form of Judaism, arrive at the conclusion that Jewish meditation must be kabbalistic. But one need not be a kabbalist to devise and practice an authentic Jewish form of meditation. In fact, the two impulses might be antithetical. Theosophical Kabbalah is a world of forms and mythos, upheavals and interaction whose closest parallel in an Eastern context is Tantric thought and mythos. The outflow of Divine energy is bedeviled by demonic forces and filled with the struggle between forces of good and forces of evil. The void, as generally posited in Kabbalah, sits at the apex of a host of seething apposite powers.[19] The person practicing a "Jewish" meditation that resembles Eastern forms would have to vault over the tumult of the kabbalistic world and into the simple, serene paradox of God's oneness. An authentically Jewish meditation would concentrate on God's essential unknowability, on the emptiness that sits at the apex of all existence and the folly of present desires.

Notwithstanding the traditions that I have described, I do not feel that there are cultures of meditation, meditation for its own sake, as in Eastern traditions, in the contemporary practice of Kabbalah, with the possible exception of certain Hasidic practices and pietistic behaviors of the early contemporaries of the Ba'al Shem Tov. Certainly there are not the methodological schools. There are not great schools of thought, social movements and a large amount of "field tested" schools of kabbalistic meditation. Moreover, the seeker after meditative practice should not assume that what is being proffered to them in the contemporary religious marketplace has veracity. Western quasi-academic fantasy romanticism notwithstanding, one cannot easily reinflate Abulafian practice. Like Aryan Christianity, Merkavah Mysticism, Qumran spirituality, Jamesian Christianity, Northern school Chan Buddhism and a lot of other movements that were historically overwhelmed and shunted aside by more ruthless schools of thought, the chain of transmission has been broken and buried in the dust.

The question of authenticity of Jewish meditation practice hinges on how authentic it can be if it has been reconstituted. Many things in Judaism have been reconstituted from time to time, the Hebrew language, settlement of the land of Israel, and some people are working on the sacrificial cult. The meditation that may have come as part and parcel of certain types of medieval Kabbalah is no longer a living tradition. The meditation traditions that are up and running, in the East, to put it rather broadly, know what they are doing, and there are not kabbalistic traditions of strict provenance that have a similar authenticity.

Portrayals of Zoharic and theosophical material as objects of meditation do not equal the developments of a meditation process. I could point out any visionary record or diary and make it the object of somebody's contemplation but that doesn't make it a meditation *system*. Visionary experience is not meditation. Prophecy may or may not be due to meditation. Hence visionary and prophetic materials are not applicable to a bona fide "meditation" system.

One could evolve an authentic Jewish meditation form without recourse to Kabbalah by simply recovering the paths that the tradition did not take, particularly in the Sufi materials and others. There is an argument to be made for the influence of Muslim mysticism in the possible development of a Jewish meditation culture. Meditation is present in the aforementioned practice of the *dikhr* in Sufism. Sufism, in turn, was central in the speculations of the philosophers whose tropes found their way into the expressions of crossover figures such as Baḥya ibn Paquda, Avraham Maimonides, Ovadiah Maimonides, Yehudah ha-Levi and R. Avraham Ibn Hasdai's translations of Al Ghazali.[20] The recovery of a pure meditation system based on the paradoxes of the inherent negative theology of classical Judaism would readdress this lost stage when the philosophical tradition drifted close to the spirituality of its Islamic host culture. That is the true seat of a search for emptiness in daily practice, and, in fact, I wouldn't be surprised if popular practice doesn't go in that direction in the coming years.

To reiterate, meditative prayer, or pure meditation, for that matter, need not draw on the specific metaphysical inheritance of the Kabbalah to be authentically Jewish or have integrity. Ultimately, the major systematic schools of meditation have evolved outside of Judaism, so that the contributors to a contemporary Jewish meditation tradition will necessarily be syncretists, recasting their core traditions through the vocabulary and intellectual constructs of another. So, it is possible that the philosophical tradition is the more appropriate vehicle for the development of an authentic Jewish meditation system, and Kabbalah, with it's attendant emphasis on symbolism and mythos, does not readily provide the locus of the quest for the underlying emptiness that characterizes conventional meditation systems.

CHAPTER 9

THE DIVINE NAMES

The thirteenth-century sage Naḥmanides observed that the whole Torah was nothing but a random collection of names of God.[1] Hence, in the kabbalistic tradition there are innumerable names of God. Sacred names are a building block of the theosophical system of the *Zohar* and make up the basis of the Lurianic system of prayer intentions. To this day, sacred names are the central feature of the doctrine of the Beit El kabbalists of Jerusalem, as well as being a salient aspect of the teachings of the Kabbalah Centre. The sacred names of God are as much the building blocks of the *Zohar*'s Kabbalah as the symbolism of the sefirot. Yet there have been few academic treatments of these doctrines, even though they are in one's face from the moment that one picks up the *Zohar*. The doctrine of sacred names, names of God that move beyond the roster in the Bible, has been the great untouchable subject in Kabbalah studies. This chapter then, will present some of the basic systems of sacred names.[2]

The names of God are interpreted and used in many ways by kabbalists in various milieus. Sacred names may be linked to some interpretation of the sefirot, or vocalized in different ways to yield different numerical coefficients. New names may be developed using kabbalistic theories and names may be recovered from the mists of antiquity, or imagined antiquity.

The sacred names signify God's existence in present reality; they are literally ways of accessing power, although kabbalists generally frowned on the use of the names for magical ends. The names accompany the emanation of the Divine into present reality and serve as instruments for channeling that emanation. Divinity flows down through the vehicle of the names. As Gershom Scholem expressed it:

> The Divine Names . . . are aroused through meditative activity directed toward them. The individual in prayer pauses over each word and fully gauges the kavvanah that belongs to it. The actual text of the prayer, therefore, serves as a kind of banister onto which the kabbalist holds as he makes his not unhazardous ascent, groping his way by the words. The kavvanot, in other words, transform the words of the prayer into holy names that serve as landmarks on the upward climb.[3]

Some of the name traditions originated deep in antiquity. The idea that God has different names originates in the Bible. The four-letter name of God, YHVH, is the most important name in the Bible. This name is followed by the names AHYH, Elohim, El Shaddai and ADNY, which are also the primary subjects of kabbalistic manipulation. Other names originated in the Talmud, Apocrypha and in the "old religion" discussed earlier.[4] Some sacred names are referenced in rabbinic writings and explained in Gaonic materials.[5] A number of traditions of letter permutation developed, such as *gematria*, a system of numerical coefficients for Hebrew letters. These led to the development of still more sacred names. Some names developed from acronyms of biblical verses, others were created through acrostics of sacred verses, and by replacing one letter of a given name with another.[6] These names were taken apart, vocalized in new forms, repeated and recombined according to different theories of Kabbalah. When appended to the prayer service, the kabbalistic mode of prayer follows this description by Joseph Dan: "it sometimes seems that where other readers would see letters and meanings in the Bible . . . (the kabbalists) would see only rows of figures and numbers, mystically connected."[7] Dan's characterization captures the essence of the use of sacred names in kabbalistic prayer.

Name traditions followed the spread of kabbalah. In the Heikhalot literature of late antiquity, sacred names accompany and underlie the workings of the Divine.[8] Names accompanied the reappearance of Kabbalah in Provence, Gerona and the Rhineland in the great resurgence of Kabbalah in the twelfth century. For example, two kabbalists who apparently had not heard of each other, Rabbi Eliezer of Worms and Isaac the Blind of Provence, both began to use the name HVYH, used "to express Divine Presence and divine will."[9]

In another section of thirteenth-century Europe, Abraham Abulafia based his mystical system on sacred names. Abulafian practice emphasized posture, breathing and bodily movement, along with the contemplation of sacred names in their permutations.[10] Moshe Idel has described Abulafian practice thus:

> Abulafia's method is based upon the contemplation of a constantly changing object: one must combine the letters and their vowel signs, "sing" and move the head in accordance with the vocalization, and even lift one's hands in the gesture of Priestly Blessing[11] . . . the letters of the Divine Name are not only a method of cleaving to God; the process of imagining the letters in the first stage precedes the vision of the letters in the final stage of the ecstatic process.[12]

Unlike Abulafia's prescriptions, the practice of sacred names in Lurianic Kabbalah is silent ("mind only") and draws on the halakhic prescriptions for prayer as its mode of implementation. The names are never enunciated, but only kept in the mind as silent objects of contemplation. The content of some name traditions, that is to say certain patterns of vocalization, survived from the Abulafian tradition to the Lurianic, while systems of breathing and movement did not.

HOW THE NAMES ARE USED

One of the core teachings of the early Kabbalah, from the early Kabbalah to the *Zohar*, is that specific names of God in the Bible may be linked to different sefirot and, in magical contexts, channel the power and influence of those sefirot. According to this view, the name ADNY, familiar to all Jews as the name that is uttered in the prayer service, is linked to the sefirah Malkhut, the realm of present reality. AHYH, the name revealed at the incident of the burning bush, is the name associated with Keter, the highest of the sefirot.[13] The name Elohim may be employed to represent the sefirot Binah or Malkhut, but is most often applied to the judgmental side of God, the sefirah Gevurah or Din.[14] The most widely parlayed name, YHVH represents the central trunk of the sefirotic tree, the sefirah Tiferet. As Moshe Cordovero put it, "All names come from YHVH."[15]

Isaac Luria linked these names to various countenances of the cosmic anthropos (parẓufim),[16] and to the circulation of the moḥin, channels of consciousness through the same anthropomorphic structure.[17] For instance, in the Lurianic system the sefirah Tiferet is replaced by the countenance Zeir Anpin. Luria embellished the status of Zeir Anpin further. He maintained that there were three levels of Zeir Anpin, which are indicated by three construct forms of the name YHVH.[18] The permutations of these basic biblical names form the basis of many subsequent Lurianic prayer intentions and formulae. By the time a master list of the combinations of AHYH, HVYH, ADNY and ELOH and ELOHIM was compiled, by the nineteenth-century Lithuanian kabbalist Shlomo Eliashiv,[19] these five names were applied in 120 combinations.[20]

MILUYYIM: THE VOCALIZATIONS OF
THE NAME YHVH

A second layer of sacred name tradition is called the *miluyyim*, which literally means "the fillings-in." The miluyyim are vocalized forms of the name YHVH. This tradition consists of the Name YHVH, transliterated. Biblical Hebrew, like all Semitic languages, is unvocalized, meaning that the vowels are seldom inflected within the structure of the written words. The miluyyim use the open consonants, such as *aleph* or *ayin*, to inflect and vocalize the name YHVH in different ways.[21] Then the technique of gematria, appending numerical coefficients for different names, is applied to the sacred name. The four miluyyim are as follows: The name "seventy-two" is based on the transliteration using the letter yu"d, as follows: YVD HY VYV HY. The name "sixty-three" makes use of the aleph in the letter vav, producing the formulation YVD HY VAV HY, forming the gematria 63. The name "forty-five" vocalizes the HV"H with the letter aleph, so as to produce YVD HA VAV HA. The name "fifty-two" makes more extensive use of the letter hey: YVD HH VV HH.[22]

Different blessings call for different vocalizations or miluyyim of the name YHVH to be substituted, in the mind of the petitioner, for the simple vocalization, depending on the particular blessing. Isaac Luria, in turn, linked the miluyyim to the four countenances that were the basis of the Lurianic system, Abba, Imma, Zeir and Nukvah. The four miluyyim represent the stages of four-worlds prayer.[23]

THE NAME OF 42 LETTERS
AND THE 72 NAMES

Two more name traditions date back to late antiquity. Perhaps the most widely reproduced of these is the 42-letter name. The 42-letter name of God[24] is discussed in the Talmud,[25] which states that states that "the 42-letter name is not to be transmitted except to one who is modest, humble, mature, never angry, never intoxicated and not arrogant." It appears in the liturgy as the acrostic of the well-known "prayer of Rav Neḥuniah ben ha-Kanah," otherwise known as *Ana be-Koaḥ*. In Jewish folklore, the 42-letter name had a protective function and appears widely on kabbalistic amulets.

A second tradition, that of the 72 names of God, has come to particular prominence in recent years. These names are constructed as an acronym originating in the three verses of Exodus 14.19–21.[26] The first letter from the first verse is combined with the last letter from the second verse and the first letter of the third verse. Hence, the first aspect of the name is w"hw, after which one begins with the second letter of the first word, the second letter from the end of the second verse and then the second letter of the third verse, making y"ly. The end result of this process comes to 72 names.

The 72 names have been revived in the activities of the Kabbalah Centres, under the direction of the Berg family.[27] Yehudah Berg has acknowledged that his affective psychological interpretation of the 72 names was influenced by an earlier tradition,[28] which associated the 42-letter name and the 72 names with the Shema' prayer. Berg drew on the eighteenth-century work *Ḥerev Pifiyyot*, which was composed by Yeshayahu Ya'akov of Alesk, a member of the kloiz of kabbalists in Brody that operated at roughly the same time as the Ba'al Shem Tov. *Ḥerev Pifiyyot* presents a psychologized version of the names, much as contemporary Hasidic works rendered a psychological interpretation of kabbalistic ideas. This psychological interpretation has been adapted by the Kabbalah Centres as one of that institution's most compelling doctrines.

NAMES AND PRAYER

In later forms of kabbalah, name speculations superseded the archetypal understanding of the sefirot, and even the advanced myth of Isaac Luria. Both the Beit El school and the Kabbalah Centre move the sacred names to the forefront in different ways. As mentioned the Kabbalah Centre emphasizes the psychological traditions associated with the names, while the Beit El tradition has made the contemplation of the names the paramount part of its prayer tradition. The Beit El emphasis on name theory is comparable to a computer user putting away her operating systems and running her computer through the sole use of DOS language. Prayers no longer have any of their exoteric meaning, but are now completely given over to esoteric formulae. The overt subject matter of the liturgy, the national and creaturely concerns that it expresses, is missing. The very idea of petitional prayer, emotional investment and the essential sense of prayer as communion and dialogue have been discarded, in favor of a faith in the most abstruse reaches of the Lurianic method, its numerology and linguistic method.

Such an emphasis on sacred names was rejected as theologically degenerate and obscurantist by the founding fathers of Hasidism. At the beginning of the Hasidic movement, special prayer books, with the prayer intentions inserted into the margins of the prayers, were spreading through Europe. The prescribed intentions for a given rite had come to include a daunting number of sacred names and associations that had to be presented on the page, linked directly to the prayer itself as it was being recited. The "prayer book with the prayer intentions of the AR"I" became the characteristic instrument for the practice of contemplative prayer.

It is unclear as to whether the disapproval of prayer intentions and sacred names began as early as the Ba'al Shem Tov, or whether it originated with his successor, the Maggid of Mezeritch. On the face of it, the Maggid abolished the practice. He argued that kavvanot could not bring about the emotional dimension necessary for cleaving to the Divine, but consisted, at best, of a rote recitation of empty formulae.[29] The thrust of the Maggid of Mezeritch's activity was to substitute emotional engagement, the stuff of Hasidic *devekut*, for the dry contemplation of sacred names. The Maggid also criticized the Lurianic system for being limited, as it specified a random selection of ideas from the *Zohar* and the speculations of Cordovero and Luria.[30] The randomness is an artificial limitation of the expressive possibilities of Kabbalah. Even Naḥman of Breslav, one generation beyond the central debate, was still compelled to polemicize against the practice of prayer intentions with sacred names:

> One of the "people of the Name" told me that he spoke with our Rebbe about the service of God as it should be. Our Teacher understood that (the adept) was engaging a bit in the mystical intentions in his prayer. Our teacher was very stringent with him, saying that he should longer engage in it, nor pray with the kavvanot. Rather, he should only pray with simple intention (even though this man had studied Luria's works according to his instructions, nonetheless he did not want him to engage in the kavvanot at all). Our teacher said to him when an unworthy person prays with the kavvanot it is like witchcraft. For it is said of witchcraft that it is studied for understanding but not for practice. The Rabbis of Blessed memory[31] explained that one does not study (witchcraft) to practice but to understand and to instruct. And the same is true with the practice of the prayer intentions. One only learns them to understand and to know, but not to practice if one is not worthy of it. For the essence of prayer is cleaving (*devekut*) . . . [32]

R. Naḥman was concerned that "unworthy people" were risking the practice of the kavvanot. Throughout early Hasidism, there was a sense that the generation was no longer worthy to practice the more recondite mystical traditions, the prayer intentions included.

The role of prayer is manifestly to bring about a tiqqun, a theurgic "fixing" in the structure of the worlds. The goal is a transitive act, bringing a change in an "other", namely God. In order to have the desired effect, the individual is called upon to negate himself, to immolate himself in joining the embraces of the *parẓufim*. This aspect of self-negation may have evolved into *bittul*, self-abnegation, a practice widely advocated in Hasidic teaching. Perhaps a subtext of the Hasidic polemics regarding prayer was an effort to jettison the apparatus of kabbalistic prayer to that time, namely, the concentration on sacred names, while keeping the spiritual experience of the earlier prayer with kavvanot, namely the experience of self-abnegation or immolation.[33]

And yet, name traditions, like so many aspects of Kabbalah, have spontaneously reappeared. Their recrudescence has occurred among two of the more emblematic populations of the late twentieth century, namely the Israeli communities of Eastern and North African provenance, as well as in the theology of the Kabbalah Centre. The mystique of the names requires total credulousness regarding the truth and validity of the most recondite and obscure parts of the Kabbalah, yet it is available in the streets of Jerusalem and any synagogue bookstore, resilient and perennial.

CHAPTER 10

KABBALAH AND CONTEMPORARY JUDAISM

How normative is Kabbalah to Judaism? It pretends to the role of being the hidden essence of the religion. At the same time, its detractors call it a kind of accretion, a fetishization of the essential, rationalistic core of Judaism. In resurging so strongly in the last half-century, there must have been a rationalistic tradition for it to challenge. This rationalistic tradition, which seems so intrinsic to Judaism, is really rather young. The forces of modernity, in both the Eastern and Western enlightenment (*haskalah*) movements, loathed kabbalistic antirationalism. Enlightened Jews, were they given to defending classical Judaism, exalted the model of Maimonides, the rationalist philosopher who disdained extraneous beliefs and metaphysics. The pendulum had swung toward Kabbalah after the Spanish persecutions of the fourteenth and fifteenth centuries and amidst the perennial enmity of European Christianity. It swung back toward rationalism with special force at the onset of modernity, into movements whose relationship with traditional Judaism could be quite tenuous: Socialism, Zionism, German Reform Judaism and the cultural forces of Jewish enlightenment in general. If pressed to define the spiritual essence of a "pure" rabbinical Judaism, most of these groups would have cited Maimonides.

It has been estimated that in the mid-nineteenth-century, two-thirds to three-quarters of the Jews in the world lived in Eastern Europe and North Africa. For this population, their default setting in the realm of Jewish metaphysics was Kabbalah. They were not full-time metaphysicians; in fact, they may have observed a reticent attitude toward such questions, but if they ever *did* think about the underlying metaphysical premises of their existence, Kabbalah would have been their source. If they wondered about what would happen after they died, or about the heavenly pantheons addressed in the liturgy and midrash, how exactly the world was created and when it would end, then their most accessible body of lore was Kabbalah. The rituals attending the observance of the Sabbath, the preparation of the dead for burial, even the muttered incantation "kein 'ayin hara" and the personal mezuzot and amulets sold in synagogue gift shops all derive from the intersection of Kabbalah and folk practice. Had emigration and the Holocaust not destroyed Eastern European Jewish culture, kabbalistic metaphysics might have survived as a mainstream core belief.

The visibility of Kabbalah has risen in the late twentieth century. There are a number of strains in the reemergence of this tradition, and they overlap and combine in ways that may even have reached the reader of these words. This chapter summarizes the major streams of contemporary kabbalistic expression; in the knowledge that, with the field still evolving, it could be out of date or refuted by history by the time these words see print or when the reader might encounter them. Here is the contemporary Kabbalah community's "lay of the land;" it may still be relevant although, increasingly, it will become something of a curio.

THE ACADEMY

One of the contexts for the emergence of Kabbalah was the academy, although it was not an immediate process. It is hard to imagine, in the swarm of Jewish Studies departments and chairs that dot the Western academic landscape, but Jewish Studies is a fairly new phenomenon in academia. There were few positions devoted to Jewish Studies in the classical academy. When the first appointments were made, they were in the fields of Bible, understandably, but also in that of Philosophy. There were a number of scholars who were authorities in medieval Arabic philosophy who also doubled in the study of Maimonides, Saadiah or Yehudah ha-Levi. These included seminal figures such as Leo Strauss and Harry Wolfson. Scholars of philosophy who handled Kabbalah with acuity, such as Alexander Altmann, were less common. Hence the old antipathy between Kabbalah and Philosophy was inadvertently imported into contemporary scholarship.

In the postwar period, the studies of Gershom Scholem began to be circulated in the Diaspora, particularly his work *Major Trends in Jewish Mysticism*, which was based on a series of lectures that Scholem gave at the Jewish Institute of Religion in Cincinnati in 1938.[1] Scholem is best compared to his older colleague Martin Buber. Each of them "dropped out" of enlightenment German society, and each of them had an interest in studying a neglected, nay, despised subject. For Scholem, it was Kabbalah, while Buber took five years to comb the traditions of Hasidism. When Scholem and Buber began their researches, the academy was largely closed to the study of Jewish religion, if not closed to Jews altogether. Enlightened Jews themselves viewed Kabbalah and Hasidism in the way that North American intellectuals might view Pentecostal snake handlers in the Florida panhandle or late night televangelists on obscure public access television channels. There was a social gap between the "enlightened" world and the world of the practitioners.

Scholem laid out the structure of the study of Kabbalah; the second chapter of this very book is indebted to his original formulation of kabbalistic history. He formulated his ideas in Germany and Jerusalem, in the eye of the storm of twentieth-century history.

Scholem saw the central driving force of Kabbalah as devolving into social messianism, which eventually found its expression in Zionism. Scholem was distinctly modern, presenting a view of history that portrays religious ideas as responses to history. In his day, Reform Judaism in Germany, Zionism, Socialism and the other great propellants of Judaism in modernity were restructuring the premises of Jewish life and he saw Kabbalah as a similar vehicle that had recast Judaism. Scholem, Buber and the seminal historian of the nineteenth century, Heinrich Graetz, portrayed changes in Jewish life as coming about in response to social trauma. Graetz had portrayed the *Zohar* as nothing but a response to Maimonidean rationalism.[2] Similarly, Scholem portrayed Lurianic Kabbalah as an emotional response to the trauma of the Spanish Expulsion. The popularity of Shabbatai Zevi's heretical messianism was widely perceived as being a response to the Chmelnitzki massacres of 1648–49. Scholem viewed the Shabbatean movement as an early stage of Judaism's evolution into modernity. In turn, he portrayed Hasidism as a response to the collapse of Shabbateanism. In the next generation, scholars, including some of Scholem's own students, would question the veracity of many of these claims.

Scholem fought to get Kabbalah a "place at the table" in the academic world. In order to bring this about, he tried to make the field palatable to the academy. He was careful to cast kabbalistic subjects in ways that made them accessible to academic discourse. For example, he seized on the notion that Kabbalah is "Jewish Mysticism," and situated himself in the study of comparative forms of mysticism. Once Kabbalah was defined as "mysticism," it could be placed in the continuum of experience defined by the academy as "mysticism."[3] As "mysticism," Kabbalah was portrayed as sharing common properties with other mystical traditions in the religions of the world. By the same token, Scholem described the Merkavah tradition as "Jewish Gnosticism," thereby placing himself in dialogue with other scholars working on the emerging study of the mystery religions and Gnostic heresies of late antiquity. The problem with defining Kabbalah as "mysticism" is necessitated forcing the square peg of Jewish metaphysics into the round hole of the Christological definition of mysticism.[4]

The field is two generations on from the Scholem's narrative. New questions are being asked, not just in response to his portrayal of the history of Kabbalah but independently. To bring but a few examples: Scholem went out of his way to impugn the authenticity of Yisrael Sarug, who sailed from the Galilee to Italy and brought Lurianic Kabbalah to the Italian Neoplatonists. Later, Ronit Meroz and Yosef Avivi determined that, in fact, Sarug's Kabbalah was authentically Lurianic with some of the terminology adapted to his new audience.[5] Scholem maintained that Isaac Luria's Kabbalah was a psychological response to the trauma of the Spanish Expulsion. Since that time, Moshe Idel, Martin Cohen and others have queried the idea of a direct relationship between Luria and the Expulsion.[6] Scholem had portrayed the concept of zimzum, or Divine withdrawal, as a novelty of Lurianic Kabbalah. Idel and Bracha Sack have demonstrated that the image of zimzum far predated Luria and was present very early in the development of Jewish mysticisms.[7] Idel has even pointed out that Gnostic ideas could very well have had their origins in Judaism and therefore the Gnostic tradition itself might really be "Gnostic Judaism."[8]

Hence, in the light of subsequent research, it is possible to seriously question the conclusions of practically every chapter of *Major Trends in Jewish Mysticism*, for quite empirical reasons. As mentioned, Moshe de Leon might have had rather little to do with the final versions of the *Zohar*. Isaac Luria might have been more influenced by his familial circumstances in the crafting of his kabbalistic system than by the recent Spanish Expulsion. Shabbatai Zevi's movement may have been better understood as a seventeenth-century phenomenon of paradigmatic change, much like the thinking of Spinoza, Luther and Newton, rather than as the natural outgrowth of Lurianic Kabbalah.[9] The possible contributing factors for the spread of Hasidism go far beyond the romanticized figure of the Ba'al Shem Tov, and may include economic and social factors outside of the influence of kabbalistic doctrine.[10] Questioning Scholem's arguments does not, as some might aver, amount to undue "anxiety of influence" on the part of the questioners! There are real problems of veracity in many of Scholem's conclusions, which lead to misconceptions that in fact have ramifications in the social realm.

Many such problems derive from Scholem's having isolated "true" Kabbalah in the historical past, as well as his troubled relationship with the active communities operating within a kilometer of his household. Boaz Huss has noted that "Scholem's meetings with contemporary kabbalists left no impression whatsoever on his vast corpus of scholarly work."[11] Scholem rejected the very possibility of studying with contemporary kabbalists, or even examining their textual record. He embraced the Zionist mythos, which required the marginalization of all previous ethnic categories and the cultural identity of Diaspora Judaism. According to the devastating critique offered by the late Arthur Hertzberg:

> Scholem was quite clearly re-evoking these fascinating shades but ultimately, to use the language of his charge against the scholars of the Wissenschaft school, in order to bury them with due respect. It was part of the Jewish past, the present was Zionism.[12]

As a result of these predilections, sometimes it seems that fairly serious students of Kabbalah, at least in the Diaspora, could not find their way around a bookstore in *Maḥaneh Yehudah*, the public market of Jerusalem, which is a seething vortex of popular Kabbalah and folk religion. There is no love lost on the other side, either. Many were the times that I heard *"Professor"* hurled as an epithet in the kabbalistic seminaries of north Jerusalem. Nonetheless, the academic establishment does not "own" Kabbalah and can't dictate its nature; it belongs to the ecclesia of Israel.

There are contemporary scholars, such as Boaz Huss,[13] Jody Myers,[14] Jonathan Meir[15] and Jonathan Garb,[16] who are performing an important scholarly task by investigating the substantial litera- ture and history of contemporary trends in Kabbalah. Jonathan Garb, in particular, has taken pains to identify the biases of the community with his distinction between the "qualitative" and the "quantitative" as ways of defining and subliminally "rating" the different contemporary movements. In the academy, and the Jewish establishment in North America, this leads to an unfortunate ten- dency to downgrade such phenomena as the Kabbalah Centre and Chabad. As social and religious phenomena, these movements' only sin may be that they are somewhat *déclassé* in the eyes of the acad- emy. In fact, in the case of American Judaism, it is a truism that the synagogue and communal "establishment" is threatened by any organization that is operating "off the grid," plucking adher- ents from outside the economic reach of the established commu- nity. The penitential Aish ha-Torah and Ohr Sameach movements, Chabad Hasidism and the Kabbalah Centre have all been targets of the community's disapprobation, even as they grow in stature and influence.

THE NEW AGE

For the last half-century, mercantilism and personal acquisition have defined life in the West. To this day, people are what they buy. Into this spiritual void, there has come a form of spirituality, known as the "New Age." This is a Western phenomenon, caused, in part, by disaffection with the institutions of formal religion. Jonathan Garb has portrayed the phenomenon of the contemporary New Age movement as the "breakdown of the modern meta-narrative in the post-modern age."[17] He sees the movement as a response to the dominance of philosophical rationalism in modern society, accom- panied by the decline in mainstream and traditional religions in their various Western host societies. It is a worldwide phenomenon, with a different tone is each society, be it American, Israel, the gen- eral Diaspora or Europe. Each of these societies has a specific sort of "New Ageism" that reflects its own religious dynamics. Followers of the New Age and its various religious options are reacting to the perceived impoverishment of Western religious traditions. Another factor is social. Some Western religions, and their institutions, are

Figure 10.1 R. Yosef Ḥayyim, the Ben Ish Hai, Chief Rabbi of Baghdad in the nineteenth century.

in decline. There might be a widespread perception of inconsistency or moral hypocrisy attaching to established religious traditions. This disaffection leads to interest in recovered traditions that are seen as more esthetic or more tolerant.

In the United States, a country of widespread religious observance, there is a sort of mainstream American Theism, what the sociologist Robert Bellah has termed "the American Civil

Religion."[18] The average lay American may reserve one day of the week to attend religious services and receive instruction. The central religious practice is attendance at an approved rite or ceremony. The other days of the week are reserved for the mall. The mall as a form of expression also underlies the phenomenon of so-called New Age spirituality. The chapel for this phenomenon is the New Age bookstore. The customary religious act of New Age spirituality is to purchase a slim volume of religious thought. The text in question is usually a streamlined abridgment of some conclusions that took a medieval mystic a lifetime of pietistic practice to reach. In this format, the teachings of this mystic are rendered free of their source disciplines, and purged of the years of struggle and torment that informed their development. These works retain, however, a tasty air of the exotic.

In late-twentieth-century American culture, in particular, "New Ageism" dovetailed with the acquisitive nature of the culture. To put it in somewhat vulgar terms, the credit card became the agent of spirituality. In the 1980s any Western bourgeois could walk into a New Age bookstore, purchase a paperback summary of some religious tradition, a crystal, some earrings and a wall hanging. Upon leaving the store and walking out into the strip mall, perhaps the buyer would reflect on the glow of the spiritual experience that they had just had. The buyer had a strong sense of having participated, albeit through a monetary transaction, with the transcendent, as well as being diverted. The biblical habitués of the cults of Ba'al in the valley of Hinnom might have had, in their day, a rather similar warm and fuzzy experience.[19]

THE KABBALAH CENTRE

The Kabbalah Centre movement has benefited from the rise of the mercantile New Age movement, as well as the financial advantages of operating off the Jewish communal grid. It originated in a small Hasidic community on the outskirts of Jerusalem, but it has become an international organization, with good prospects for enduring for some time. The Kabbalah Centre has its origins in the activities of an obscure Hasidic Rebbe, Rabbi Yehudah Ashlag, who led an impoverished circle in the Givat Shaul quarter, then a bleak industrial district of mandate-era Jerusalem. Ashlag was affected by Marxism and the other social currents of the twentieth century. He wrote voluminously, interpreting the *Zohar* according to Cordoverean and Lurianic Kabbalah, often plagiarizing large blocs of text from earlier commentaries for his own, which he called the "Sulam" or ladder. Upon his death, his students continued his work. Their visibility grew in the latter part of the twentieth century with the work of Rabbi Philip Berg and his sons. The Berg family's activity has been successful at both a popular and a "high" level. In latter terms, their kabbalistic prayer book with kabbalistic intentions, *Tefilah le-Oni*, is a particularly erudite work.

In this regard, the success of the Kabbalah Centre should be unsurprising; it was a case of "something to sell meets something to buy." From the point of view of the Kabbalah Centre, there was no dissonance in this practice. The "Kabbalah Research Centre" was originally a nonprofit organization, licensed by the Israeli government to print and distribute the works of Rabbi Yehudah Ashlag. In the punitively socialist economic environment of Israel in the 1960s, forming such a corporation was the only way to make a go of any business venture. The group had its origins in marketing, and as it hit its stride, its marketing strategies became more enterprising. So they marketed their trademark red strings, which were adopted from Jewish and Palestinian folk tradition. The selling of mineral water may have been inspired by Rabbi Yisrael Abuḥaẓeira (the Baba Sali) and his practice of blessing water for his supplicants. Is it nefarious to sell Kabbalah water? It's a scam to sell *any* bottled water!

The practices of the Kabbalah learning centre that have caused such hysteria in the Jewish community are pretty much normative kabbalistic practices that, isolated in the harsh light of day, could be sensationalized when portrayed unsympathetically. Take, for example, the Kabbalah Centre's advocacy of "scanning" pages of the *Zohar*, reading the blank syllables of the Aramaic text with no attempt to understand their meaning. Isaac Luria advocated this practice for the penitents (*ba'alei teshuvah*) of his era. These were probably reformed conversos[20] who were trying to work their way back into Judaism. To assist in their rehabilitation, Luria advocated that they read dozens of pages of *Zohar* a day. The process of reading vast amounts of text with relatively little understanding is also common in Breslav Hasidism, and the practice is advocated in the later Breslav writings. These are the origins of the Kabbalah Centre's "scanning" practice.[21] Of course, the guaranteeing of positive outcomes, especially for the ill, is ethically dubious.

In the 1990s, the Kabbalah Centres had rather a stormy encounter with the mainstream Jewish community, who gathered whatever disapprobation they could generate and heaped it, as best they could, on Rabbi Berg and his staff and supporters. This brought about a break with formal Judaism on the part of the centres and the formulation of what amounted to a mission to the gentiles. This change took place after an unseemly short period, compared to that of early Christianity. Since that time, the mainstream Jewish community has cleverly rid itself of the Kabbalah Centres, their Sabbath and Holiday services, as well as their wide enrollment of expatriate Israelis and other disaffected Jews. All of these souls are now off the mainstream community rolls. To what end, if not to spite the Jewish community's face?

In fact, the application of Kabbalah outside of normative Judaism is not unusual in Jewish history. It has happened many times over the centuries. Paradoxically, Kabbalah has always been a crossover phenomenon. At its inception, the Merkavah mystics applied the Gnostic mysteries of "the Old Religion" to Judaism. In the thirteenth century, there may have been contact between the Gnostic Catharites of Lanquedoc and the early Kabbalists of Provence. Yisrael Sarug brought Lurianic Kabbalah to the Italian Neoplatonists and the contemporary scholar Moshe Idel is demonstrating that the Ba'al Shem Tov drew on traditions of pneumatic holy men in the Ukraine who operated in a number of religious traditions. So Kabbalah has always been a crossover phenomenon and there is really no reason to *shrei gevalt* when such crossover occurs in the strip malls of America.

MUTATIONS OF HASIDISM

The Nazis killed a million and a half ḥasidim. Moving first into Poland, the cradle of Hasidism, they tore out the heart of the movement. In the vacuum formed after the war by the destruction of the main dynasties, less influential but no less complex figures rose to the fore, such as Rabbi Yoel Teitelbaum of Satmar (Satu Mare), in present day Romania. Escaping the Nazis, Teitelbaum first immigrated to Mandate Palestine and then, in 1949, left Israel for Williamsburg, Brooklyn where many surviving ḥasidim, whose leaders had perished, began to coalesce around him. Leaders such as the Satmar *Rebbe* had been known for their recidivist positions and now, in the eyes of their followers, they had been vindicated by the ruthless savagery of the gentiles. In other courts, however, the tone and character of the Hasidic movement changed, for a while, after the war. New forms of the movement asserted themselves and some Hasidic sects began to evolve, in their own ways, toward modernity.

Chabad Hasidism, founded by a disciple of the Maggid of Mezeritch, R. Schneur Zalman of Liadi, White Russia (1745–1812), in White Russia (Belarus), always had a specific character. It was ideological in nature and prized itself on its theoretical literature, as opposed to being based on a subjective relationship with the Rebbe, as in the case of most Hasidic courts. In that way, Chabad, or Lubovitch synagogues might be set up in far climes without the Rebbe's constant attendance to them. The core of Chabad teaching was a doctrine of the soul, of the resilience and independent existence within and apart from the body. This doctrine of the soul, over the years, proved to be a compelling draw for Chabad Hasidism, vindicating its own premise by drawing acolytes from the ranks of the Hasidic world and converts and penitents from the secular realm. The soul doctrine was augmented by a view of history, which saw the gathering of souls as leading to the coming of the Messiah. Messianic elements defined Chabad Hasidism well before the activities of the last Rebbe, Menachem Mendel Schneerson.[22]

In the postwar period, Chabad Hasidism began a long, slow arc away from Haredi mores and toward the larger Jewish community and the world. A simplistic explanation for these policies of outreach would be that Rabbi Menachem Mendel Schneerson, known simply as the "Rebbe," was more educated and worldly than his contemporary Rebbes. His predecessor fled the Soviet Union and established his court in the Eastern Parkway section of Brooklyn, but it was R. Menachem Mendel who truly understood the possibilities of America and of twentieth-century modernity as well, to advance the Chabad cause.

The Lubovitcher Rebbe developed a program of open proselytizing within the Jewish community. This was scandalous to the Hasidic establishment but faithful to the original teachings of the Baal Shem Tov. The lifestyle and religious beliefs of Chabad remained well within the Haredi fold, even though their presentation and accessibility to the rest of the Jewish community made them, socially, something other than conventional Haredi. They seemed to abandon the furtive and reclusive nature of Haredi communities, as well as those communities' passive-aggressive, dissembling manner of dealing with their host countries. Chabad was having none of that; they embraced American and Israeli culture and, in effect, created a situation in which the Lubavitcher Rebbe became, in their estimation, the default Rebbe for the Jewish world, which is another way of saying that he became the *Zaddik ha-Dor*, the leading light of his generation for the entire Jewish community.

One might surmise that the large number of penitents, or Ba'alei Teshuvah, in the Chabad communities swayed the movement toward Western mores. After all, the most modern part of the trope "We want Moshiach now!" is the word "now;" it speaks to the culture of gratification and entitlement that is particularly Western, if not American. In fact, Wolfson's thorough research has demonstrated the strong current of mystical relativism and pragmatic messianism that evolved over the arc of the Rebbe's voluminous written record. Samuel Heilman and Menachem Friedman have also shown that the notion of the Rebbe as a once and future king, whose "death" is merely a withdrawal to a higher plane of existence, did not originate with the death of the last Rebbe but was actually a Chabad principle for several generations.[23]

Today, the vast movement perseveres in the wake of the Rebbe's death in 1995. Some branches have added a few lines celebrating the coming of the Messiah at certain points in the liturgy; others are more circumspect. It was the Rebbe's genius to have decentralized financial control and power in the movement so that each district or city has its own budget, leaving little to fight over in the headquarters in Brooklyn. For the first 20 or so years since the Rebbe's death, the Chabad community has held together without, thus far, being rent by a major schism.

More tellingly, with the exception of some individual decriers of the messianic doctrine, the Jewish community as a whole has not shunned Chabad, even when extravagant claims are made for the paranormal powers of the Rebbe as the once and future Messiah. The Jewish community, as a body politic, seems unwilling to forgo the services that Chabad institutions provide, their network of religious schools, synagogues, college chaplaincy, drug rehabilitation centers, meat processing and distribution and the myriad ways that Chabad puts itself out there. The evidence for the "messianic heresy" was laid before the Jewish community and met with a shrug. This is perhaps the way it has always been with messianic movements in Judaism; they rise, fail, and the remnants are reabsorbed into Judaism and become part of its normal structure.[24]

Breslav Hasidism is a second form that has mutated out of the Hasidic community into a force that stands between secular and religious culture. The components of this development are manifold, and the story is far from over. It was the aim of its progenitor, Rabbi Naḥman of Breslav, through his radical self-consciousness and displacement of the inner demons that impelled his thought, to not leave a successor. At the same time, the cult of personality for the dead young Rebbe (he died at age 39 of complications from tuberculosis) was perhaps unsurpassed in Hasidism. In the ensuing years, the sect quarreled with the locals, particularly the courts of Chernobyl and the Talner Hasidism, who tormented and persecuted the Breslaver ḥasidim unmercifully.[25] At the same time, the picaresque literary nature of Breslav ḥasidim made them darlings of the nineteenth-century Jewish enlightenment, the secular neo-Hasidic movement in the early part of the twentieth century and contemporary Jewish renewal. According to legend, the first communal settlement in Palestine, Degania, borrowed its inflection of the word "collective," *kibbutz*, from a group of Breslaver ḥasidim who had taken in a few errant *kibbutzniks* on the eve of Rosh ha-Shanah. This crossover interest continued from the Yiddish theater into the counter-culture. Martin Buber's first reworking of Hasidic material was a free adaptation of the tales of Rabbi Naḥman. Breslaver Hasidism remained a point of intake in the early days of the movement of "return" to Orthodoxy. The saintly Rabbi Gedaliah Kenig aggressively worked the remnants of the first House of Love and Prayer in Jerusalem after it burned down in 1970, and many products of the original San Francisco counter-culture are scattered among the good burghers of Kiryat Mattersdorf, Ramot and other established Haredi enclaves in Jerusalem.

Modern Breslav Hasidism entered a new phase with the "revelation" of a mysterious and unknown figure Rav Yisroel Odesser, henceforth known as the *Ba'al ha-Petek*. Odesser claimed to have discovered a note written in Naḥman's hand in an old book he possessed. The note was signed "Na, Nah, Nahma, Nahman me-Uman" and counseled the repetition of the formula as a sort of mantra. This note, which came to light in 1922, was accredited to R. Naḥman, who died in 1810. Whatever its veracity, an ecstatic wing of mostly Israeli penitents formed around the cult of the note. They are known for dancing wildly on the streets of Israeli urban centers (and at weddings, for a fee).

The mutations of Chabad and Breslav are such that they no longer conform, in many respects, with the social models of the rest of Hasidic society, although they maintain the same stringency in their halakhic observance. Their distinctiveness shows itself largely in the social realm. Each of these groups has extended itself into some sort of dialogue with secular, and, in the case of Chabad, even non-Jewish society. If such discourse is considered anathema by the rest of Haredi society, then one might say that the very standards of observance of these two groups have softened. In any case, there is certainly a distinction between style and content in these groups' self-portrayal to the world when compared to the remainder of the Haredi world. For the present, the effect of these mutated forms of Hasidism in contemporary Israeli society is to render the barriers between secular and religious Jews far more porous than they had been. These groups, together with the forces of religious Zionism, serve as gateways between secular and Haredi society, even though both Breslav and Chabad remain solidly within the Haredi fold.

The religious Zionism of Rav Kook has its origins in the Kabbalah and brings a metaphysical understanding to politics and the social realm. Rav Kook drew his ideas from the kabbalistic tradition, and his musings on the soul, the ecclesiastical soul of the people Israel and the dynamics of messianism are couched in Kabbalistic terms,[26] which he brings to the discourse from his own background. This command of the Rav Kook tradition at its theoretical level is a particular strength of Jonathan Garb's earlier study on the uses of power in Kabbalah.[27] He portrays the evolution of Kook's original mystical Zionism, a "Messianism without a Messiah" into the political milieu of the violent expressions of the extremist wing of Religious Zionism, and, by association, the inner mystique of the later-day settlers' movement. No doubt Kook's writings bear the scrutiny; he was a voluminous legalist and social theologian, constantly portraying contemporary history in classical and apocalyptic terms, always employing the biblical and rabbinic tropes in the service of his inclusive vision.

JEWISH RENEWAL

Another element in the late-twentieth-century evolution of Kabbalah is the inception of the Jewish Renewal movement, which combines a number of contemporary social forces. Renewal is a multifaceted phenomenon, operating in a number of venues. I suggest tracing the Renewal movement to two progenitors. The first, Rabbi Shlomo Carlebach, a German-Jewish refugee and rabbinic scion, emerged from the postwar yeshivas of New York and New Jersey, acclaimed as a prodigy (*ilui*) in his youth. His career as a Talmudist was followed by an affiliation with Chabad. In 1948, the sixth Lubavitcher Rebbe sent Carlebach and Zalman Schachter to Brandeis University in an early experiment with campus outreach. Contact with the burgeoning counter-culture of Greenwich Village in the early 1960s set him on another course, however, as a traveling musician, and that is how he plied his trade for most of his life. Carlebach was, theologically, a mercurial genius. As the youth culture of the Western world erupted, he rode the wave, always teaching, gathering disciples, forming the distinctive "House of Love and Prayer" in San Francisco and Jerusalem, teaching out of his father's synagogue on the upper west side in New York and eventually chartering a communal farm in Modi'in, Israel. Besides the activities of Chabad, these houses were the first concerted effort at Orthodox outreach, which would become dynamic in the late twentieth century through other institutions. Although not of Hasidic background, Carlebach made strong use of Hasidic and kabbalistic texts, based on his considerable genius with sources. He was unsystematic and undisciplined, and by no means a systematic institution-builder. The road was his home and where he died, on a plane traveling to an engagement.

Carlebach's youthful "buddy," Rabbi Zalman Schachter-Shalomi did much more to set up the institutions of Jewish Renewal, and thus his activity is easier to categorize. A product of Chabad training in the postwar period, Schachter-Shalomi's activities are best compared to other postwar figures who were schooled in one tradition and acquired expertise in others. Such figures include Thomas Merton (with whom Schachter-Shalomi was a friend and correspondent), who drifted from a Bohemian background into Catholicism, eventually becoming a Trappist monk. Toward the end of his life (he died in a tragic accident in Bangkok in 1968), Merton developed

Figure 10.2 R. Shlomo Carlebach (Photo courtesy R. Mimi Feigelson).

a strong interest in Buddhism, which he incorporated into his Catholic practice. Another changeling of the period was Alan Watts, who oscillated between Anglican Christianity, Zen Buddhism and, eventually, Taoism. In the course of his academic activities, he was exposed to some of the earliest experiences with the spiritual possibilities of psychedelic drugs, which colored his later thinking. Each of these figures was reared in the Beat generation and then became leaders in the burgeoning counter-culture of the 1960s.

Unlike Shlomo Carlebach, Zalman Schachter-Shalomi maintained a career linked with academia, first as the director of the Orthodox student organization Yavneh in the early 1960s, then as a Hillel Chaplain and finally winning academic appointments at the University of Winnipeg, Temple University, the Reconstructionist Rabbinical College and the Naropa Institute in Boulder, Colorado. His teaching venues also formalized into a series of conclaves known as the Jewish Renewal movement, the Aleph Rabbinical School program, and other formal venues in which the Jewish Renewal movement coalesced.

It was in these contexts that Schachter-Shalomi developed his notion of the "paradigm shift," a popular theological term, borrowed from the hard sciences. The premise of the idea was that kabbalistic ideas may be pursued in a new context that is outside of the old paradigms of Jewish law that are patriarchal, racially insular or otherwise no longer relevant. Renewal circles therefore tend to be religiously liberal, in contrast to the circles founded and left by Carlebach, which generally pledge fealty to conventional Orthodoxy. Schachter-Shalomi's institutions, Aleph, the Elat Chayyim center and other wings of the movement have continued to function but seem to lack a second or third generation that can take over and provide future leadership. However, as the community of baby-boomers in the Renewal movement dissolves, it flavors and influences the activities of the whole rest of the liberal Jewish community.

Another influential surge of activity in the communal acceptance of kabbalistic ideas came from the members of the "Chavurah" communal movement of the early 1970s. This activity centered community of scholars in the Boston area in the late 1960s, particularly students of Professor Alexander Altmann at Brandeis University, who were more often than not products of the Conservative movement's camping experience of the 1960s. That generation formed a core group of academics, led by Professor Arthur Green, who were most influential in the American academic study of Kabbalah and formed a counterweight to the activities of the Israeli scholars in the wake of Scholem's passing. This group was distinguished, as well, by its sense of communal responsibility and it has not been uncommon for members of that scholarly circle to leave the purely scholarly track in favor of doing affective work with the general population, usually under the banner of some wing of Jewish Renewal.

Green has also produced a number of works of contemporary theology which are notable for their incorporation of kabbalistic ideas and for the soulful authenticity of their content, a quality otherwise lacking in much contemporary liberal Jewish theology.[28]

NON-ASHKENAZI KABBALAH

Paradoxically, the most obscurantist, recondite forms of Kabbalah flourish today as street religion. The Jewish populations of North Africa and the Middle East (*Sefardim* and *Edot ha-Mizraḥ*), forcibly repatriated to Israel in the postwar period, guarded their traditions. In an atmosphere of neglect from the socialist power structure, they nurtured a social class of religious leaders, who, by the 1980s had become synonymous with the emerging political muscle of those populations. R. Israel Abuḥaẓeira, the "Baba Sali," held court from the development town of Netivot. From the alleys of Machaneh Yehudah and the Bukharian Quarter, R. Mordechai Shar'abi and the venerable Hakham Kadourie held court, giving advice, dispensing cures and performing the odd miracle. The presence of these figures in the late twentieth century established an ethic of veneration of living saints among the displaced North African and Middle Eastern populations that paralleled the popular devotion of ḥasidim to their "ẓaddik."

In the veneration of these living saints, certain disparate kabbalistic values became normative. One factor which leaps out at the onlooker is a formal obeisance to holy men who are perceived as occupying the classic stance of the thaumaturge, one foot in present reality and one foot out. From Tel Aviv to Los Angeles, it is not uncommon to enter a business and see, in one corner, a small shrine containing talismans, a few volumes of the *Zohar* and pictures of these saints, living and dead, displayed as icons of the Holy.

I evoked a little of the feeling of this devotionalism in an earlier book on the subject:

I began to write this book[29] as an expression of *ga'agu'im*, my yearning for the Jerusalem that I first experienced as a young Rabbi, fresh from an orthodox seminary, ensconced in the old Bukharian quarter of Jerusalem, which was at the time still largely central Asian in its population. There the locals would point out to me the attic of the *Shoshanim le-David* synagogue, where Ya'akov Ḥayyim Sofer had sat and composed the voluminous kabbalistic law code *Kaf ha-Ḥayyim*. In the large multiplex synagogue founded by the family Moussaieff, I would hear tell of the nearby Yissacharoff synagogue and the circle of kabbalists who had moved there, Ḥayyim Shaul Dweck and the Rehovot ha-Nahar community. Throughout the neighboring communities, stretching in an "L" shape from the Bukharian quarter, into the hasidic suburb of Geulah and thence to the area around Jerusalem's large open-air market, Maḥaneh Yehudah, there were kabbalistic synagogues. The Beit El synagogue, vacated during the fall of the old city of Jerusalem, had moved to the border of the two latter neighborhoods and still held a circle of initiates, led by members of the Hadaya family.

In those days, when I was a younger man, I had gone for a blessing to the saint R. Mordechai Shar'abi, who was not, despite his name, a lineal descendent of Shalom Shar'abi. He lived in a large facility off the main promenade of the open-air market. It was a crisp morning, and I sat in the courtyard and watched as his young wife fed the cats. After a while I was shown into a darkened room. Shar'abi sat in robes, cross-legged on a divan, swaying from side to side like a blind man. And indeed, he seemed not to see me. "Who is it?" he cried. Next to him sat a burly

Figure 10.3 The traditional seal of the kabbalists of Beit El, Jerusalem.

young man, in the garb of any run of the mill yeshivah student. Perhaps it was a young Benyahu Shmueli, I can't remember now. "He is coming with a question!" called out the burly young man, though Shar'abi was sitting not three feet away from him. "Let him ask," called Shar'abi in an equally loud voice. He swayed from side to side in a trance, smiling and staring blindly out into the room. I asked my question and he answered with a certain brusque optimism. And I walked out into the morning light with a good feeling, as if I had encountered somebody who existed between two worlds, this one and the next, and he had leaned down from his other world and brought my needs into it. Now Shar'abi has passed, with his generation of holy men, and the house that I visited is now the Nahar Shalom Yeshivah, where a new generation pursues the Beit El practice.

For the North African and Middle Eastern communities, the *Zohar* is far more a piece of national literature than it is, by and large for the Ashkenazi population. This may be because the residual presence of Arabic in those communities, which could help with fluency in the *Zohar*'s Aramaic. Certain traditional families also keep up traditions of religious poetry, or *piyyut*, at the Sabbath table and in synagogue life. The *Zohar*, in its original form, is more widely circulated among those populations. I have observed the custom of reciting the *Zohar*'s *Idra Rabbah* at a prayer quorum on the anniversary of a death, as well as widespread Zohar study among these populations.

The graves of the saints of the *Zohar* and Talmud are also venerated by Sefardim and Edot ha-Mizraḥ, with a pilgrimage often being the object of a vow at times of illness or danger. Saints from Morocco and Iraq receive honorary gravesites in Israel, which then become pilgrimage sites. This phenomenon has been described as a means of acquisition of the space by benighted populations. In that regard, Jews and Muslims often share many sacred gravesites.[30] They even have practices in common, such as the custom for women to tie a piece of cloth or leave an article of clothing at the saint's grave as a keepsake or remembrance.

Studies of Sefardic, North African and Middle Eastern Kabbalah have been hindered by another factor. The academy is the lineal child of the Jewish enlightenment, or "haskalah," which skimmed the intellectual cream of traditional European society, east and west, in the nineteenth and twentieth centuries. To this day, there is far less attention paid to the history and kabbalistic traditions of the Sefardic, North African and Middle Eastern Jewish communities. The reasons for this reticence to confront North African and Middle Eastern manifestations of Kabbalah are social and historical, dictated by the mores of the academy, as well as the internal politics of Kabbalah study. Kabbalah scholars have largely represented a certain stratum of Israeli society, often (but not always, as in the enthralling work of Havivah Pedaya and Avraham Elkayam) separated from practitioners by social, ethnic and religious barriers. The alienation of non-Ashkenazic and Ashkenazic studies preceded and mirrors the alienation of contemporary Western culture from Islam. This problem was forecast in Scholem's reference to Beit El as the expression of "the Sefardic and arabized tribes,"[31] evidence of his social distance from the pulsing kabbalistic activity going on less than a kilometer away from any of his Jerusalem homes.

FUTURE DEVELOPMENTS

Chabad, The Kabbalah Centre, Breslav Hasidism, and the Renewal movement represent late, manifestly inelegant interpretations of aspects of the kabbalistic tradition, shaped by modernity yet emerging from within the closed walls of each sect. All of these circles are arguably "popular," as they have been embraced by broader elements of the modern Jewish community beyond the traditional closed circles of classical Kabbalah. The new incarnation of Breslav, in particular, has made inroads in the Israeli youth culture. Many Israeli youth visit India after their army service and have been returning with an internalized sensitivity to Eastern spirituality, which they apply to Jewish models back home. The evangelical groups, by which I mean Orthodox organizations devoted to outreach in the secular world, as well as neo-Breslav and Kabbalah Learning Centre have also served to blur the traditionally rigid lines between religious and secular in Israeli society. They operate "off-the-grid" and pose threats to various elements for which the grid is a comfort and a shield.

The reality is that Kabbalah provided the form and basis of conventional Judaism. Without Kabbalah, Judaism would not have the Friday night service in its present form, nor the inviting of the guests, or *ushpizin*, into the *Sukkah*, or the *Tashlikh* service on the afternoon *Rosh ha-Shanah*. These practices are kabbalistic in their essence; they have no other identity. The real impediment to the incorporation of Jewish mysticism into one's lifestyle is that if one doesn't live in an intensely Jewish, and Jewishly literate way, then the process won't work. The stricture against studying Kabbalah before the age of 40 wasn't because the material was inherently dangerous, but because the mind had to be steeped in Jewish symbols and associations for the imagery of the *Zohar* to make any sense at all. The *Zohar* is completely informed by the tropes and symbols of Judaism, building on the concrete form of the sacred texts in their original. It was only when the student had a "full belly" of the Bible and Talmud that the Jewish mysticism would make any sense.

In this way, Kabbalah resembles other forms of mysticism. Religious systems that jettison their traditional structures, that "dumb down" and reduce themselves to a few ideas or unifying images, do not generally produce mystics. For instance, there have been very few examples of Protestant mysticism. As Gershom Scholem pointed out, Kabbalah has a conservative nature; it doesn't rock the boat or attempt to restructure traditional Judaism. There is more profound Jewish experience, potentially, in the *shema'* said well, with a contrite and empty spirit, than in all the meditation retreats in California.

In context, the practices of Jewish mysticism are neither stringent nor obscure. A kabbalistic practice requires an embodied Judaism, in which religious life is part of one's physical place in the world and the *miẓvah* is part of the consciousness of the individual. The *Zohar*, the classical work of Kabbalah, claims to have been written in the period after the Jewish revolt, and the stringency of the laws is not much different from that observed at the median level of Conservative or Liberal Judaism. The *Zohar* polemicized for basic Jewish practices, such as praying with *tefillin* or reciting the grace after meals. A kabbalist need not be ultra-Orthodox, but he or she has to be conventionally observant. A kabbalistic lifestyle doesn't depend on which Temple one attends, but more on how one gets to it, how intensely one prays there and whether one observes the laws of *kashrut*.

Nonetheless, on a macro level the Jews are where they have always been, in a mortal struggle for their existence against a ruthless, ceaselessly morphing opponent. The seething, stormy world

Figure 10.4 R. Yehudah Petayyah, influential kabbalist of Baghdad and Jerusalem, d. 1937.

of the Kabbalah, with its forces of good struggling to get free from the impediments of forces of evil, remains an accurate reflection of reality. Yet, there is something to be said for those Jews who are evolving to the point, as must be reached in each life, when the struggles that are generated from within give way to the equanimity that points to a path through the clear water beyond.

NOTES

2 KABBALAH: A BRIEF HISTORY

1   See Alon Goshen-Gottstein, "Is Ma'aseh Bereishit Part of Ancient Jewish Mysticism?" *Journal of Jewish Thought and Philosophy* 4: 185–201; Gershom Scholem, *Major Trends in Jewish Mysticism*, third edition, rev. New York: Schocken, 1961, pp. 20, 42, 55, 73, 75.
2   Scholem, *Major Trends in Jewish Mysticism*, pp. 40–79.
3   See Mark Verman, *The Books of Contemplation: Medieval Jewish Mystical Sources*, Albany, NY: State University of New York Press, 1989.
4   Ronit Meroz, "The Middle Eastern Origins of Kabbalah," *The Journal for the Study of Sephardi and Mizrahi Jewry* (February 2007): 39–57.
5   See Scholem, *Major Trends in Jewish Mysticism*, pp. 205–86. Among useful full-length studies of the *Zohar*, notable are Melila Hellner-Eshed, *A River Flows from Eden*, Palo Alto, CA: Stanford, 2009 and Yehudah Liebes, *Studies in the Zohar*, Albany, NY: State University of New York Press, 1993. Of the many works of Elliot Wolfson, *Venturing Beyond* is largely concerned with the *Zohar*, although the *Zohar*'s thought pervades most of Wolfson's recent writing.
6   Elliot Wolfson, "The Anonymous Chapters of the Elderly Master of Secrets—New Evidence for the Early Activity of the Zoharic Circle," *Kabbalah* 19 (2009): 143–278.
7   Boaz Huss, Like the Radiance of the Sky: Chapters in the Reception History of the Zohar and the Construction of its Symbolic Value (Hebrew), Jerusalem: Bialik, 2008; Yehudah Liebes, "How was the Zohar Written?" in Studies in the Zohar, Albany, NY: State University of New York Press, 1993; Ronit Meroz, "Zoharic Narratives and their Adaptations," Hispania Judaica Bulletin 3 (5760/2000); idem, "The Middle Eastern Origins of Kabbalah"; Daniel Abrams, "Zohar, Book and 'the Book of the Zohar': A History of the Assumptions and Projections of Kabbalists and Scholars"; Kabbalah 19 (2009); Avraham Elkayam, "Shabbatai Tzvi's Manuscript Copy of the Zohar," Kabbalah 3, Los Angeles, 1998, 343–87.
8   Abulafia's limited and rather insular career has enlivened the study of Kabbalah since Gershom Scholem introduced him back into the discourse (*Major trends in Jewish Mysticism*, pp. 119–55). When the popular writer Aryeh Kaplan began to write about him (Kaplan,

Meditation and Kabbalah, York Beach, ME: Weiser, 1982, pp. 55–115), Abulafia's works remained in manuscript. Moshe Idel then published his groundbreaking studies of Abulafia's thought and method (*Language, Torah and Hermeneutics in Abraham Abulafia*, Albany, NY: State University of New York Press, 1989; idem, *The Mystical Experience in Abraham Abulafia*, Albany, NY: State University of New York Press, 1989; idem, *Studies in Ecstatic Kabbalah*. This work has recently been augmented by a full length study of Abulafia by Elliot Wolfson (*Abraham Abulafia: Kabbalist and Prophet*, Los Angeles, CA: Cherub Press, 2000).

9 Such is the agreement of the works of Moshe Idel and Mark Verman, as well as the popular works of Aryeh Kaplan, namely that the core of the contemplative, or, for Kaplan, "meditative" impulse in Kabbalah is in the concept of "hitbodedut" (Verman, *The History and Varieties of Jewish Meditation*, New York: Jason Aronson, 1996, p. 39).

10 Idel, "Hitbodedut as Concentration in the Ecstatic Kabbalah," in *Jewish Spirituality* I, ed. Arthur Green, New York: Crossroads, 1986, pp. 412–13, 428.

11 Idel, "Hitbodedut as Concentration in the Ecstatic Kabbalah," pp. 415–18.

12 Idel, "Hitbodedut as Concentration in the Ecstatic Kabbalah," pp. 427–8;

13 Idel, "Hitbodedut as Concentration in the Ecstatic Kabbalah," p. 431.

14 The most complete study of Luria is Lawrence Fine's *Physician of the Soul, Healer of the Cosmos*, Stanford, CA: Stanford University Press, 2003. See also Fine's article "The Contemplative Practice of Yihudim," in *Jewish Spirituality* II, ed. Green, pp. 64–98, and Scholem, *Major Trends in Jewish Mysticism*, pp. 284–6. A somewhat deeper study is Shaul Magid's *From Metaphysics to Midrash: Myth, History, and the Interpretation of Scripture in Lurianic Kabbala*, Indiana: Indiana University Press, 2008.

15 Scholem, *Major Trends in Jewish Mysticism*, p. 286.

16 See Pinchas Giller, *Shalom Shar'abi and the Kabbalists of Beit El*, New York: Oxford University Press, 2008.

17 Allan Nadler, *The Faith of the Mithnagdim: Rabbinic Responses to Hasidic Rapture*, Baltimore, MD: Johns Hopkins University Press, 1997.

3 KABBALISTIC METAPHYSICS

1 *Tiqqunei ha-Zohar* 123a–b, *Zohar* III (*Ra'aya Meheimna*) 109b; also *Zohar* I 103b, 245a, III 152a, 159a for the *Zohar*'s paradigm of the soul. See Moshe Hallamish, *An Introduction to the Kabbalah*, Albany, NY: State University of New York Press, 1999, pp. 121–66.

2 This idea first appears in Azril of Gerona's *Commentary to the Aggadot*, *Perush ha-Aggadot le-Rabbenu Azriel*, ed. Isaiah Tishby, Jerusalem, 1945, p. 118.

3 *Ma'arekhet ha-Elohut*, chapter 7; Tishby, *The Wisdom of the Zohar*, p. 234.
4 See Daniel Matt, "*Ayin*: the Concept of Nothingness in Jewish Mysticism," in *Essential Papers in Kabbalah* ed. Lawrence Fine, New York: University Press, 1995, pp. 67–108;
5 Boaz Huss, *Ketem Paz . . .*, pp. 158–9; Bracha Sack, "Prayer in the Teachings of Moshe Cordovero," 6.
6 The complete presentation of the development of the four worlds traditions remains Gershom Scholem's "The Development of the Tradition of the Worlds," (Hebrew), *Tarbiẓ* 2: 415–42; 3: 33–66; Tishby, *The Wisdom of the Zohar*, p. 557.
7 See Wolfson, *Luminal Darkness*, Oxford: Oneworld, 2007, pp. 57–110.
8 See, for example, Idel, *Hasidism: Between Ecstasy and Magic*. Albany, NY: State University of New York Press, 1995, pp. 45–53.

4 LURIANIC KABBALAH

1 These three names seem to be interchangeable in the Zohar, however, Isaac Luria differentiated then and had them standing for different aspects of the Divine.
2 See Giller, *Reading the Zohar*, New York: Oxford University Press, 2000, pp. 113–22.
3 *Zohar* II 88b, III 288b.
4 Two far more thorough portrayals of the Lurianic system in its excelsis are Shaul Magid's *From Metaphysics to Midrash* and Lawrence Fine's *Physician of the Soul, Healer of the Cosmos*.
5 Tishby, *The Wisdom of the Zohar*, p. 555.
6 See Daniel Abrams, "When Was the Introduction to the Zohar Written?" (Hebrew) *Assufot* 8 (1994).
7 *Zohar* I 15a–b; cf. Wolfson, *Luminal Darkness*, pp. 50 n29, 117, 138 n34; Daniel C. Matt, *Zohar: The Book of Enlightenment*, New York: Paulist Press, 1984, pp. 49–50; Ḥallamish, *An Introduction to the Kabbalah*, pp. 183–201. On the more popular implications of this idea, see Matt, *God & the Big Bang: Discovering Harmony Between Science & Spirituality*, New York: Jewish Lights, 1998.
8 *Tiqqunei Zohar Ḥadash* 122a. The original text and *Kav ha-Middah* were glossed by the authors of *Tiqqunei ha-Zohar (Tiqqunei ha-Zohar* 19a–20b, 37b) and the compositions called the *Matnitin*, or "Mishnahs."
9 . . . and therefore, sharing few commonalities with Christianity, giving the lie to the fallacy of there being a "Judeo-Christian tradition."
10 See Alexander Altmann, "The Gnostic Background of the Rabbinic Adam Legends," in *Studies in Religious Philosophy and Mysticism*, Ithaca, NY: Cornell University Press, 1969, pp. 1–16, 161–79.
11 Babylonia Talmud Shabbat 146a; Avodah Zarah 22b; Yevamot 103b; Ecclesiastes Rabbah 1:4.

12 See Giller, *The Enlightened Will Shine*, Albany, NY: State University of New York Press, 1993, p. 35.
13 See Neuman, *The Great Mother*, Princeton, NJ: Bollingen, 1964, pp. 147–203.
14 TZ 115a–b; TZH° 110b; I (TZ) 23a. See also Altmann, "The Gnostic Background of the Rabbinic Adam Legends," pp. 1–16; Idel, *Kabbalah: New Perspectives*, New Haven, CT: Yale University Press, 1988, pp. 117–19, 131, 183, 330n; Scholem, *Kabbalah*, New York: Meridian, 1978, p. 164.
15 *Sanhedrin* 38b, *Zohar* I 38b,*Tiqqunei ha-Zohar* Z 99b, 100a, 116b, 128b; *Tiqqunei* ZH 114c.
16 Tishby, *The Doctrine of Evil and the "Kelippah" in Lurianic Kabbalism* (Hebrew), Jerusalem: Magnes, 1984.
17 See Wolfson "Left Contained in Right: A Study in Zoharic Hermeneutics," *Association for Jewish Studies Journal* 11 (1987): 27–32.
18 In the classical midrash, see: *Bereshit Rabbah* 3:7–9, 9:2; *Kohelet Rabbah* 3:11; *Shoher Tov* 34:1. In the *Zohar*, see: I 154b, 262b; III 135a–b, 292b. In the *Tiqqunim*, see: *Zohar* I (*Tiqqunei ha-Zohar*) 24b, 252b–53a, III 61a, 292b, *Tiqqunei Zohar Hadash* 108a, 110a–b, 114b–d.
19 Sha'ar Ma'amarei RaShB"Y, p. 107.
20 The Castilean kabbalist Yosef Gikatilla implied that the account was too esoteric for general circulation, maintaining to his audience that "if you are worthy, you will hear tremendous traditions regarding this from mouth to mouth, things that represent the furnace of the world." *Sha'arei Orah* 98b; cf. Avi Weinstein's translation, *Gates of Light*, San Francisco: HarperCollins, 1994, p. 346.
21 Midrash Genesis Rabbah 3.7, 15.1, Ecclesiastes Rabbah 3.11.
22 Giller, *Reading the Zohar*, pp. 242–57.
23 Sarug, *Limmudei Azilut* 11b.
24 Yosef Avivi, *Binyan Ariel* (Hebrew), Jerusalem: Misgav Yerushalayim, 1987, pp. 349–53, 371–411; Meroz, "Redemption in the Lurianic Teaching," p. 27.
25 Sha'ar Ma'amarei RaSHB"Y ve-RaZ"L, p. 274.
26 Israel Weinstock, "R. Yosef Ibn Tabul's Commentary on the Idra" (Hebrew), *Temirin* 1, Jerusalem: Mossad ha-Rav Kook, 1982, p. 139.
27 *Zohar* II 96a, III (RM) 109b; ShMR, pp. 190, 192, 217–18; Sarug, *Limmudei Azilut* 4b, 7d; *Ez Hayyim* II, pp. 345–9; Likkutim Hadashim me-ha-AR"I Z"L u-me-Hayyim Vital Z'"L, p. 18; Avivi, *Binyan Ariel*, pp. 252, 359.
28 This is from an early composition by Vital, the "drush to Sagis," *Likkutim Hadashim me-ha-AR"I Z"L u-me-Hayyim Vital Z"L*, pp. 19–20, 22.
29 The image of God as a cosmic potter is presented in Jeremiah 18.6.
30 *Likkutim Hadashim me-ha-AR"I Z"L u-me-Hayyim Vital Z"L*, p. 20.
31 Vital, Sha'ar Ma'amarei RaSHB"Y ve-RaZ"L, p. 186; Sha'ar ha-Hakdamot, pp. 16–18.
32 Giller, *Reading the Zohar*, pp. 48, 159.
33 Avivi, *Binyan Ariel*, pp. 166–7.

NOTES

34 See Menachem Kallus, "The Theurgy of Prayer in Lurianic Kabbalah," Ph.D. Thesis; Hebrew University, 2002.
35 Avivi, *Binyan Ariel*, pp. 171–256; Meroz, "Redemption in the Lurianic Teaching," pp. 120, 164.
36 See Vital, Sha'ar Ma'amarei RaShBY, pp. 249, 267, 269–70.
37 On the origins of this term see Ze'ev Gries, in *Jewish Spirituality* Volume II, ed. Green, pp. 157–205.
38 *Tiqqunei ha-Zohar* 50b.
39 *Tiqqunei ha-Zohar* 107b, 130a, 140b.
40 Avivi, *Binyan Ariel*, p. 349; idem "Luria's Writings in Italy to 1620," *Alei Sefer* 11 (1984): 121–2.
41 See above p. 68–77. Vital, *Eẓ Ḥayyim I*, p. 24; Sarug, *Limmudei Aẓilut* 4d, 6a–b, 12d.
42 Meroz, "Redemption in the Lurianic Teaching"; Avivi, *Binyan Ariel* (Hebrew), *Kabbalat Ha-AR"I* (Hebrew), Jerusalem: Makhon Ben Zvi, 2008.
43 See above Chapter 1 p. 61, Isaiah Tishby documented the patterns of that success, although Moshe Idel has challenged whether Cordovero's teachings fell quite so deeply from disfavor (Idel, *Hasidism: Between Ecstasy and Magic*, pp. 33–43).
44 See p. 165.
45 Naḥman of Breslav, *Likkutei Moharan I* #64, p. 290.
46 Scholem, *Major Trends in Jewish Mysticism*, Schocken, 1948, pp. 245, 246, 286.
47 Idel, "The History of the Concept of Ẓimẓum in Kabbalah Research," *The Kabbalah of the AR"I : Jerusalem, Studies in Jewish Thought* 10: 89.
48 Idel, *Kabbalah: New Perspectives*, p. 265.

5 THE SOUL

1 See Giller, "Recovering the Sanctity of the Galilee: the Veneration of Sacred Relics in the Classical Kabbalah," *The Journal of Jewish Thought and Philosophy* 4: 150–69; Moshe Ḥallamish, *An Introduction to the Kabbalah*, pp. 83–4, 247–80.
2 See J. A. A. Wijnhoven, "The Zohar and the Proselyte," in *Texts and Responses: Studies Presented to N. Glatzer*, ed. Michael Fishbane, Leiden: E. J. Brill, 1957, pp. 120–40; Giller, *Reading the Zohar*, pp. 46–8; Wolfson, *Luminal Darkness*, pp. 268–72.
3 *Shivḥei ha-AR"I* #5, brought in Lawrence Fine, "The Contemplative Practice of Yiḥudim," in *Jewish Spirituality* II, p. 89; Ḥallamish, *An Introduction to the Kabbalah*, pp. 280–309.
4 Vital, *Sha'ar Ruaḥ ha-Kodesh*, p. 109.

6 MYSTICAL PRACTICE AND THE MIẒVOT

1 Scholem, "The Meaning of the Torah in Jewish Mysticism," in *On the Kabbalah and Its Symbolism*, New York: Schocken, 1965, p. 32.

2 Scholem, "Religious Authority and Mysticism," in *On the Kabbalah and Its Symbolism*, pp. 5–31.
3 See Wolfson, *Sefer ha-Rimmon*.
4 Giller, *The Enlightened Will Shine*, p. 89.
5 Matt, "The Mystic and the Miẓwot," in *Jewish Spirituality* I, ed. Arthur Green, New York: Crossroads, 1987, pp. 370–6.
6 See Maimonides' The Guide for the Perplexed, ed. Y. Kapach, Jerusalem: Merkaz ha-Rav Kook, 1977, 3.47; Scholem, *Jewish Gnosticism, Merkabah Mysticism and Talmudic Tradition*, p. 11.
7 *Tiqqunei ha-Zohar* 140a. See Tishby, *The Wisdom of the Zohar*, pp. 890–2.
8 Giller, *The Enlightened Will Shine*, pp. 89–105; Ḥallamish, *An Introduction to the Kabbalah*, pp. 167–82.
9 "The Mystic and the Miẓwot," in *Jewish Spirituality* I, p. 388.
10 Matt, "The Mystic and the Miẓwot," pp. 370–2.
11 *Mishneh Torah*, Laws of Circumcision 3.8.
12 See Tishby, *The Wisdom of the Zohar*, pp. 464–5, 531, 538–41.
13 *Zohar (Ra'aya Meheimna)* III 280a.
14 *Zohar (Ra'aya Meheimna)* III 125b. 15 See Giller, *The Enlightened Will Shine*, pp. 83–9; Tishby, *The Wisdom of the Zohar*, pp. 447–546.
16 *Zohar* I (*Tiqqunei ha-Zohar*) 27b.
17 Giller, *The Enlightened Will Shine*, pp. 84–9.
18 *Tiqqunei ha-Zohar* 62b.
19 *Tiqqunei ha-Zohar* 23b; *Zohar* III (*Ra'aya Meheimna*) 111a.
20 *Tiqqunei ha-Zohar* 1b, *Zohar (Ra'aya Meheimna)* II 114b, III 222b.
21 See Giller, *The Enlightened Will Shine*, pp. 21–32.
22 *Tiqqunei ha-Zohar* 49b, 52a, 100b, 101a.
23 The treatment of messianism is a vast topic in the academic study of Kabbalah, particularly in Gershom Scholem's *The Messianic Idea in Judaism*, New York: Schocken, 1971 and *Shabbatai Zevi: The Mystical Messiah*, Princeton, NJ: Bollingen, 1973. In recent times the work of Matt Goldish (*The Sabbatean Prophets*) and David Halperin (*Sabbatai Sevi: Testimonies to a Failed Messiah*) have further addressed the phenomenon of Shabbateanism.
24 *Tiqqunei ha-Zohar* 112b, 69b, 85a, 142a.
25 *Zohar (Ra'aya Meheimna)*, II 42a, 114b, 121a, III 123a, 215a, 222b, 271a; *Tiqqunei ha-Zohar* 1b.
26 *Tiqqunei Zohar Ḥadash* 102d, 107c.
27 *Zohar* II 96a.
28 *Tiqqunei Zohar Ḥadash* 119a.
29 *Zohar (Ra'aya Meheimna)* III 16b; *Tiqqunei ha-Zohar* 59a.
30 Giller, *The Enlightened Will Shine*, p. 51; *Zohar* III (*Ra'aya Meheimna*) 277a–b.
31 See Yiẓḥak Baer, *A History of the Jews in Christian Spain* I, translated by Louis Schoffman, Philadelphia, PA: Jewish Publication Society, 1978, pp. 243–305.
32 *Zohar (Ra'aya Meheimna)* III 89b.
33 See Tishby, *The Wisdom of the Zohar*, pp. 1335–1406.

34 *Tiqqunei ha-Zohar* 134a, *Tiqqunei Zohar Ḥadash* 114d; *Zohar* 1 55b, III 109b.

35 Talmud *Baba Meẓia* 59a; *Tiqqunei ha-Zohar* 30b, 126b; see Tishby, *The Wisdom of the Zohar*, pp. 1355–1409.

36 *Tiqqunei ha-Zohar* 84a.

37 *Tiqqunei ha-Zohar, Tiqqunei ha-Zohar* 19a, 25b, 55b, *Zohar* III 256b.

38 *Tiqqunei ha-Zohar* 22a–b; *Zohar* (*Ra'aya Meheimna*) III 276a, 277a.

39 This is found in the Talmud, *Berachot* 5b, 7a; *Ta'anit* 7a; *Zohar* I 18b, 170b, II 117b, III 168a, 231a, 276a; *Tiqqunei ha-Zohar* 82b, 84a, 90b, 130a.

40 Talmud *Eruvin* 63b; *Tiqqunei ha-Zohar* 99b; Talmud *Ketubot* 62b; *Tiqqunei ha-Zohar* 61a, 78a.

41 *Zohar* (*Ra'aya Meheimna*) III 226a.

42 *Tiqqunei ha-Zohar* 23a.

43 *Zohar* II 94a–114a; see Giller, *Reading the Zohar*, pp. 35–68; Melila Hellner-Eshed, *A River Flows Out of Eden*, pp. 146–50, 157–65; Wolfson, "Beautiful Maiden Without Eyes," in *Luminal Darkness*, pp. 55–110.

44 Yehudah Liebes, "How was the *Zohar* Written?" in *Studies in the Zohar*, pp. 86–8.

45 *Zohar* II 102a.

46 *Zohar* II 102a. An instance of this type of conflict is detailed in R. Elijah ha-Kohen of Izmir's eulogy for Jacob Hagiz (1674), which is reproduced in Marc Saperstein's *Jewish Preaching*, New Haven, CT: Yale, 1993, pp. 320–2.

47 *Zohar* II 102b.

48 *Zohar* II 102b. Theoretically, were the widow to visit the gravesite, with the *ruaḥ* of her husband in her and the *nefesh* at the grave, her presence would be an eroticized kind of union.

49 *Zohar* I 188a, 219b.

50 *Tiqqunei ha-Zohar* 133a.

51 *Tiqqunei Zohar Ḥadash* 114d; *Tiqqunei ha-Zohar* 30b, 126b. See Wolfson, *Language, Eros and Being*, New York: Fordham University Press, 2005, pp. 296–332.

52 See Giller, "Elliot Wolfson and the Study of Kabbalah in the Wake of Scholem," pp. 23–8; Wolfson, *Luminal Darkness*, pp. 151–6, 204–9, 275–80; *Through a Speculum That Shines*, pp. 326–92; "From Sealed Book to Open Text: Time, Memory and Narrativity in Kabbalistic Hermenutics," in *Interpreting Judaism in a Postmodern Age* ed. Steven Kepnes, New York: N.Y.U. Press, 1996, pp. 145–80.

53 Vital, *Zohar ha-Raki'a* 100c.

54 Vital, *Zohar ha-Raki'a* 99a, 102c.

55 *Zohar* II 103a.

56 See Giller, *The Enlightened Will Shine*, p. 152n; Yiẓḥak Baer, *A History of the Jews in Christian Spain* 1, pp. 243–305; *Zohar* II 111a.

57 See p. 66.

58 See David Biale, *Eros and the Jews*, Berkeley: University of California, 1992, pp. 121–49.

59 Talmud *Beẓah* 16a; *Zohar* II 204a–b; Tishby, *The Wisdom of the Zohar*, pp. 1290–5.
60 Wolfson, *Luminal Darkness*, pp. 144–8.
61 Green, "The Ẓaddiq as *Axis Mundi* in Later Judaism," *Journal of the American Academy of Religion* 45 (1977): 327–47.
62 Talmud *Shabbat* 119a, *Baba Kama* 32b.
63 *Zohar* II 88a–b; Tishby, *The Wisdom of the Zohar*, pp. 1286–90. See also Joel Hecker, *Mystical Bodies, Mystical Meals: Eating and Embodiment in Medieval Kabbalah*, Ann Arbor, MI: Wayne State University Press, 2005, pp. 137–9; Wolfson, *Luminal Darkness*, pp. 157–9.
64 On this point, see Boaz Huss, "*Sefer ha-Zohar* as a Canonical, Sacred and Holy Text: Changing Perspectives of the Book of Splendor between the Thirteenth and Eighteenth Centuries," *The Journal of Jewish Thought and Philosophy* 7 (1997): 257–307.
65 Hallamish, *An Introduction to the Kabbalah*, p. 63.
66 Treatments of the Sabbath as a temporal form of sacred space include Abraham Joshua Heschel, *The Sabbath*, New York: Farrar Straus Giroux, 2005 and Elliot Ginzburg, *The Sabbath in Classical Kabbalah*, Albany, NY: State University of New York Press, 1989.
67 *Sha'ar ha-Kavvanot* II pp. 224, 227.
68 See Giller, *Shalom Shar'abi and the Kabbalists of Beit El*, pp. 131–2, 143–4.
69 *Sha'ar ha-Kavvanot* I p. 206; II p. 220.
70 *Sha'ar ha-Kavvanot* II pp. 220, 228–30.
71 *Sha'ar ha-Kavvanot* II p. 231; See Giller, *Shalom Shar'abi and the Kabbalists of Beit El*, pp. 67–71, 142–4.
72 *Zohar* III 103b–104a, Tishby, The *Wisdom of the Zohar*, pp. 130–8.
73 Tishby, The *Wisdom of the Zohar*, pp. 103b–104a.
74 *Sha'ar ha- Kavvanot* (Jerusalem p. 84) as interpreted by Shar'abi (*Nahar Shalom* 35b, 35d).
75 Shmuel Vital, *Siddur Ḥemdat Yisrael* 207b; see Giller, *The Enlightened Will Shine*, p. 54.
76 See p. 140.
77 See Giller, *Shalom Shar'abi and the Kabbalists of Beit El*, pp. 67–82.
78 See Daniel Remer, *Tefilat Ḥayyim*, Betar: Tzrur ha-Chaim, 2004, pp. 242–3.
79 Giller, *Shalom Shar'abi and the Kabbalists of Beit El*, pp. 74–7.

7 PRAYER

1 Shaul Magid, "Conjugal Union, Mourning and Talmud Torah in R. Isaac Luria's *Tikkun Ḥaẓot*," *Daat* 36 (1996): xxiii.
2 Scholem, "The Concept of Kavvanah in the Early Kabbalah," in *Studies in Jewish Thought*, ed. Alfred Jospe, Detroit, MI: Wayne State University Press, 1981, pp. 167, 171–4.
3 Jonathan Garb, *Manifestations of Power in Jewish Mysticism* (Hebrew), Jerusalem: Magnes, 2005, pp. 142–247.

4 The theme of mystical union formed the crux of a debate between Gershom Scholem and Moshe Idel. See Idel, *Kabbalah: New Perspectives*, pp. 59–73; Scholem, *Origins of the Kabbalah*, pp. 299–309 (esp. p. 302, "*Debhequth* is . . . not *unio* but *communio*."); idem, *Major Trends in Jewish Mysticism*, pp. 140–1; idem, *The Messianic Idea in Judaism*, pp. 226–7; Tishby and Lachover, *The Wisdom of the Zohar*, p. 947; Menachem Kallus, "The Theurgy of Prayer in the Lurianic Kabbalah," p. 165 note 110; Wolfson, "Mystical Theurgical Dimensions of Prayer in *Sefer ha-Rimmon*," in *Approaches to Medieval Judaism*, ed. D. R. Blumenthal, Atlanta, GA: Scholars Press, 1988, pp. 43, 66 note 16.

5 Maimonides, *Book of Miẓvot*, Positive *Miẓvot* 2.

6 *Zohar* II 57a.

7 Isaiah ha-Levi Horowitz, *Siddur Sha'ar ha-Shamayim* 1:329; Meir Ibn Gabbai, *Avodat ha-Kodesh* (Jerusalem 1973), p. 222; (Jerusalem 1992), p. 404.

8 See *Zohar* II, 262a–b, expanded by Cordovero, *Tefillah le-Moshe* 101a–b.

9 Shalom Shar'abi, *Nahar Shalom* 39a.

10 Ḥallamish, "LeShem Yiḥud and its Generations in Kabbalah and Halakhah," in *Kabbalah: In Liturgy, Halakhah and Customs* (Hebrew), Ramat Gan: bar Ilan, 2000, pp. 45–70.

11 *Sha'ar ha-Kavvanot* I pp. 188–91, 195.

12 *Sha'ar ha-Kavvanot* I pp. 249–53; Menachem Kallus, "The Theurgy of Prayer in the Lurianic Kabbalah," pp. 153 note 69, 155.

13 Translated from the *Commentary on the Aggadah of Rabbi Azriel*, as published by Y. Tishby, Jerusalem 1983, pp. 39–41.

14 Thanks to Chava Weissler for pointing this out to me.

15 See pp. 57–9.

16 Menachem Kallus, "The Theurgy of Prayer in the Lurianic Kabbalah," p. 135.

17 Joseph Weiss, *Studies in Eastern European Jewish Mysticism*, Oxford: Oxford University Press, 1985, p. 96.

18 Menachem Kallus, "The Theurgy of Prayer in the Lurianic Kabbalah," pp. 123, 169, 173.

19 Vital, *Sha'ar ha-Kavvanot* I p. 78.

20 Vital, *Sha'ar ha-Kavvanot* I pp. 77–9, 93; *Pri Eẓ Ḥayyim* I p. 2; Menachem Kallus, "The Theurgy of Prayer in the Lurianic Kabbalah," p. 261.

21 See Menachem Kallus, "The Theurgy of Prayer in Lurianic Kabbalah," p. 72: "Among the novel dynamic features in the functional structure of the AR"I theurgic practice in daily prayer which are absent in Cordoverean practice; particularly the ascending-descending Four-Worlds structure of the liturgy, which made its first appearance only in the Lurianic Kabbalah" (ibid. note 143).

22 See Tishby, *The Wisdom of the Zohar*, pp. 597–614.

23 The main *Heikhalot* texts are to be found in *Zohar* I 38a–48a; II 245b–266b.

24 Vital, *Sha'ar ha-Kavvanot* I p. 216.

25 *Zohar* II 211b, III 102b; Vital, *Sha'ar ha-Kavvanot* I pp. 78–81.
26 Hallamish, "Luria's Status as a Halakhic Authority," in *Kabbalah: In Liturgy, Halakhah and Customs*, pp. 199–200.
27 Vital, *Sha'ar ha-Kavvanot* I pp. 106–7; *Pri Ez Hayyim* I p. 139; Adam Afterman, *The Intention of Prayers in Early Ecstatic Kabbalah: A Study and Critical Edition of an Anonymous Commentary to the Prayers* (Hebrew), Los Angeles: Cherub Press, 2004, p. 13.
28 Vital, *Sha'ar ha-Kavvanot* I p. 106.
29 Hallamish, "Luria's Status as a Halakhic Authority" (Hebrew) *The Kabbalah of the AR"I: Jerusalem, Studies in Jewish Thought* 10, eds Yehudah Liebes and Rachel Elior, Jerusalem: Magnes, 1992, p. 284.
30 Immanuel Etkes, *The Master of the Name*: *The BeSH"T: Magic, Mysticism, Practice*. (Hebrew), Jerusalem: Zalman Shazar, 2000, pp. 138–9, 146.
31 Ya'akov Yosef of Polnoye, *Ketonet Passim* 43b.
32 See Idel, *Hasidism: Between Ecstasy and Magic*, pp. 1–44.
33 Etkes, *The Master of the Name*, pp. 169–78; Joseph Weiss, *Studies in Eastern European Jewish Mysticism*, pp. 9, 27–46, 96–7; Rivka Schatz-Uffenheimer, *Hasidism as Mysticism: Quietistic Elements in 18th Century Hasidic Thought*, Jerusalem: Magnes, 1993, p. 217.
34 Kallus, "The Theurgy of Prayer in the Lurianic Kavvanot," pp. 122–3 note 23.
35 Steven Katz, *Mysticism and Religious Traditions*, Oxford: Oxford University Press, 1983, p. 24.
36 Eitan Fishbane, "Tears of Disclosure: The Role of Weeping in Zoharic Narrative," *The Journal of Jewish Thought and Philosophy* 11:1 (2002): 25–47; Idel, *Kabbalah: New Perspectives*, pp. 74–111.

8 THE QUESTION OF MEDITATION

1 The states of mind described by Patanjali in the Yoga sutras, the Theravadan *Satipattana Sutta* or the Lu Dongbin's *Secret of the Golden Flower*, the Buddhist schools of *shamatha* and *vipassana*, which respectively turn the mind inward and outward, all focus directly on the contemplative act. See Lewis Lancaster and Whelan Lai, eds, *Early Chan in China and Tibet*, Berkeley, CA: Asian Humanities Press, 1983, Introduction, pp. xi–xiv.
2 See, in particular, Katz' introductions to two of his edited volumes, *Mysticism and Philosophical Analysis* and *Mysticism and Religious Traditions*.
3 Further discussions of this theme, when expressed in terms of the cross-cultural value of *unio mystica* have formed the crux of a debate between Gershom Scholem and Moshe Idel. See Idel, *Kabbalah: New Perspectives*, pp. 59–73; Scholem, *Origins of the Kabbalah*, pp. 299–309 (esp. p. 302, "*Debhequth* is . . . not *unio* but *communio*."); idem, *Major Trends in Jewish Mysticism*, pp. 140–1; idem, *The Messianic Idea in Judaism*, pp. 226–7; Tishby and Lachover, *The Wisdom of the Zohar*,

p. 947; Kallus, "The Theurgy of Prayer in the Lurianic Kabbalah," p. 165 note 110; Wolfson, "Mystical Theurgical Dimensions of Prayer in *Sefer ha-Rimmon*," pp. 43, 66 note 16.

4   On the subject of power, see Rebecca Macy Lesses, *Ritual Practices to Gain Power: Angels, Incantations and Revelation in Early Jewish Mysticism*, Harrisburg, PA: Trinity Press International, 1998; Garb, *Manifestations of Power in Jewish Mysticism*.

5   See Daniel Matt, *"Ayin*: the Concept of Nothingness in Jewish Mysticism."

6   See, for example, Jeremy Stolow, *Orthodox by Design: Judaism, Print Politics and the Artscroll Revolution*, Berkeley: University of California Press, 2010.

7   Verman, *The History and Varieties of Jewish Meditation*, p. 2.

8   Verman, *The History and Varieties of Jewish Meditation*, p. 62; Arthur Green, *"Three Warsaw Mystics," Jerusalem Studies in Jewish Thought* 13 (1966): 1–58.

9   Verman, *The History and Varieties of Jewish Meditation*, pp. 5, 53, 62, 119, 174–5;.

10   Verman, *The History and Varieties of Jewish Meditation*, p. 39

11   At the time (the 1970s and early 1980s) that Aryeh Kaplan began to write about him, Abulafia's works remained in manuscript. Moshe Idel had not yet published his groundbreaking studies of Abulafia's thought and method, not to mention the full-length study of Abulafia by Elliot Wolfson which was followed by the article "Kenotic Overflow and Temporal Transcendence: Angelic Embodiment and the Alterity of Time in Abraham Abulafia,"

12   Idel, "Hitbodedut as Concentration in the Ecstatic Kabbalah," p. 428.

13   Idel, "Hitbodedut as Concentration in the Ecstatic Kabbalah," pp. 415–18, 421, 427–8; Hallamish, *An Introduction to the Kabbalah*, pp. 50, 55.

14   Idel, "Hitbodedut as Concentration in the Ecstatic Kabbalah," p. 428; Cordovero, Or Yaqar ms Cincinatti, 45b.

15   Idel, "Hitbodedut as Concentration in the Ecstatic Kabbalah," p. 431.

16   Idel, "Hitbodedut as Concentration in the Ecstatic Kabbalah," pp. 412–14, 424–5; Kaplan, *Meditation and Kabbalah*, p. 113; Hallamish, *An Introduction to the Kabbalah*, p. 53. On the Isaac of Acre, see Eitan Fishbane, *As Light Before Dawn: The Inner World of a Medieval Kabbalist*, Palo Alto, CA: Stanford, 2009.

17   See Ephraim Kanarfogel, *Peering Through the Lattices: Mystical, Magical and Pietistic Dimensions in the Tosafist Period*, Detroit, MI: Wayne State University Press, 2000.

18   See Whelan Lai, "Inner Worldly Mysticism: East and West," in *Zen and Hasidism*, ed. Harold Heifetz, New York: K'tav, 1996, pp. 186–207.

19   See Daniel C. Matt, *"Ayin*: the Concept of Nothingness in Jewish Mysticism," pp. 67–108.

20 Idel, "Hitbodedut as Concentration in the Ecstatic Kabbalah," pp. 408–9; Moshe Ḥallamish, *An Introduction to the Kabbalah*, p. 11. See Diana Lobel's important studies in this regard: *Between Mysticism and Philosophy: Sufi Language of Religious Experience in Judah Ha-Levi's Kuzari*, Albany, NY: State University of New York Press, 2000 and *A Sufi-Jewish Dialogue: Philosophy and Mysticism in Bahya ibn Paquda's Duties of the Heart*, Philadelphia: University of Pennsylvania Press, 2006.

9 THE DIVINE NAMES

1 Naḥmanides, Commentary to the Torah, Introduction; Wolfson, *Abraham Abulafia: Kabbalist and Prophet*, Los Angeles, CA: Cherub Press, 2000, pp. 58, 73–4; Scholem, "The Name of God and Linguistic Theory of the Kabbalah," *Diogenes* 79–80 (1972); Giller, *The Enlightened Will Shine*, chapter 1 note 29.
2 See also Giller, *Shalom Shar'abi and the Kabbalists of Beit El*, pp. 39–53.
3 Scholem, *Kabbalah*, p. 177.
4 See above pp. 12–15.
5 Idel, *The Mystical Experience in Abraham Abulafia*, p. 15.
6 *Sha'ar ha-Kavvanot* I, pp. 247, 271.
7 Joseph Dan, "The Emergence of Mystical Prayer," in *Jewish Mysticism: The Middle Ages*, p. 229.
8 Idel, *The Mystical Experience in Abraham Abulafia*, p. 14.
9 Joseph Dan, *Jewish Mysticism: The Middle Ages*, pp. 142, 157; idem, "The Emergence of Mystical Prayer," p. 229; see Idel, *The Mystical Experience in Abraham Abulafia*, p. 23.
10 Idel, *The Mystical Experience in Abraham Abulafia*, p. 28; Wolfson, *Abraham Abulafia: Kabbalist and Prophet*, p. 57; Afterman, *The Intention of Prayers in Early Ecstatic Kabbalah*, pp. 20, 26.
11 Idel, *The Mystical Experience in Abraham Abulafia*, p. 40; idem, *Language, Torah and Hermeneutics in Abraham Abulafia*, p. x.
12 Idel, *The Mystical Experience in Abraham Abulafia*, p. 34; Kallus, "The Theurgy of Prayer in the Lurianic Kabbalah," p. 176 note 135.
13 *Sha'ar ha-Kavvanot* I, p. 114; *Pri Eẓ Ḥayyim* I, p. 152.
14 *Zohar* II 22a, III 183a; see Wolfson, *Abraham Abulafia: Kabbalist and Prophet*, pp. 102–3.
15 Moshe Cordovero, *Elimah Rabbati* 89a.
16 Vital, Ḥayyim, *Sha'ar ha-Kavvanot* I, pp. 101, 151, 277; *Sha'ar Ma'amarei RaSHB"Y*), pp. 155–6, 198, 222, 254, 272, 276.
17 *Sha'ar ha-Kavvanot* I, p. 194.
18 The first is YHVH AHYH, the second level is YHVH Elohim and the third level is YHVH ADNY.
19 *Eẓ Ḥayyim*, Tel Aviv 2, pp. 335–6; Warsaw 99a–d.
20 *Eẓ Ḥayyim*, Tel Aviv 2, p. 342; Warsaw 100a; see Idel, *The Mystical Experience in Abraham Abulafia*, p. 92; Wolfson, *Abraham Abulafia: Kabbalist and Prophet*, p. 62; Giller, *Shalom Shar'abi and the Kabbalists of Beit El*, p. 42.

NOTES

21 Kallus, "The Theurgy of Prayer in the Lurianic Kabbalah," pp. 134–5.
22 Fine, *Physician of the Soul, Healer of the Cosmos*, p. 213; Kallus, "The Theurgy of Prayer in the Lurianic Kabbalah," pp. 182 note 137, 184 note 142, 206.
23 See above pp. 137–9. *Sha'ar ha-Kavvanot* I, pp. 79, 118, 241, 276; *Pri Ez Hayyim* I, pp. 9–11; Kallus, "The Theurgy of Prayer in the Lurianic Kabbalah," p. 135.
24 ABG YTZ KRA STN NGD YKhS BTR ZTG HKB TNA YGL PZK SKV ZYT.
25 Kiddushin 71a.
26 Idel, *The Mystical Experience in Abraham Abulafia*, pp. 15, 32, 35, 38.
27 See, in particular, *Yehudah Berg, The 72 Names of God: Technology for the Soul*.
28 Lvov 1786, rep. Jerusalem 2001. This information is gleaned from a discussion between Professors Joel Hecker and Boaz Huss on the E-Idra list, March 3, 2004.
29 Rivka Schatz-Uffenheimer, *Hasidism as Mysticism*, pp. 214–41; see also Kallus, "The Relationship of the Baal Shem Tov to the Practice of Lurianic Kavvanot in Light of his Comments on the *Siddur Rashkov*," *Kabbalah: Journal for the Study of Jewish Mystical Texts*, eds Daniel Abrams and Avraham Elqayam, Los Angeles, CA: Cherub Press, Volume 2, 1997; Moshe Idel, *Hasidism: Between Ecstasy and Magi*, pp. 149–56.
30 The Maggid, *Or ha-Emet* 77b and *Liqqutei Yeqarim* 15a, brought in Rivka Schatz-Uffenheimer, *Hasidism as Mysticism*, p. 218.
31 B. T. Shabbat 75a, Rosh Ha-Shanah 24b, Sanhedrin 68a.
32 Liqqutei Moharan II 120.
33 Vital, *Sha'ar ha-Kavvanot* I, pp. 78–80, 195–6, 220–9, 233; *Pri Ez Hayyim* I, pp. 6, 9–11; Kallus, "The Theurgy of Prayer in the Lurianic Kavvanot," pp. 122–3 note 23.

10 KABBALAH AND CONTEMPORARY JUDAISM

1 Gershom Scholem, *Major Trends in Jewish Mysticism*.
2 See Heinrich Graetz, *History of the Jews*, Philadelphia, PA: Jewish Publication Society, 1894, vol. 4, pp. 10–22.
3 Admittedly, this phenomenon had begun well before Scholem arrived on the scene by such figures as Adolph Jellenik, who termed Kabbalah "Jewish Mysticism" in 1853. Buber echoed this view in his initial studies of R. Naḥman of Breslav, which he terms "Die Judische Mystik," in 1906 (Moshe Idel, "On Aharon Jellenik and Kabbalah," 15–22).
4 Huss has explored the association of Kabbalah with mysticism in his article "The Metaphysics of Kabbalah and the Myth of 'Jewish Mysticism.'"
5 Meroz, "Was Israel Sarug a Student of the AR"I?—New Research"; Avivi, "Luria's Writings in Italy to 1620."

6 Scholem, *Major Trends in Jewish Mysticism*, pp. 245–6 and 286.
7 Idel, "The History of the Concept of Ẓimẓum in Kabbalah Research," in Liebes and Elior, *The Kabbalah of the AR"I: Jerusalem, Studies in Jewish Thought* 10, p. 89; Bracha Sack, "R. Moshe Cordovero's Doctrine of Ẓimẓum."
8 Idel, *Kabbalah: New Perspectives*, pp. 30–2.
9 This is but one of Matt Goldish's conclusions in his study *The Sabbatean Prophets*.
10 See in particular Glen Dynner's study *Men of Silk: The Hasidic Conquest of Polish Jewish Society*, New York: Oxford University Press, 2008 and the various works of David Assaf, including *Untold Tales of the Hasidism: Chapters of Crisis and Discontent in the History of Hasidism*, Waltham, MA: Brandeis, 2010.
11 Boaz Huss, "Ask No Questions," *Modern Judaism* 25: 2005 2: 141.
12 Arthur Hertzberg, "Gershom Scholem as Zionist and Believer," *Modern Judaism* 5 (1985): 12.
13 "The New Age of Jewish Mysticism" (Hebrew), *Modern Jewish Studies* 6:2 June (2007).
14 *Kabbalah and the Spiritual Quest: The Kabbalah Centre in America*, Santa Barbara, CA: Praeger, 2007.
15 "The Revealed and the Revealed within the Revealed: On the Opposition to the 'Followers' of Rabbi Yehudah Ashlag and the Dissemination of Exoteric Literature" (Hebrew), *Kabbalah* 16 (2007); idem, "New Discoveries Concerning R. Judah Leib Ashlag" (Hebrew), *Kabbalah* 20 (2009).
16 *The Chosen Will Become Herds: Studies in Twentieth Century Kabbalah*, trans. Yaffah Berkovits-Murciano, New Haven, CT: Yale University Press, 2009.
17 *The Chosen Will Become Herds*, p. 2.
18 See "Civil Religion in America," *The Robert Bellah Reader*, pp. 225–45.
19 Jody Myers (*Kabbalah and Spiritual Quest*) brings an extensive bibliography of scholarship on contemporary New Age religion, particularly the work of Wouter Hanegraaf (*New Age Religion and Western Culture: Esotericism in the Mirror of Western Thought*, Albany, NY: State University of New York Press, 1998). Most of my analysis, however, is undocumented and off the cuff.
20 The more widespread term, *marranos*, is pejorative.
21 Jody Myers, *Kabbalah and the Spiritual Quest*, p. 127; Boaz Huss, "*Sefer ha-Zohar* as a Canonical, Sacred and Holy Text," 295–9.
22 Heilman and Friedman, *The Rebbe*, pp. 29–64; Wolfson, *Open Secret: Postmessianic Messianism and the Mystical Revision of Menahem Mendel Schneerson*, pp. 161–99.
23 Heilman and Friedman, *The Rebbe: The Life and Afterlife of Menachem Mendel Schneerson*, Princeton, NJ: Princeton University Press, 2010, pp. 61–3.
24 David Berger's *The Rebbe, The Messiah, and the Scandal of Orthodox Indifference* (Oxford: Littman Library, 2001) attempted to raise a hue

NOTES

and cry about the evils of Chabad but was met with indifference, scandalously.

25 Assaf, *Untold Tales of the Hasidim*, pp. 120–42.
26 Garb, *The Chosen Will Become Herds*, pp. 35–59.
27 Garb, *Manifestations of Power in Jewish Mysticism* (2005).
28 See, in particular, Green's recent *Radical Judaism: Rethinking God and Tradition* (The Franz Rosenzweig Lecture Series).
29 Giller, *Shalom Shar'abi and the Kabbalists of Beit El*, pp. 15–16.
30 See Giller, "Recovering the Sanctity of the Galilee," 155–7.
31 Scholem, *Devarim be-Go* (Hebrew), Tel Aviv: Am Oved, 1975, p. 71.

WORKS CITED

PRIMARY

Anonymous. *Sefer Ma'arekhet ha-Elohut 'Im Perush he-Hayyat.* Mantua 1568.

Azriel of Gerona. *Perush ha-Aggadot le-Rabbenu Azriel.* Edited by Isaiah Tishby. Jerusalem, 1945.

—. *Tefillah le-Moshe.* Premishla, 1892.

De Leon, Moshe. *Sefer ha-Rimmon.* Edited by Elliot Wolfson. Atlanta, GA: Scholars Press, 1988.

Gikatilla, Yosef. *Sefer Sha'arei Orah.* Warsaw, 1883.

Horowitz, Isaiah ha-Levi. *Siddur Sha'ar ha-Shamayim.* Jerusalem, 1998.

Ibn Gabbai, Meir. *Avodat ha-Kodesh.* Jerusalem, 1973.

—. *Avodat ha-Kodesh.* Jerusalem, 1992.

Maimonides, Moses. *Moreh Nevukhim* (Guide for the Perplexed) Y. Kapach, ed. Jerusalem: Merkaz ha-Rav Kook, 1977.

—. *Sefer ha-Miẓvot,* trans. with notes by C. B. Chavel. London and New York: Soncino, 1967.

Margaliot, Reuven, ed. *Sefer ha-Zohar* 3 vols. 4th edition. Jerusalem: Mossad ha-Rav Kook, 1964.

—. ed. *Tiqqunei ha-Zohar.* Jerusalem: Mossad ha-Rav Kook, 1978.

—. ed. *Zohar Hadash.* Jerusalem: Mossad ha-Rav Kook, 1978.

Matt, Daniel. *Zohar: The Pritzker Edition,* vols. 1–5. Palo Alto, CA: Stanford University Press, 2003–2009.

Naḥman of Breslav. *Likkutei Moharan.* Benei Barak: Keren Hadpasa de-Hassidei Breslav, 1964.

Remer, Daniel, ed. *Sefer Tefilat Ḥayyim.* Betar: Tzrur ha-Chaim, 2004.

—. *Siddur Tefilat Ḥayyim.* Betar: Tzrur ha-Chaim, 2004.

Sarug, Yisrael. *Limmudei Aẓilut.* Munkacz, 1897.

Shar'abi, Shalom. *Nahar Shalom.* Jerusalem, 1910.

Vital, Ḥayyim. *Eẓ Ḥayyim.* Jerusalem, 1910.

—. *Eẓ Ḥayyim.* Tel Aviv, 1961.

—. *Ketavim Ḥadashim me-Rabbeinu Ḥayyim Vital.* Jerusalem: Ahavat Shalom, 1988.

—. *Likkutim Ḥadashim me-ha-AR"I Z"L u-me-Ḥayyim Vital Z"L.* Jerusalem, 1985.

—. *Sha'ar ha-Hakdamot .* Tel Aviv, 1961.

—. *Sha'ar ha-Kavvanot.* Tel Aviv, 1961.

—. *Sha'ar Ma'amarei RaSHB"Y ve-RaZ"L.* Tel Aviv, 1961.
—. *Siddur Ḥemdat Yisrael.* Munkacz 1901. Wildmann, Yitzḥak Eizik Ḥaver. *Pitḥei She'arim.* Warsaw, 1888.
Ya'akov Yosef of Polnoye. *Ketonet Passim.* New York, 1950.

SECONDARY

Abrams, Daniel. "The Invention of the Zohar as a Book-On the Assumptions and Expectations of the Kabbalists and Modern Scholars," *Kabbalah* 19 (2009): 7–142.
—. "When Was the Introduction to the Zohar Written?" (Hebrew), *Assufot* 8 (1994): 211–26.
Afterman, Adam. *The Intention of Prayers in Early Ecstatic Kabbalah: A Study and Critical Edition of an Anonymous Commentary to the Prayers* (Hebrew). Los Angeles, CA: Cherub Press, 2004.
Assaf, David. *Untold Tales of the Hasidism: Chapters of Crisis and Discontent in the History of Hasidism.* Waltham, MA: Brandeis, 2010.
Altmann, Alexander. "The Gnostic Background of the Rabbinic Adam Legends," in *Studies in Religious Philosophy and Mysticism.* Ithaca, NY: Cornell University Press, 1969, pp. 1–16, 161–79.
Avivi, Yosef. *Binyan Ariel* (Hebrew). Jerusalem: Misgav Yerushalayim, 1987.
—. *Kabbalat Ha-AR"I* (Hebrew). Jerusalem: Makhon Ben Zvi, 2008.
—. "Luria's Writings in Italy to 1620" (Hebrew), *Alei Sefer* 11 (1984): 91–134.
Baer, Yiẓhak. *A History of the Jews in Christian Spain.* 2 vols. Translated by Louis Schoffman. Philadelphia, PA: Jewish Publication Society, 1978.
Bellah, Robert. *The Robert Bellah Reader.* Chapel Hill, NC: Duke University Press, 2006.
Berger, David. *The Rebbe, The Messiah, and the Scandal of Orthodox Indifference.* Oxford: Littman Library, 2001.
Biale, David. *Eros and the Jews.* Berkeley: University of California, 1992.
Boyarin, Daniel. *Carnal Israel: Reading Sex in Talmudic Culture.* Berkeley: University of California, 1995.
Chajes, J. H. *Between Worlds: Dybbuks, Exorcists and Early Modern Judaism.* Philadelphia: University of Pennsylvania Press, 2003.
Dan, Joseph. *Jewish Mysticism: The Middle Ages.* Northvale, NJ: Jason Aronson, 1998.
Dynner, Glen. *Men of Silk: The Hasidic Conquest of Polish Jewish Society.* New York: Oxford University Press, 2008.
Elior, Rachel. *The Paradoxical Ascent to God: The Kabbalistic Theosophy of Habad Hasidism.* Albany, NY: State University of New York Press, 1993.
—. *Temple and Chariot, Priests and Angels, Sanctuary and Heavenly Sanctuaries in Early Jewish Mysticism.* Jerusalem: Magnes, 2002. English edn *The Three Temples.* Oxford: Littman Library, 2004.

Elkayam, Avraham. "Shabbatai Tzvi's Manuscript Copy of the Zohar," *Kabbalah* 3, Los Angeles, 1998.

Etkes, Immanuel. *The Master of the Name: The BeSH"T: Magic, Mysticism, Practice* (Hebrew). Jerusalem: Zalman Shazar, 2000.

Fine, Lawrence. "The Contemplative Practice of Yichudim," in *Jewish Spirituality* II, Arthur Green, ed. New York: Crossroads, 1987, pp. 64–98.

—. *Physician of the Soul, Healer of the Cosmos: Isaac Luria and His Kabbalistic Fellowship.* Stanford, CA: Stanford University Press, 2003.

Fishbane, Eitan. *As Light Before Dawn: The Inner World of a Medieval Kabbalist.* Palo Alto, CA: Stanford, 2009.

—. "Tears of Disclosure: The Role of Weeping in Zoharic Narrative," *The Journal of Jewish Thought and Philosophy* 11:1 (2002): 25–47.

Garb, Jonathan. *The Chosen Will Become Herds-Studies in Twentieth Century Kabbalah.* Yaffah Berkovits-Murciano, trans. New Haven, CT: Yale University Press, 2009.

—. *Manifestations of Power in Jewish Mysticism* (Hebrew). Jerusalem: Magnes, 2005.

Giller, Pinchas. *The Enlightened Will Shine: Symbolization and Theurgy in the Later Strata of the Zohar.* Albany, NY: State University of New York Press, 1993.

—. *Reading the Zohar: The Classic Text of the Kabbalah.* New York: Oxford University Press, 2000.

—. "Recovering the Sanctity of the Galilee: the Veneration of Sacred Relics in the Classical Kabbalah," *The Journal of Jewish Thought and Philosophy* 4 (1994): 147–69.

— . *Shalom Shar'abi and the Kabbalists of Beit El.* New York: Oxford University Press, 2008.

Ginsburg, Elliot K. *The Sabbath in the Classical Kabbalah.* Albany, NY: State University of New York Press, 1989.

Goldish, Matt. *The Sabbatean Prophets.* Cambridge: Harvard University Press, 2004.

Goshen-Gottstein, Alon. "Is Ma'aseh Bereishit Part of Ancient Jewish Mysticism?" *Journal of Jewish Thought and Philosophy* 4(1994): 185–201.

Green, Arthur. *Ehyeh: A Kabbalah for Tomorrow.* New York: Jewish Lights, 2003.

—. *Radical Judaism: Rethinking God and Tradition* (The Franz Rosenzweig Lecture Series). New Haven, CT: Yale University Press, 2010.

—. "*Three Warsaw Mystics,*" *Jerusalem Studies in Jewish Thought* 13 (1966): 1–58.

—. "The Zaddiq as *Axis Mundi.* in Later Judaism," *Journal of the American Academy of Religion* 45 (1977): 327–47.

Green, Arthur, ed. *Jewish Spirituality* I & II. New York: Crossroads, 1986, 1987.

Gries, Ze'ev. "Hasidic Conduct Literature," in *Jewish Spirituality* II, Green, Arthur, ed. pp. 157–205.

Ḥallamish, Moshe. *An Introduction to the Kabbalah*. Albany, NY: State University of New York Press, 1999.

—. *Kabbalah: In Liturgy, Halakhah and Customs* (Hebrew). Ramat Gan: bar Ilan, 2000.

—. *Kabbalistic Customs of Shabbat* (Hebrew). Jerusalem: Orḥot, 2006.

Halperin, David. *Sabbatai Sevi: Testimonies to a Failed Messiah*. Oxford: Littman Library, 2007.

Hanegraaf, Wouter. *New Age Religion and Western Culture: Esotericism in the Mirror of Western Thought*. Albany, NY: State University of New York Press, 1998.

Hecker, Joel. *Mystical Bodies, Mystical Meals: Eating And Embodiment In Medieval Kabbalah*. Ann Arbor, MI: Wayne State University Press, 2005.

Heifetz, Harold. *Zen and Hasidism*. New York: K'tav, 1996.

Heilman, Samuel and Friedman, Menachem. *The Rebbe: The Life and Afterlife of Menachem Mendel Schneerson*. Princeton, NJ: Princeton University Press, 2010.

Hellner-Eshed, Melila. *A River Flows from Eden*. Palo Alto, CA: Stanford, 2009.

Hertzberg, Arthur. "Gershom Scholem as Zionist and Believer," *Modern Judaism* 5 (1985): 12.

Heschel, Abraham Joshua. *The Sabbath*. New York: Farrar Straus Giroux, 2005.

Huss, Boaz. "Ask No Questions: Gershom Scholem and the Study of Contemporary Jewish Mysticism," *Modern Judaism* 25.2: 141–59.

—. "Ketem Paz- The Kabbalistic Doctrine of Rabbi Simeon Lavi in his commentary to the Zohar" (Hebrew) Ph.D. dissertation, Hebrew University, 1992.

—. *Like the Radiance of the Sky: Chapters in the Reception History of the Zohar and the Construction of its Symbolic Value* (Hebrew). Jerusalem: Bialik, 2008.

—. "The Metaphysics of Kabbalah and the Myth of 'Jewish Mysticism'" (Hebrew), *Peamim* no. 110 (Winter 2007): 9–30.

—. "The New Age of Jewish Mysticism" (Hebrew), *Modern Jewish Studies* 6.2 (June 2007).

—. "*Sefer ha-Zohar* as a Canonical, Sacred and Holy Text: Changing Perspectives of the Book of Splendor between the Thirteenth and Eighteenth Centuries," *The Journal of Jewish Thought and Philosophy* 7(1997): 257–307.

Idel, Moshe. *Abraham Abulafia: An Ecstatic Kabbalist: Two Studies*. Lancaster, CA: Labarinthos, 2002.

—. *Hasidism: Between Ecstasy and Magic*. Albany, NY: State University of New York Press, 1995.

—. "The History of the Concept of *Ẓimẓum* in Kabbalah Research" (Hebrew), in Liebes and Elior, *The Kabbalah of the AR"I: Jerusalem*, Studies in Jewish Thought 10 (1992).

—. "Hitbodedut as Concentration in the Ecstatic Kabbalah," in *Jewish Spirituality* I, ed. Green, Arthur. New York: Crossroads, 1986, pp. 405–38.

—. *Kabbalah: New Perspectives*. New Haven, CT: Yale University Press, 1988.

—. *Language, Torah and Hermeneutics in Abraham Abulafia*. Albany, NY: State University of New York Press, 1989.

—. *The Mystical Experience in Abraham Abulafia*. Albany, NY: State University of New York Press, 1989.

—. "On Aharon Jellenik and Kabbalah" (Hebrew), *Peamim* 100 [2004]: 15–22.

—. *Studies in Ecstatic Kabbalah*. Albany, NY: State University of New York Press, 1989.

Kallus, Menachem. "The Relationship of the Baal Shem Tov to the Practice of Lurianic Kavvanot in Light of his Comments on the *Siddur Rashkov*," *Kabbalah: Journal for the Study of Jewish Mystical Texts* eds. Daniel Abrams and Avraham Elqayam, Vol. 2. Los Angeles, CA: Cherub Press, 1997, pp. 151–68.

— "The Theurgy of Prayer In Lurianic Kabbalah." PhD. Thesis; Hebrew University, 2002.

Kanarfogel, Ephraim. *Peering Through the Lattices: Mystical, Magical and Pietistic Dimensions in the Tosafist Period*. Detroit, MI: Wayne State University Press, 2000.

Kaplan, Aryeh. *Jewish Meditation*. New York: Schocken, 1995.

—. *Meditation and Kabbalah*. New York: Weiser, 1989.

—. *Meditation and the Bible*. New York: Weiser, 1978.

Katz, Steven, ed. *Mysticism and Language*. Oxford: Oxford University Press, 1992.

—. *Mysticism and Philosophical Analysis*. Oxford: Oxford University Press, 1978.

—. *Mysticism and Religious Traditions*. Oxford: Oxford University Press, 1983.

—.*Mysticism and Sacred Scripture*. Oxford: Oxford University Press, 2000.

Kepnes, Steven. *Interpreting Judaism in a Post-Modern Age*. New York: New York University Press 1995.

Lancaster, Lewis and Lai, Whelan, eds. *Early Chan in China and Tibet*. Berkeley, CA: Asian Humanities Press, 1983.

Lesses, Rebecca Macy. *Ritual Practices to Gain Power: Angels, Incantations and Revelation in Early Jewish Mysticism*. Harrisburg, PA: Trinity Press International, 1998.

Liebes, Yehudah. "Sabbath Meal Hymns of the Holy AR"I" (Hebrew), *Molad* 4 (1972): 540–55.

—. *Studies in the Zohar*. Albany, NY: State University of New York Press, 1993.

Lobel, Diana. *Between Mysticism and Philosophy: Sufi Language of Religious Experience in Judah Ha-Levi's Kuzari*. Albany, NY: State University of New York Press, 2000.

—. *A Sufi-Jewish Dialogue: Philosophy and Mysticism in Bahya ibn Paquda's Duties of the Heart*. Philadelphia: University of Pennsylvania Press, 2006.

Magid, Shaul. "Conjugal Union, Mourning and Talmud Torah in R. Isaac Luria's Tikkun Hatzot," *Daat* 36 (1996): xvii–xlv.

—. *From Metaphysics to Midrash: Myth, History, and the Interpretation of Scripture in Lurianic Kabbala*. Indiana: Indiana University Press, 2008.

Matt, Daniel. *"Ayin*: the Concept of Nothingness in Jewish Mysticism," in *Essential Papers in Kabbalah*, ed. Lawrence Fine. New York: University Press, 1995, pp. 67–108.

—. *God & the Big Bang: Discovering Harmony Between Science & Spirituality*. New York: Jewish Lights, 1998.

—. "The Mystic and the Miẓwot," in *Jewish Spirituality* I, ed. Arthur Green. New York: Crossroads, 1987, pp. 367–404.

—. *Zohar: The Book of Enlightenment*. New York: Paulist Press, 1984.

Meir, Jonathan. "New Discoveries Concerning R. Judah Leib Ashlag" (Hebrew), *Kabbalah* 20 (2009): 345–68.

—. "The Revealed and the Revealed within the Revealed: On the Opposition to the 'Followers' of Rabbi Yehudah Ashlag and the Dissemination of Exoteric Literature" (Hebrew), *Kabbalah* 16 (2007): 151–268.

Meroz, Ronit. "The Middle Eastern Origins of Kabbalah," *The Journal for the Study of Sephardi and Mizrahi Jewry* (February 2007): 39–57.

—. "Redemption in the Lurianic Teaching" (Hebrew). PhD. Thesis; Hebrew University, 1988.

—. "Was Israel Sarug a Student of the AR"I?—New Research" (Hebrew), *Da'at* 28 (1992): 41–56.

—. "Zoharic Narratives and their Adaptations," *Hispania Judaica Bulletin* 3 (5760/2000): 3–63.

Myers, Jody. *Kabbalah and the Spiritual Quest: The Kabbalah Centre in America*. Santa Barbara, CA: Praeger, 2007.

Nadler, Allan. *The Faith of the Mithnagdim: Rabbinic Responses to Hasidic Rapture*. Baltimore, MD: Johns Hopkins University Press, 1997.

Neumann, Erich. *The Great Mother*. Princeton, NJ: Bollingen, 1964.

Pedaya, Havivah. "Seized with Speech: Clarifying the Ecstatic Prophecy of the Early Kabbalists," *Tarbitz* 65 (1996): 565–637.

Sack, Bracha. "Prayer in the Teachings of Moshe Cordovero." (Hebrew) *Da'at* 9 (1982): 5–12.

—. "R. Moshe Cordovero's Doctrine of Ẓimẓum" (Hebrew), *Tarbiz* 58 (1989): 207–37.

Saperstein, Marc. *Jewish Preaching*. New Haven, CT: Yale, 1993.

Schatz-Uffenheimer, Rivka. *Hasidism as Mysticism: Quietistic Elements in 18th Century Hasidic Thought*. Jerusalem: Magnes Press, 1993.

Scholem, Gershom. "The Concept of Kavvanah in the Early Kabbalah," in *Studies in Jewish Thought*, ed. Alfred Jospe. Detroit, MI: Wayne State University Press, 1981, pp. 162–80.

—. Hebrew version: *Tarbiẓ* 2: 415–42; 3: 33–66 (1932).

—. *Jewish Gnosticism, Merkabah Mysticism and Talmudic Tradition* . New York: Jewish Theological Seminary of America, 1960.

—. *Kabbalah.* New York: Meridian, 1978.

—. *Major Trends in Jewish Mysticism.* Third edition, rev. New York: Schocken, 1961.

—. *The Messianic Idea in Judaism.* New York: Schocken, 1971.

—. "The Name of God and Linguistic Theory of the Kaballah," *Diogenes* 79–80 (1972): 59–80, 164–94.

—. *On the Kabbalah and Its Symbolism.* New York: Schocken, 1965.

—. *Origins of the Kabbalah.* Princeton, NJ: Jewish Publication Society and Princeton University Press, 1987.

—. *Sabbatai Sevi: The Mystical Messiah.* Princeton, NJ: Bollingen, 1973.

Stolow, Jeremy. *Orthodox by Design: Judaism, Print Politics and the Artscroll Revolution.* Berkeley: University of California Press, 2010.

Tishby, Isaiah, and Fischel Lachover. *The Wisdom of the Zohar.* Translated by David Goldstein, Oxford: Littman Library 1991.

Verman, Mark. *The Books of Contemplation: Medieval Jewish Mystical Sources.* Albany, NY: State University of New York Press, 1989.

—. *The History and Varieties of Jewish Meditation.* New York: Jason Aronson, 1996.

Weinstein, Avi. *Gates of Light.* San Francisco, CA: HarperCollins, 1994.

Weinstock, Israel. "R. Yosef Ibn Tabul's Commentary on the Idra" (Hebrew), *Temirin* 1. Jerusalem: Mossad ha-Rav Kook, 1982: 123–62.

Weiss, Joseph. *Studies in Eastern European Jewish Mysticism.* Oxford: Oxford University Press, 1985.

Wijnhoven, J. A. A. "The Zohar and the Proselyte," in *Texts and Responses: Studies Presented to N. Glatzer,* ed. Michael Fishbane. Leiden: E. J. Brill, 1957, pp. 120–40.

Wolfson, Elliot. *Abraham Abulafia: Kabbalist and Prophet.* Los Angeles, CA: Cherub Press, 2000.

—. "The Anonymous Chapters of the Elderly Master of Secrets—New Evidence for the Early Activity of the Zoharic Circle," *Kabbalah* 19 (2009): 143–278.

—. "From Sealed Book to Open Text: Time, Memory and Narrativity in Kabbalistic Hermenutics," in *Interpreting Judaism in a Postmodern Age,* ed. Steven Kepnes. New York: N.Y.U. Press, 1996, pp. 145–80.

—. "Kenotic Overflow and Temporal Transcendence: Angelic Embodiment and the Alterity of Time in Abraham Abulafia," *Kabbalah: Journal for the Study of Jewish Mystical Texts* 18 (2008): 133–90. Revised version in *Saintly Influence: Edith Wyschogrod and the Possibilities of Philosophy of Religion,* 113–49. Edited by E. Boynton and M. Kavka. New York: Fordham University Press, 2009.

—. *Language, Eros, Being.* New York: Fordham University Press, 2005.

—. *Luminal Darkness: Imaginal Gleanings from Zoharic Literature.* Oxford: Oneworld, 2007.

—. "Mystical-Theurgical Dimensions of Prayer in *Sefer ha-Rimmon,*" in *Approaches to Medieval Judaism* 3: 41–80. Edited by D. R. Blumenthal. Atlanta, GA: Scholars Press, 1988.

WORKS CITED

——. *Open Secret: Postmessianic Messianism and the Mystical Revision of Menahem Mendel Schneerson.* New York: Columbia University Press, 2009.

——. *Through a Speculum That Shines: Vision and Imagination in Medieval Jewish Mysticism.* Princeton, NJ: Princeton University Press, 1994.

——. *Venturing Beyond: Law and Morality in Kabbalistic Mysticism.* New York: Oxford University Press, 2006.

INDEX